Traveling to Vietnam

Syracuse Studies on Peace and Conflict Resolution
Harriet Hyman Alonso, Charles Chatfield, and Louis Kriesberg, *Series Editors*

Traveling to VIETNAM

American Peace Activists and the War

Mary Hershberger

Syracuse University Press

First Edition 1998
98 99 00 01 02 03   6 5 4 3 2 1

The paper used in this publication meets the minimum requirements of American National Standard for Information Sciences—Permanence of Paper for Printed Library Materials, ANSI Z39.48-1984. ∞™

Library of Congress Cataloging-in-Publication Data

Hershberger, Mary.
    Traveling to Vietnam : American peace activists and the war / Mary Hershberger. — 1st ed.
      p. cm. — (Syracuse studies on peace and conflict resolution)
    Includes bibliographical references and index.
    ISBN 0-8156-0517-X (cloth : alk. paper)
    1. Vietnamese Conflict, 1961–1975—Protest movements—United States.   2. Pacifists—United States.   3. Vietnam (Democratic Republic)—Description and travel.   I. Title.   II. Series.
DS559.62.U6H47   1998
959.704'3—DC21   98-10651

Manufactured in the United States of America

To Dave

Mary Hershberger teaches at Capital University in Columbus, Ohio.

Contents

Illustrations

Acknowledgments

This work owes much to the writings and recollections of individuals who traveled to Vietnam during a time when such travel was unpopular. I wish especially to thank Joseph Elder for papers that he generously provided and Staughton Lynd for thoughtful comments about his experiences in Vietnam. I am grateful for Elizabeth Boardman's vivid recollections of her sea trip to Hanoi. Warm thanks also to inveterate activist David Dellinger, who, at the age of eighty-one, traveled to my hometown of Columbus to lend his inspiring presence to local efforts to refocus Columbus Day celebrations and took time to talk about earlier travels to Vietnam. Thanks to Mary Clarke for her readiness to answer questions about the first of these many trips to Vietnam, and to Doug Hostetter and Joy Carol for additional information.

At the Swarthmore College Peace Collection archivists Wendy Chmielewski, Kate Myer, and Barbara Addison provided help with numerous document collections, and Wilma Mosholder guided me through the Fellowship of Reconciliation papers. At the archives of the American Friends Service Committee in Philadelphia, Jack Sutters and Joan Lowe proved invaluable in locating relevant materials. The LBJ Foundation provided a grant for research at the Lyndon Baines Johnson Library, where archivists Mike Parrish and Regina Greenwell were unfailingly diligent in identifying collections containing significant documents. Requests to Washington for declassification of other government documents on citizen travel to Vietnam were almost all rejected in favor of continued secrecy, a policy that stands in contrast to the openness of the travelers.

Thanks to those persons who read all or parts of the manuscript. At the University of Georgia, thanks to Bill Stueck, Bob Pratt, Jean Friedman, Bill Leary, and Numan Bartley for their thoughtful reading and challenging comments. At Syracuse University Press Cynthia Maude-Gembler, Mary Selden Evans, John Fruehwirth, and Joyce Atwood offered expert advice and patient help. Harriet Alonso also provided helpful comments and suggestions. Heartfelt thanks go to Charles Chatfield for his interest in the work, his astute observations, and his continued encouragement.

Above all, thanks to my husband, Dave Kraybill, for cheerful inspiration and thoughtful conversation. To our daughters, Jessica and Erica, thank you for your encouragement and your love.

Abbreviations

AFSC	American Friends Service Commmittee
APW	American Prisoners of War in Southeast Asia
AQAG	A Quaker Action Group
CC	*Christian Century*
CFR	Committee on Foreign Relations
CFSC	Canadian Friends Service Committee
COR	Committee of Responsibility
CORE	Congress of Racial Equality
CNVA	Committee for Non-Violent Action
CR	Congressional Record
DRV	Democratic Republic of Vietnam
FOR	Fellowship of Reconcilation
HUAC	House Committee on Un-American Activities
IPC	Indochina Peace Campaign
IVS	International Voluntary Service
JE	Papers of Joseph Elder
LBJL	Lyndon Baines Johnson Library
NLF	National Liberation Front
NSA	National Student Association

Abbreviations

NYT	*New York Times*
SANE	Committee for a Sane Nuclear Policy
SDSP	Students for a Democratic Society Papers
SNCC	Student Nonviolent Coordinating Committee
TNR	*The New Republic*
WIN	Workshop in Nonviolence
WSP	Women Strike for Peace

Introduction

This is the story of Americans who traveled to Hanoi during their nation's war in Southeast Asia. There were over two hundred of them in all, usually traveling in small groups of three or four at a time and averaging, by 1969, about one group a month. Some groups were made up of a collection of individuals going on their own; others involved delegates from specific organizations or a coalition of organizations. There are detailed reports on some of the trips; for many others there are few available documents. Many individuals did not keep records of their journeys; others wrote detailed reports that were published in the antiwar press at the time or placed in the files of their sponsoring organization. Because the travels were not coordinated, records were scattered through the papers of many organizations, some of which no longer exist.

The travelers were not easy to catagorize because they came from diverse backgrounds and institutions. Still, there are a number of characteristics that these individuals shared. One was a belief in the efficacy of individual effort in bringing about large-scale reform. Hence, many of these travelers were affiliated with organizations within the long American reform tradition: peace reform, racial reform, the women's movement. The first travelers to Hanoi, for example, came from Women Strike for Peace, an organization devoted to ending the threat of nuclear war. Two other groups that sponsored a number of trips to Vietnam were the American Friends Service Committee and the Fellowship of Reconciliation, well-established organizations long attuned to national and international issues. Many of the travelers were also affiliated with churches or synagogues throughout the nation. They were highly intergenerational, ranging in age from early twenties to early eighties, though most were middle-aged and came from professional occupations. Almost all of them were, long before this war crept into their consciousness, concerned with issues of international conflict, particularly those involving nuclear weapons testing, Cold War enmities, and the scores of newly independent nations in the wake of the breakup of the traditional colonial order. Before going to Vietnam, many of them immersed themselves in the available literature on Southeast Asia's past, so they were generally more informed about Vietnam's history than was the average antiwar activist.[1]

Many of those who went to North Vietnam had been keenly disappointed by the quick resumption of international hostilities after the burdens of World War II. The nuclear arms race poured radioactive wastes into the earth's atmosphere, and Cold War interests overrode the Third World's quest for genuine independence and economic development. Because of these global realities, activists had formed organizations to end the arms race and foster diplomacy between national enemies. Disturbed by colonialism and its continuation across the century, they sympathized with the struggles of the anticolonialists. When American bombs began to rain on Vietnam, it appeared to many activists as more of a conflict rooted in the legacy of colonized and colonizer than a necessary fight against communism.

Many of the travelers were active in domestic social issues as well as international ones. A number of them were seasoned civil rights activists, participating in national or local organizing to end discrimination and segregation. Activism in the civil rights movement provided experiences with opposition and harassment that left them more willing to challenge conventional wisdom on other official policies, such as the war in Vietnam itself. Indeed, Frances Herring of Women Strike for Peace articulated a widely held perception among activists when she referred to "the

1. In 1965, most Americans knew practically nothing about Vietnam. This was true for the mass public, which generally knew little about nonwestern regions. It was true of the diplomatic corps because the reflexive anticommunism of the Cold War had purged the State Department of officials who were knowledgeable about Asian affairs and had replaced them with officials whose primary credential was their anticommunism. Had the State Department wished to bring in people knowledgeable about Vietnam, it would have been hard pressed to find them. In 1970, after two decades of American military commitment to Vietnam, there was not a single scholar in the United States who focused on current affairs in North Vietnam. There was no full professor specializing in Vietnamese studies at any American university. Only six schools offered instruction in the Vietnamese language and they collectively enrolled fewer than thirty students.

interrelated problem of civil rights and liberties in this country and the right of all peoples to self determination" (Herring 1965, SCPC). Black civil rights figures faced a dilemma that their white counterparts seldom encountered; the Johnson administration put heavy pressure on them to keep silent on Vietnam in return for official support for civil rights legislation at home. Almost all of the travelers, then, were white.

From the beginning, most of the travelers to Hanoi shared some level of opposition to America's involvement in the war. Some of them opposed it on moral grounds, seeing the war itself as rooted in western imperialism. Some opposed it on humanitarian grounds, objecting to its cost in lives and the environment; some opposed it for reasons of history and international law, viewing the American war in Vietnam as violating the Geneva Accords signed in 1954. Some were disturbed that, as the war progressed, the United States became ever more isolated in world opinion. They believed that waning support for the war from America's closest allies should have counted for something in Washington.

Those who traveled to Hanoi were consistently open about their travel. They made concerted efforts through the national media to publicize their journeys, presenting their travel itineraries, inviting interviews with the White House, and offering information they had gleaned in conversations in Hanoi. Washington officials seldom granted them interviews. When travelers urged national newspapers and periodicals to cover their travels, report on their findings, and take their information seriously, the media responded with suspicion, preferring its conventional news sources from administration officials. The travelers' own local newspapers usually were more willing to interview them and print straightforward accounts of their travels throughout North Vietnam than was the national media. The detailed reports that some travelers wrote of their visits to the countryside of North Vietnam and of their conversations with Vietnamese officials were published primarily in the antiwar media and disseminated through the countless public meetings they held upon their return.

Many of the travelers to Vietnam came from professions that prided themselves on taking a "balanced view" that identified at least two perspectives and dispassionately weighed the pros and cons of each. In the face of the carnage that the United States was inflicting on Vietnam, many of the Americans who went there came to believe that Vietnam belonged to a lopsided category like concentration camps, genocide, and the Inquisition. The bombing of Vietnam left the United States, they thought, with little claim to moral superiority over anyone. No other country had ever exploded so many bombs on another—there was no military equivalence between the two countries. When he was in Vietnam, the Fellowship of Reconciliation's A. J. Muste wrote:

> We do not simply equate any case of resort to violence with any other. We have an obligation, as do others, to analyze specific situations as best we can and to make political judgments. We do not equate the violence employed in final desperation by people who have been subjugated, exploited and oppressed by great and heavily armed nations and whose nonviolent efforts to achieve change are brutally suppressed, with the violence used against them by their oppressors or by foreign powers which intervene in their domestic affairs. (Muste 1966, 5)

Washington officials tried to block travel to North Vietnam while searching for some conspiracy behind it. The White House wanted to prove that the visits to Hanoi were directed by the Soviet Union and sent the Central Intelligence Agency on a fruitless quest for such evidence. At the same time, the Justice Department seized passports of returned travelers, threatened them with imprisonment and fines, and sought to prohibit future journeys both through legislation and by refusing to issue passports to prospective travelers. The ensuing legal tangle left many of the travelers confined within their nation's borders and, for a time, cut off nearly all the journeys. Ultimately, however, the nation's courts sided with the travelers, and they won the right to travel.

Officials in Hanoi did little either to encourage or to increase the visits. They took the travelers seriously, however, and granted them wide latitude in visiting rural areas or towns under active bombardment if their requests were persistent. Government officials appeared most concerned that Americans not be harmed or fall ill while in their country, so they insisted that a doctor accompany the group if older people were along or if the group traveled in an area subject to bombing. Not infrequently, Premier Pham Van Dong or President Ho Chi Minh would ask the visitors to convey some message to Presidents Johnson or Nixon, messages that invariably reiterated North Vietnam's public position on the issues surrounding the American military presence in Vietnam.

From the beginning, activists frequently discussed with Hanoi officials America's antiwar movement. They stated forcefully in many of their meetings that Hanoi would be badly mistaken to rely on the antiwar movement to end the war. They consistently presented that movement to the North Vietnamese officials as relatively small and no match for the overwhelming firepower of the American military in Vietnam. Officials in Hanoi agreed with that assessment—they were avid connoisseurs of the American media and could repeat verbatim Richard Nixon's vow not to be the first American president to lose a war. Americans would never turn against a war that they were winning on the battlefield, they believed, but they were clearly gratified that some Americans, early in the war, were not against them. Indeed, as the war ground on, they believed that it was the United States government, not their own, that became more and more isolated in world opinion. There were many other visitors to Hanoi from countries traditionally allied with the United States—Canada, England, France, the Netherlands, West Germany—who went to see the war firsthand. Vietnamese officials saw those visitors, along with the Americans, as representative of broadening international support.

Vietnamese civilians occasionally appeared hostile, but they generally treated the American visitors with hospitality. In heavily bombed areas, villagers were often eager to tell their stories; repeating their experiences under the bombardments, recounting their losses, saying the names of the dead to these visitors from the same country that had sent the bombs appeared to be, for some, a healing ritual. It was also in these moments that American visitors experienced their own deepest emotions. After his trip to North Vietnam, political scientist Richard Falk wrote in a letter to the *New York Times* on 9 September 1972:

> as any visitor to North Vietnam will confirm, the experience is a compelling one in human terms. To turn aside in silence from such desolation would require the most callous and self-interested state of mind. Americans in Hanoi have almost all felt shame over what their country has done and a strong patriotic impulse, in the best sense, to convey an impression to the people and leaders of Vietnam that we, as a nation, do not stand behind our Government's war policies.

The response of the American public to these travels was mixed. In the many meetings across the United States that returned travelers held, reaction ranged from sympathetic to hostile. For example, contributions to cover the costs of the travels often came from local citizens who attended the returnees' meetings. On the other hand, scheduled gatherings for returned travelers were sometimes canceled because of hostile community reaction. Most of the travelers received vitriolic letters and phone calls denouncing them as communists and traitors after accounts of their travels were published in local papers. Reprisals ranged from minor to consequential. When Elizabeth Boardman returned from a sea voyage that carried medicines and pharmaceuticals to Hanoi, her local auto mechanic refused to work on the family car. Yale University denied tenure to historian Staughton Lynd after his trip to Hanoi, and five other universities then refused to hire him, effectively ending his teaching career. Many of the early travelers found themselves engaged in lengthy and costly legal efforts to recover their passports. Over time, however, traveling to Hanoi became "mainstream," and by 1971, scientists, professionals, and academics traveled to Hanoi with few repercussions.

Whenever people would find out that I was researching the story of American activists who traveled to Vietnam during the war there, the response would invariably involve a comment about Jane Fonda. It may come as some surprise, then, that there is very little about Fonda in this study. The popular perception of Jane Fonda's two visits to Hanoi is at some variance with those events themselves, a not unusual phenomenon in historical memory. Fonda went to Hanoi late in the war in July 1972, more than seven years after American groups began to travel to North Vietnam, just as the last American combat units were being withdrawn from Vietnam, and only six months before the Paris Agreement of January 1973. In North Vietnam, Fonda filmed the effects of American bombing of the dikes along the Red River, which was then raising international concerns about consequent massive flooding, disease, and death. Some politicians, particularly a few who were facing tough reelection bids, criticized her, but the trip did not attract unusual negative attention at the time. Indeed, Secretary of State Henry Kissinger even invited her to meet with him at the White House when she returned, an invitation she declined. In 1974 Fonda returned to North Vietnam with a film crew. After her two visits there, she produced a film about the effects of the war on everyday life in Vietnam, which she called *Introduction to the Enemy*. Film critic Nora Sayre called the film, which focused on the personal rather than the political side of the war in Vietnam, "quiet, modest . . . pensive and moving" with a "mood of restrained optimism."

Although it was unknown to many of them at the time, the travelers to Vietnam were heirs to a long, still-seldom-heralded tradition of American travel to "enemy" territory during times of crisis. Beginning with antislavery activist John Woolman's perilous journey to Indian towns on the Wyalusing River in 1763, during settler wars against those towns, there came a stream of citizen-based efforts to rise above national interests that

took the nation to war, and to make serious efforts to engage the perceived enemy in peaceful resolutions. In 1799, in response to Philadelphia farmer George Logan's successful peacemaking journey to France
during the hysteria over the XYZ affair, the new United States government banned these citizen-based efforts at diplomacy. In the twentieth
century, during the early Cold War, Washington began withdrawing passports, or refusing to issue them, as a means of controlling citizen travel to
areas it declared held national "enemies." It was little wonder that, in addition to involving themselves in matters of this particular war, the first
American travelers to Vietnam soon found themselves embroiled in legal
suits to recover their passports and to gain the right to travel, a right that
they eventually won for all Americans.

In addition to addressing this legal issue, the travelers brought to the
early antiwar movement a focus that endured: a call for an end to the
American bombing of Vietnam and a withdrawal of American forces from
that country. They developed personal relationships with Vietnamese officials that resulted in regular, reliable letter and package delivery between
the American prisoners of war in North Vietnam and their families in the
United States. They repeatedly pressed the North Vietnamese government to release some American prisoners of war, eventually bringing
home twelve of them. At the same time, they succeeded in delivering
modest amounts of medical and pharmaceutical materials to the North
Vietnamese. After the war was over, they continued to maintain an American humanitarian presence in Vietnam, assist in wartime reconstruction,
and work for normalized relations between the two nations.

In seeking out communication with the other side, these activists
helped identify key officials with whom Washington could have held fruit-
ful discussions. In his study of the negotiating strategies of Washington
and Hanoi during the Johnson administration, Wallace Thies concluded
that Washington remained "by and large ignorant of who was really in
control of DRV policy toward the war in the South" (1980, 403). Thies
noted that the North Vietnamese official most interested in arranging a
negotiated settlement of the war was Premier Pham Van Dong, though
Washington officials seemed not to know this and paid him scant attention. Pham Van Dong was the official who consistently met with American travelers in Hanoi. His repeated messages to them were messages that
he hoped Washington would hear and answer. They became the center
point of the negotiations that finally ended the war after years of bombing
and millions of deaths. Washington had, from 1965 on, if it had paid at-

tention, a direct channel to Hanoi through these Americans who went there and listened.

The first three chapters of the book cover journeys to Hanoi from 1965 to the end of 1967, a period in which almost all of the travelers' objectives were to bring back eyewitness information about the war's effects and foster a diplomatic solution to the war. Most of these groups went to North Vietnam, but when some groups feared that Washington's harassment made it too difficult or dangerous to go there, they went to Saigon instead. Some of those trips, especially the ones that resulted in extended contacts with opposition figures in the south, are discussed as well. The first groups to go to Vietnam came away from that experience and their reading in Vietnam's history with the belief that a negotiated settlement of the war could only take place after the United States ended the bombing of North Vietnam and agreed to withdraw its troops. It was a message that they emphasized in their media reports and in the numerous public meetings they held upon their return. It was a new perspective for many developing antiwar activists, who believed, in 1965, that a cease-fire and negotiations could and should get underway with American troops remaining in South Vietnam for the indefinite future. Over time, the travelers' two basic points became the rallying cry of the growing antiwar movement, and eventually their own government did end the bombing of North Vietnam and withdraw its troops.

In the meantime, as the war escalated, some of the travelers turned to organizing humanitarian aid for the North Vietnamese. These efforts are discussed in the fourth chapter. Various groups brought in medicines and pharmaceuticals to North Vietnam's hospitals and clinics, but the American Friends Service Committee, already known for its efforts to administer to all sides impartially during wars, developed the most enduring relationship with the medical establishment in North Vietnam, arranging donations of medical equipment, penicillin, and other medicines. After the war's end, other Americans, many of them previous travelers to Hanoi, raised funds to rebuild structures destroyed in the bombing, including the Bach Mai Hospital.

The fifth and sixth chapters deal primarily with efforts to help American prisoners of war in Hanoi. From the beginning, many of the travelers requested meetings with the POWs, almost all of whom were downed while on bombing missions over the country. The activists urged Hanoi to release at least some of the prisoners early, and eventually twelve were released. Washington's cool response to Hanoi's gesture appeared designed to discourage other releases. Indeed, American officials seemed to use the occasion of each release as a means of deepening mistrust between the two nations. Washington also did little to facilitate mail service between the prisoners and their families in the United States, and, in response to family requests, a group of travelers organized a committee to move mail quickly and reliably between families and the prisoners in Hanoi. Although Washington discouraged this effort as well, the travelers persisted and were able to secure an official list of American war prisoners from Hanoi and to compile their own list based on the letters that flowed through their mail service.

The last chapter carries these activities up to the war's end and beyond. By presenting a face of America that countered their government's military image in Vietnam, the activists offered an alternative model to that of international violence. Their persistence in bringing back eyewitness reports of the bombing, their attention to the Vietnamese perspective, their diligent efforts to provide humanitarian aid, and their intercession for war prisoners and their mail service for them and their families, helped lay the groundwork for an eventual reconciliation between the two countries. When the war was over at last in Vietnam, this alternative image of Americans endured, fostering a new relationship between the two countries in which some American veterans joined the activists in working to rebuild a small part, at least, of what their country had once destroyed.

Traveling to Vietnam

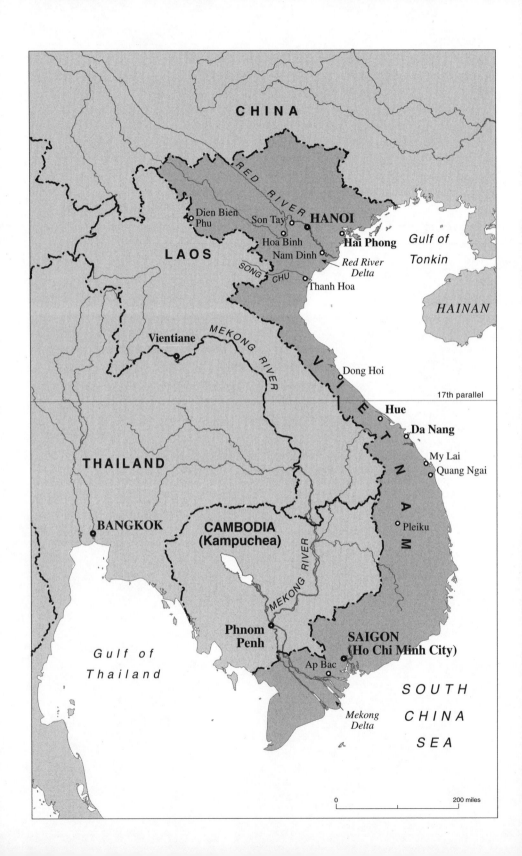

CHINA

RED RIVER

Dien Bien
Phu

Son Tay

HANOI

LAOS

Hoa Binh

Hai Phong

Gulf of
Tonkin

Nam Dinh

Red River
Delta

SONG

CHU

Thanh Hoa

HAINAN

Vientiane

MEKONG RIVER

Dong Hoi

17th parallel

Hue

Da Nang

V
I
E
T
N
A
M

My Lai

Quang Ngai

THAILAND

Pleiku

BANGKOK

CAMBODIA
(Kampuchea)

MEKONG RIVER

Phnom
Penh

SAIGON
(Ho Chi Minh City)

Gulf of
Thailand

Ap Bac

SOUTH

CHINA

SEA

Mekong
Delta

0

200 miles

The First Travelers in Hanoi

A mericans who first reached out to Vietnamese officials on "the other side" did so before a national movement against the war in Vietnam coalesced in the United States. They came from Women Strike for Peace (WSP), a group born in late 1961 when fifty thousand women in sixty communities across the nation walked off their jobs and out of their kitchens for a one day "strike" against testing nuclear weapons in the earth's atmosphere. WSP attacked nuclear testing for contaminating the milk supply upon which the nation's children depended. Jerome Weisner, science advisor to President Kennedy, said that WSP was more influential than the arms "experts" as the president negotiated the Limited Test Ban Treaty of 1963 (Hamilton 1970). As public pressure rose in support of a ban on atmospheric testing, WSP members looked beyond the arms race to the doctrine of containment that nourished it, and they set out to put a human face on the enemy. Women Strike for Peace was not a tightly structured organization, and members were free to pursue their own specific projects within the larger goal of ending the nuclear threat and fostering dialogue between nations. To that end, some of them visited the Soviet embassy in Washington, D.C., where they developed cordial personal relationships with Nedezhda Khimatch, the Cultural Attaché for Women there. In turn, she invited them to participate in international peace conferences in Moscow.

Traveling to Moscow and calling for peace in the frost of the Cold War marked Women Strike for Peace as heretics to the anticommunist creed. The Federal Bureau of Investigation charged that WSP was "infiltrated" by communists. In late 1962, the House Committee on Un-American Activities (HUAC) summoned WSP and demanded the name of anyone in their organization who had ever been a member of the Communist party in the United States. WSP refused to buckle before HUAC; the group did not root out anyone because of ideological labels, members told the Committee. Anyone who was concerned with peace and willing to work peaceably for it, was welcome to join—even communists. "Unless everybody in the whole world joins us in this fight, then God help us," WSP member Dagmar Wilson told HUAC (McGrory 1962). Historian Charles DeBenedetti (1980, 178) concluded that the position WSP adopted at the hearings "did not end the Congress's preference for treating private peace actions as subversive. But it did help break the petrified anti-Communism of Cold War American politics and gave heart to those reformers who conceived peace as more than military preparedness."[1]

In February 1965, President Johnson announced Operation Rolling Thunder, a massive bombing campaign aimed at North Vietnam. In April, the first American ground troops were dispatched to South Vietnam. The escalating American war in Vietnam, especially the heavy bombing of the North, grabbed the attention of some Americans, many of whom were barely aware of Vietnam's existence. There was some very early opposition to growing American military actions in Southeast Asia, the most dramatic of which came just days after the president's announcement of the bombing campaign. Helga Alice Herz, a seventy-nine-year-old German immigrant who had spent several years in detention in wartime Germany, set herself afire on a street corner in Detroit in protest of the American bombing in Vietnam. Herz was a founding member of the Detroit Women Strike for Peace and a long-time member of the Women's International League for Peace and Freedom (WILPF). "I am not doing this out of despair," Herz wrote in her last note, "but out of hope for mankind." She called on Americans to take action to end the war before it was too late: "Yours is the responsibility to decide if this world shall be a good place to live for all human beings or if it should blow itself up to oblivion" (Swerdlow 1993, 130).

Self-immolation horrified American activists, but it was a traditional form of resistance among Buddhists, and when Herz chose this form of protest, it touched the Vietnamese deeply. North Vietnam's newspapers carried accounts of her action, noting both of her antiwar affiliations as

---

1. Eric Bentley concluded that "in the 1960s a new generation came to life. As far as HUAC is concerned, it began with Women Strike for Peace" (1971, 951).

they were reported in the American media. Herz's fiery death lent a face
and a name to the prior presumption in Vietnam that some Americans
might be on their side. A North Vietnamese newspaper, the *Vietnam
Courier*, published a supplement on 18 March devoted to Herz and
reprinted the note she left behind in which she protested President Johnson's "use of his high office in trying to wipe out smaller nations." Herz's
action, the paper said, demonstrated that Americans themselves could see
that this war was "a blemish on the American people's reputation." The
same paper carried a message to Herz's family and published an open letter from the Vietnam Women's Union to American women saying that
Vietnamese women were deeply moved by her act, which had called international attention to the war that "stains the honour and tradition of the
freedom and equality-loving American people."

In May, several months after Herz's death, two Women Strike for
Peace activists, Mary Clarke and Lorraine Gordon, went to Moscow for
commemorations of the twentieth anniversary of the end of World War
II. There they asked to meet with representatives from North Vietnam
and the National Liberation Front (NLF) and, on the spot, proposed to
them a future meeting between American women and Vietnamese
women. That Herz had belonged to the same organization that these
women came from prompted a warm response from the Vietnamese, who
invited the two activists to Hanoi to meet with the North Vietnamese
Women's Union. There they could plan a larger, official meeting between
women from Vietnam and the United States.[2] Clarke and Gordon flew
directly from Moscow to China and on to Hanoi. On their first attempt
to fly to Hanoi from China, the pilot was forced to turn back at the border because American bombers were in the air corridor to Hanoi. After a
second night in Beijing, the plane flew safely on to Hanoi, and the first
citizen-initiated contacts with the North Vietnamese were underway.

Clarke and Gordon spent three days in and around Hanoi. They were
startled by the burgeoning construction of air raid shelters there; streets
everywhere were lined with cylindrical one-person bomb shelters set in
the ground at ten-foot intervals. Made of concrete with two-inch thick
lids left slightly ajar for quick occupancy, the shelters could be used in-

---

2. North Vietnam had a strong Women's Union, and the vitality of the NLF as a mass-
based rural movement stemmed in part from the large number of women participating at all
levels. See Wiegersma 1988.

stantly by pedestrians during air raids. American planes were already blanketing areas south of Hanoi with bombs, and the Vietnamese were preparing for the bombing to move over Hanoi itself.

Vietnamese officials told Clarke and Gordon that the meeting with WSP representatives should not be in Hanoi. They expressed two concerns, one for the Americans' physical safety during the bombing, and the other over Washington's reaction should it learn of the presence of Americans in Hanoi. This latter concern was so great that they provided lodging for Clarke and Gordon in private homes rather than in the international hotel where foreign guests and journalists stayed. Nor did Clarke and Gordon, at first, want this visit publicized, because it was not an official WSP trip: it had come entirely at their personal initiative in Moscow, and they hesitated to publicly involve WSP in a meeting that the organization had not planned. In addition, their passports carried the warning that they were not valid for travel to North Vietnam. In discussing a future meeting between American and Vietnamese women, they left the meeting site up the Women's Union in Vietnam. Hanoi had far fewer air links to areas around the world than did New York or Los Angeles. "It was relatively easy for us Americans to go anywhere in the world to meet with them," Clarke said in an interview on 3 March 1995. "But it was more difficult for them, so we wanted them to suggest a location that they found convenient." Vietnamese Prime Minister Pham Van Dong proposed Jakarta as a possible site. He would contact the Indonesian government if they agreed, he told the Americans, and perhaps they could arrange a meeting there.

Before they left Hanoi, Clarke and Gordon visited a hospital in Hanoi where they saw patients, including children, who had been napalmed by American planes. Some of the patients had been wounded by cluster bombs. Standing there before the hospital beds, silently watching the bandaged and scarred war victims, Clarke said she suddenly imagined this tragedy happening to her family. In that case, she would hope that someone would do something about it. Working in the antiwar movement was, she believed, something that she could do about it. It was a scene and a response that repeated itself over the coming years as more and more Americans came to Hanoi.

When Clarke and Gordon returned to the United States from Hanoi, their hesitation about publicizing the trip was confirmed to some extent. Some WSP members objected, at first, to a meeting with Vietnamese representatives because it made their antinuclear activities and contacts with

Soviet officials look almost conventional by contrast. It went far, perhaps too far, some felt, beyond the heretofore daring travel to Moscow. The image of American citizens traveling to Vietnam, a country against whom American troops were actively deployed, called up a mixture of cultural and political taboos that included treason. In the immediate sense, however, the fact that the planned meeting was to be held outside Vietnam, in Indonesia, muted these early concerns about meeting directly with this "enemy," and, as members of WSP learned more about Vietnam and the Vietnamese through their travels and their readings, concerns about the political safety of these encounters lessened.

Vietnamese misgivings about contacts with Americans in Hanoi lessened as well. Apart from concerns over safety issues, Vietnamese officials soon openly welcomed Americans in Hanoi, for a number of reasons. To begin with, Washington ignored the first visits and, by the time the administration did take note and object, the contacts were sufficiently established to endure political repercussions. In addition, Vietnamese political rhetoric already drew a distinction between American citizens and their government, and even hinted at potential solidarity between the citizens of both countries. In a letter to the American publication *Minority of One* in June 1964, for example, Ho Chi Minh wrote that his early travels in America had left him with a positive perception of the American people that shaped his response to this war:

> The Vietnamese people are well aware that the American people want to live in peace and friendship with all other nations. I have been to the United States, and I understand that the American people are a talented people who are strongly attached to justice. The Vietnamese people never confuse the justice-loving U.S. people and the U.S. Governments which have committed numerous crimes against them in the past ten years. Those very saboteurs of our nation's independence and freedom are also the people who have betrayed the Declaration of Independence of the United States.

Throughout the war, Vietnamese government officials and intellectuals reiterated this distinction between American citizens and their government. It was Johnson and then Nixon, they insisted, who kept the war going. Vietnamese periodicals frequently characterized the war as a stain on America's own ideals, a depiction that subtly placed the best in American history on the side of Vietnam. Public spaces in Hanoi that commemorated the long struggle against foreign rule linked Vietnam's revolt

against colonialism to America's own struggle for independence. Vietnamese officials pointedly held up the American Declaration of Independence as the inspiration for their own similar document. For example,
behind a large bust of Ho Chi Minh in the Revolutionary Museum in
Hanoi, inscribed in gold on a red background, was the Vietnamese Declaration of Independence. It began with a phrase taken from the American
declaration: "We believe this to be true, that all men are naturally free,
and they have the right to life, liberty, and happiness." Moreover, public
figures and the media in Vietnam often depicted this latest war as the last
phase of Vietnam's fight against colonialism rather than as a new war alto-
gether. In this light, the United States invasion was less a unique threat
than simply the latest one in a long period of nationalist struggle.

The *Vietnam Courier,* a biweekly English-language publication devoted entirely to coverage of the war, began publishing in Hanoi in April
1964. It carried reports of bombing strikes and chemical warfare and
photos of captured American pilots, and it relied heavily on Western
sources: Reuters, United Press International, *Newsweek, Time,* and the
New York Times. These sources provided Vietnamese officials with insight
to official American thinking, including the extent to which some Americans thought the United States should go in order to win. American visitors to Hanoi were often surprised at Vietnamese knowledge about
American opinion about the war. Nguyen Duc Thua, the assistant director of the Polytechnic University in Hanoi, once repeated to Joseph
Elder, a visiting sociology professor from Madison, Wisconsin, General
Curtis LeMay's recommendation for bombing Vietnam back to the Stone
Age. Despite the massive bombing, Thua told Elder as they surveyed
the university grounds, they could both see that "this isn't the Stone
Age" (Elder 1969c).

Christians in North Vietnam sometimes explained the war using images and stories from the Bible, a text that Americans knew well. One
American visitor noticed that, whereas the Vietnamese public generally
talked about the United States in terms of "aggression," the Christians
there used the language and stories of their faith—they referred to the
United States as "Satan." During an impassioned exegesis on the Massacre of the Innocents one Christmas evening in 1967, a pastor in a small
North Vietnamese village told his American guest, an Episcopal minister,
that "nobody can keep us Evangelicals from comparing Lyndon Johnson
to King Herod" (Brown 1968, 20).

After Mary Clarke and Lorraine Gordon returned from Hanoi in

May 1965, Women Strike for Peace quickly organized a ten-person delegation for Jakarta. The delegates prepared for their journey by reading what they could find of the then-limited material on Vietnam in the United States, conferring with Congressman George Brown of California and Senator Ernest Gruening of Alaska, and raising money for their travel expenses. They distributed press releases about their upcoming visit, hoping to draw maximum public attention to the issues of the war. The women in the delegation were Clarke; Esther Jackson, a black civil rights activist in Los Angeles who had attended Lyndon Johnson's inaugural ball that January; Phyllis Schmidt from Southern California; Aline Berman, former news editor of the Voice of America; Bernice Steele, social worker and WSP liaison to the United Nations; Margaret Russell, chair of the Washington Area Council of the United Nations; Shirley Lens, political activist from Chicago; Frances Herring, from the Institute of Government Studies at Berkeley; Nanci Gitlin, a Students for a Democratic Society (SDS) activist at Ann Arbor; and Beverley Axelrod, attorney and civil rights activist from San Francisco. Reporters pressed HUAC for its reaction to the upcoming trip, and at first it professed no interest in the visit. "There are thousands of things like this going on all the time," the committee's staff director, Francis McNamara, said, "and we don't have time to look into all of them." But he insisted, without specifying why, that the women's mission was "obviously injurious" to the United States and possibly violated the Logan Act. Then he raised the ultimate alarm used to discredit peace initiatives. "In many cases their position parallels the Communist line," he told reporters (U.S. Women 1965, SCPC).[3]

On 12 July 1965, the WSP delegation arrived in Jakarta for talks with nine women from the Vietnam Women's Union and the National Liberation Front. With the help of three interpreters, the group held eight-hour sessions for five days. The WSP delegates made it clear from the beginning that they did not represent typical American opinion and emphasized that American support for their nation's foreign policy was generally strong. But they characterized support for the war as generally passive

3. McNamara's response was, by 1965, a time-honored one. Lieberman (1992) shows how many Americans were suspicious of any position that coincided with that of the American communists: opposition to nuclear testing and civil defense drills, American involvement in Southeast Asia, a commitment to civil rights—all causes that warranted public discussions and appealed to many people in their own right. The State Department vigorously used its power to deny visas and passports to those involved in international peace conferences.

rather than actively supportive because they believed that "most Americans are unclear as to the origin and purposes of the war." They predicted that exposure to the reality of the war in Vietnam would, in time, lessen support for it. The Vietnamese were interested in the broad attitudes of Americans toward their nation's war in Vietnam, but they were also fascinated by something else: the Civil Rights movement in the United States. They plied their American visitors with questions about the nature of equality in their country and about the mass mobilization tactics that characterized the ongoing struggle for equal rights in the United States.

Meeting with "the enemy" and hearing from them what the partition of their country and the war on their soil meant for their personal and professional lives was profoundly moving for the Americans. The National Liberation Front cadres provided vivid descriptions of American bombing raids on villages, "search and destroy" missions, forests and fields defoliated by American herbicides, and the deliberate creation of refugees through the pacification program. In Jakarta, the abstract arguments from Washington that appealed to a "domino theory," or to the necessity of honoring agreements made with allies to combat communism, gave way to a depiction of the brutality that those abstractions wrought in everyday life.

Some of the Vietnamese delegates that the Americans met in Jakarta became long-term contacts. One of them, Vo Thi The, was subsequently arrested and imprisoned in Saigon, and WSP members began an international campaign on her behalf, sending letters to the Saigon government and bombarding the American embassy with requests for her safety and release until she was eventually freed. Another representative, Nguyen Thi Dinh, was unknown to the international community at the time, but she became the NLF's foreign minister and then its delegate to the Paris Peace Talks.

In Jakarta, the Americans saw scant evidence of the political ideology that Washington officials insisted characterized resistance to American power in Vietnam. The Vietnamese appealed to history. The path to peace, they emphasized, lay in the same agreement that they had wrested from the French in 1954. Vietnam's colonial history had to be reversed. The Vietnamese appeal to their history, a history undeniably laced with the burdens of colonialism, lent their arguments a credibility among Western audiences that an ideological appeal could not have matched. The bitterness of the Western betrayal of the Geneva Accords and a determination never again to sign a peace agreement that left foreign troops on

Vietnamese soil were starkly evident throughout the talks in Jakarta. Peace could only come to Vietnam when the bombing ended and foreign troops left. These two conditions, an end to the bombing in the North and withdrawal of foreign troops throughout the country, introduced a theme that Americans in Hanoi would repeatedly hear during the coming years. These principles had first been articulated in the Geneva Accords in 1954, and the Vietnamese viewed them as summing up precisely the requirements for an end to colonial habits (Memorandum on an Informal Meeting 1965, SCPC).

At their final meeting in Jakarta, all the delegates signed an agreement concluding that "the implementation of the Geneva Accords constitutes the only honorable solution to terminating hostilities in Vietnam." As the newspaper *La Wisp* reported in August 1965, the Americans returned from Jakarta bringing with them two focused demands: the United States must cease bombing North Vietnam and must withdraw all its troops from the region. These demands from Jakarta came to provide a rallying point for disparate elements of the antiwar movement as it grew over the coming years. At the time of the Jakarta meeting, there were other calls from the emerging antiwar movement. The Committee for a Sane Nuclear Policy (SANE), for example, took the position that American troops should stay in place in Vietnam until a negotiated settlement was worked out, which would have produced a negotiating situation much like the process that had, in 1954, led to the failed Geneva Accords. Imbedded in SANE's position was the implication that both sides were equally "aggressive." Increasingly, the antiwar movement came to see the two sides as most unequal. Hanoi was not bombing the United States, there were no Vietnamese soldiers on American soil, and Vietnam was one country—the United States was the invader. The Vietnamese at Jakarta insisted that the lesson of the Geneva Accords was that negotiations could produce nothing new until the United States was willing to end the bombing and withdraw its troops. The call for an end to the bombing and American troop withdrawal became a focused demand for all sectors of the antiwar movement, both domestic and international, because it made eminent sense to those who viewed the conflict as a case of late colonialism and of misplaced global politics, two points on which the antiwar movement, diverse as it was, could agree.

Before the Jakarta meeting, WSP opposed the war in Vietnam on the grounds that its tactics were destructive and inhuman. The meeting with the Vietnamese set them against Washington's goals in Vietnam as well.

Visits to North Vietnam had this effect on most activists. Many of them came to Hanoi already opposed to the tactics of bombing and the pacification program in the South. Journeying to Vietnam itself convinced them that Washington's larger goals were out of joint, that Vietnam's struggle was rooted in the historical condition of colonization and that it posed no danger to the world, only to the colonizers who resisted full independence for colonized areas. If the Cold War was to be waged in a poor country struggling to build a nation out of the imperial delineations of the nineteenth century, then, for the travelers to Hanoi, the whole basis of the Cold War was suspect. Strip away the anticommunist rhetoric, they believed, and reveal the colonial roots of the war, and other Americans would join them in opposing Washington's military pursuit of a divided Vietnam with an American-maintained government in the South. Traveling to Hanoi and meeting with Vietnamese in other parts of the world provided WSP members with the information they needed to challenge the formal and informal ban on contacts with Vietnamese officials. Examining the issues of the war and surveying the landscape in North Vietnam for themselves eroded what little credibility they found in Washington's pronouncements about the character of the war and the character of the Vietnamese.

"The outreach of this Djakarta trip is greater than from any previous project of Women Strike for Peace," Frances Herring wrote (1965, SCPC) upon her return after she herself had been "besieged" with requests for speaking engagements. The White House turned down WSP's request to meet with the president, saying that his schedule was too full. The delegates requested meetings with members of Congress, but those meetings often left them with a greater sense of foreboding than before because the representatives, who had recently voted for the Gulf of Tonkin resolution, appeared to know so little about Vietnam. "It would be hard to exaggerate the paralysis of leadership the women encountered," a disappointed Frances Herring (1965, SCPC) wrote about the representatives. "They almost to a man refrain from public opposition to Administration decisions. They seem to have abdicated their traditional exclusive right to declare war."

WSP members were never noted for their reticence, and they continued to press officials at the White House and State Department for meetings on any level to discuss the specifics of the administration's policy in Vietnam. Administration officials were not accustomed to dealing with persistent, all-female groups on issues of foreign policy and it showed.

During a meeting with Chester Cooper, an aide to National Security Advisor McGeorge Bundy, some WSP members tried to discover the White House perspective on Vietnam's colonial past. How did the president and his advisors interpret French colonialism and its impact on Vietnam? Could the White House acknowledge that the ongoing struggle there might be a continuation of Vietnam's long determination to end foreign dominance? And, if so, where did that leave America's growing commitment to the Saigon regime, itself largely composed of Catholic collaborationists in a heavily Buddhist country? Cooper told the women that these questions were not relevant; the only relevant issue was that communism was a threat in Vietnam. After the meeting, Cooper wrote WSP a letter intended to discourage further contacts, and he implied that they were women incapable of seasoned political judgment. "I spend a great deal of time with representatives of various groups," the advisor wrote, "including groups taking a much more belligerent line with respect to the war in Vietnam and the Government, but this has been the first and only occasion when I felt it pointless to proceed with any further discussion" (Cooper to Good, 1965, LBJL). It was not an unusual response to women's groups during the war. Navy officials were soon telling women married to captured pilots not to talk to the press because they "wouldn't be themselves in their present emotional state" (Keenan 1986, 95).

WSP members redoubled their efforts to encourage news coverage of the trip. They prepared press releases, held news conferences, and contacted individual members of the press. The national press dismissed the trip outright as a communist-inspired venture. On 19 July the *New York Times* carried the women's press conference under a headline that read, "10 Americans Join Vietnam Reds." WSP's appeal for a negotiated end to the war "echoed Hanoi's propaganda line," the reporter concluded. Right-wing commentators covered the trip in the same spirit. In his "Washington Report" on 27 July, nationally syndicated columnist Fulton Lewis, Jr., paired the WSP trip with the American Communist party's 1961 call to intensify "work for peace." Because WSP was a peace organization that had been investigated by HUAC, and because the Communist party called for peace, Lewis concluded that WSP must be controlled by the Communist party.

All ten members of the WSP delegation were inundated with requests to hold public meetings upon their return. They spoke at churches, women's clubs, colleges and universities, civil rights meetings, trade union meetings, town meetings, teach-ins, local demonstrations against the war, and meetings in the homes of their neighbors. Public responses to this journey anticipated the responses that travelers to Vietnam would receive over the next several years. WSP delegate Nanci Gitlin spoke to numerous and diverse audiences about the Jakarta trip, and she soon began to notice how the composition of the audience predicted its response. In New Haven, Connecticut, she spoke to a hall filled with university-affiliated intellectuals about her trip and the discussions that the WSP delegation held with the Vietnamese. She placed the Vietnamese in the context of a historical struggle with which her highly educated audience was somewhat familiar. Many of them knew of recent developments in the war, even before their meeting with Gitlin, and they responded to her positively (Gitlin 1965, SCPC).

In Cleveland, Ohio, Gitlin spent a day talking with people in a white working-class neighborhood. It was "a totally different experience," she noted. Most "did not know anything about the war," and although all were interested, "none was greatly concerned. . . . All thought the purpose of the war was to keep the Russians and Chinese from taking us over. Most also thought that one could not oppose his government without being a traitor." One women who "had to keep asking the name of the country in which we were fighting," felt sorry for the president because "he looked worried on TV." Another respondent thought Johnson was just "gutless" for not finishing off the war quickly. Still, members of her audience agreed that they did not want their family members going to Vietnam. Even while maintaining that the president should be supported and that the war was a fight against communism, they blamed Johnson for the war itself and believed President Kennedy would never have let it happen. Her audience had no historical understanding of the war, Gitlin said, and "talking about the Geneva Agreements was impossible." Compared to her meeting in New Haven, the Cleveland meeting was "very difficult" (Gitlin 1965, SCPC).

The following day, Gitlin spoke in a black working-class neighborhood in Cleveland and got a somewhat different response. Many in the audience readily declared that the United States had no business in Vietnam, but they also expressed concern that if the United States left now, "the Communists will take over." Gitlin was able to find common ground with her audience when she discussed the historical context of the war in Vietnam along with her audience's own historical experience at the hands of government policy. "The analogy between the fate of Negroes in this country and peasants in Vietnam and wars of liberation in general struck a chord with most of them," Gitlin noted (1965, SCPC).

Student responses lay somewhere between that of the New Haven intellectuals and the audiences in working-class neighborhoods, though they were closer to the latter. After a ten-day swing through Virginia and Georgia, where Gitlin spoke at a number of colleges and universities, including the University of Virginia and Emory University in Atlanta, she felt that the "whole trip was depressing because the major concern was Communism here and in Asia. I found a certain kind of amorality in people who refused to be concerned with the war and its brutality. They refused to step out of the game and could only deal with questions of how to win it. All too many thought the whole population of Vietnam should be destroyed as the only sure way to rid the world of the Vietcong" (Gitlin 1965, SCPC).

Despite a mixed reception from the public, the meeting with Vietnamese representatives in Jakarta had a profound impact on the women of WSP. In the United States, warfare was depicted as essentially men's work and men's concern. America's modern wars were fought far beyond America's own borders, in the cities and the villages of other women, not those of American women. In the twentieth century, American women were not drafted into battle, and war did not come to them. Only young males were drafted, only young males were groomed as warriors. Women were traditionally "dis-armed," and because of this were perceived as lacking the authority on matters of national force and violence that all men, by virtue of their sex, held. A barely concealed fiber of disdain for women who involved themselves in international matters of war and peace had always run through media and official responses to women's antiwar activism. The journey to Vietnam, and the shared experience in Jakarta with Vietnamese women who were themselves active participants in the political and military struggle in Vietnam, inspired Women Strike for Peace with self-confidence and a sense of legitimacy. It marked a point from which they could begin to use their own voices to oppose the war.

Women Strike for Peace contacts in North Vietnam grew out of international networks women had developed in response to twentieth century militarism. Other groups who followed them in forging links to "the other side" also had networks in place that aimed to transcend national divisions. It was, admittedly, much safer, politically and legally, to travel to Saigon during that time, and some groups chose that route. The same

month that WSP delegates went to Jakarta, the Fellowship of Reconciliation, an established international peace organization, sent a delegation to
South Vietnam to make contact with religious and government figures
there in hopes of providing some basis for a negotiated settlement of the
war. As a broad-based pacifist organization, FOR had long involved itself
in international reconciliation efforts and had nurtured national organizations devoted to peace and justice. In 1942, for example, FOR provided
the funds to organize the Congress of Racial Equality (CORE). The two
organizations sponsored the first Freedom Ride into the South in 1947,
an early effort that netted these riders arrest, imprisonment, and scant national attention.[4]

The FOR-sponsored trip to Saigon in July 1965 grew out of concern
about Lyndon Johnson's campaign of bombing North Vietnam. Operation Rolling Thunder's objectives were to end Hanoi's support of the National Liberation Front in South Vietnam and shore up falling morale in
Saigon (Tilford 1993; Thompson 1980). The administration's reasoning
in executing the bombing campaign was also based on a determination to
keep Vietnam divided, even if Saigon's leaders wanted reunification.
William Bundy, assistant secretary of state for Far Eastern Affairs, wrote a
memo to Secretary of State Dean Rusk on 6 January 1965 that without
massive bombing of the north, there was the distinct possibility of "a government of key groups starting to negotiate covertly with the Liberation
Front or Hanoi, perhaps not asking in the first instance that we get out,
but with that necessarily following at a fairly early state. In one sense this
would be a 'Vietnam solution,' with some hope that it would produce a
Communist Vietnam that would assert its own degree of independence
from Peiping and that would produce a pause in Communist pressure in
Southeast Asia" (Senate Committee 1984, 684).

Bundy argued against reunification of North and South Vietnam. If
there would be a "Vietnam solution," he confidently prophesied, it was
"virtually certain" that Laos would become "untenable," Cambodia
"would accommodate" in some way and "the Thai" would "lose confidence" in the United States (Senate Committee 1984, 684). Bundy's rec-

4. The 1947 trip was called the Journey of Reconciliation. These first freedom riders,
drawn from the ranks of internationalists and racial reformers, were arrested and imprisoned
in the South. Three of them served twenty-two days on convict road gangs. See Meier and
Rudwick 1973.

ommendation was to bomb the North to reassure the Saigon government that Washington was firmly behind a divided Vietnam.

There were obvious public relations problems inherent in carrying out such a strategy. The American public and the international community were likely to grow critical of this bald justification for a massive bombing campaign of North Vietnam. When Lyndon Johnson therefore announced Operation Rolling Thunder to the American public on 13 February 1965, he gave no indication that the bombing campaign in the North was intended to deter the Saigon government from talking to Hanoi. Instead, he framed the bombing campaign in the context of aggression from North Vietnam. It had not been easy to dredge up this story. Chester Cooper had been working for months to pull together a presentable justification for bombing the North. He wrote to Bundy late in January 1965 that "we will have a catalogue of sins and Hanoi's culpability by the end of the week, if possible. . . . D.O.D. [Department of Defense] is preparing a justification for further early strikes in the event there are not additional spectaculars in the next few days." Cooper's "catalogue" appeared as the White House's White Paper on Vietnam in mid-February (Kahin 1986, 290).

By July, the same month that WSP held its Jakarta meeting, Secretary of Defense Robert McNamara concluded that the only clear success of the four-month bombing campaign in North Vietnam had been to lift morale temporarily in South Vietnam, but, "with the failure of the situation to improve—morale in South Vietnam is not discernibly better than it was before the program began." Consequently, McNamara told President Johnson, the United States now had to keep bombing the North, despite its strategic failure there because "South Vietnam is now 'addicted' to the program; a permanent abandonment of the program would have a distinct depressing effect on the morale in South Vietnam" (Thompson 1980, 43, 73).

At the time, the American public knew nothing of this official reasoning. From Washington it heard only that the American bombing in Vietnam was a reasonable, if regrettable, response to "communist aggression." In 1965, the years of bombing that lay ahead were beyond the imagination of the administration's worst critics. But the first bombs over North Vietnam were real, and they alarmed many in the religious community. When he first heard about Operation Rolling Thunder in February 1965, Alfred Hassler, executive director of the Fellowship of

Reconciliation, drafted a statement in response. The statement, eventually signed by 2,700 ministers, rabbis, and priests, appeared as a full-page letter to the president in the *New York Times* on 4 April 1965. Its headline read: "MR. PRESIDENT, In the Name of God STOP IT!"

"We had touched a sensitive nerve," Hassler said later. Letters poured in from around the country. A few were hostile, but most writers thanked Hassler for opposing Operation Rolling Thunder and asked that their names be added to the letter. "I thought the millennium had come," wrote one advocate, "ministers daring to take a stand against war!" (Vietnam Crisis 1965, SCPC). The FOR sent the White House telegrams and letters urging negotiations to end the war and informing it of upcoming public actions. If the White House had ignored the women of WSP, it took notice of these men. When Johnson delivered a speech on Vietnam at Johns Hopkins University three days after the ad appeared, a State Department official called Hassler to ask him what he had thought about the president's speech. What Hassler thought was that it was time for FOR to go to Vietnam to get information for itself (Hassler 1970, 5).

The FOR's first trip to South Vietnam demonstrated how quickly elements of the religious "establishment" lined up in some sort of opposition to the war. The Civil Rights movement had already legitimized political protest by drawing people to domestic social activism through their churches. The early consensus by the large religious institutions on the "wrongfulness" of the war in Vietnam was noted by even the *New York Times* in a 15 February 1966 article, which concluded that, since the reaction to the war "has now involved thousands of clergymen throughout the country," who could hardly be characterized as radical, "the current clergy protest is not so much the emergence of a 'new left' within the churches as the stirrings of what may become the 'new center.'" Still, it would be a mistake to overemphasize the early differences between Washington and mainstream American religious institutions over Vietnam policy. It is generally safe to say that, in 1965 and well into 1966, most religious figures supported the broad assumptions of the Cold War, which were that containment was a good policy and that the rhetorical division of the world into "communist" and "free," backed by military firepower and war, was both accurate and represented a proper policy position. The war in Vietnam weakened this consensus on containment; when some members in the religious community questioned the tactics of the containment doctrine in Vietnam, they began to question its global assumptions as well.

The Fellowship of Reconciliation's first trip to Vietnam pulled together a group of thirteen individuals who came from Protestant, Jewish, and Catholic backgrounds, laity and clergy, women and men, many of them long-time activists on civil rights and international issues. Annalee Stewart, former president of the Women's International League for Peace and Freedom, and James Lawson, who had studied the tactics of nonviolent resistance in India and then taught it to the students of the Nashville sit-ins of 1960, joined Hassler and ten other American delegates for a journey to Saigon, Cambodia, and Thailand. Robert Browne, professor of economics at Fairleigh Dickinson University, who became an advisory editor of *Viet-Report,* accompanied the FOR group as a representative of the Inter-University Committee for Debate on Foreign Policy. Browne had been in Vietnam as a United States Operations Mission team member from 1958 to 1961, and he was the only group member who spoke Vietnamese. The other delegates were Harold Bosley, former dean of Duke University Divinity School; William Crittenden, Episcopal Bishop, vice president of the National Council of Churches and chair of the Episcopal Peace Advisory Committee; Edwin Dahlberg, former president of the American Baptist Convention and National Council of Churches; Dana McLean Greeley, president of the Unitarian-Universalist Association; Elmira Kendricks, president of the National Student Christian Federation; Edward Murray, consulter to the Archdiocese of Boston; Elsie Schomer of the Women's International League for Peace and Freedom; Howard Schomer, president of Chicago Theological Seminary; and Jacob Weinstein, president of the Central Conference of American Rabbis. Two European FOR members, internationally renowned for their opposition to fascism during World War II, joined the group: Pastor Martin Niemoeller, imprisoned by the German government during the Second World War, and André Trocmé, whose French village of Le Chambon-sur-Lignon had protected the Jewish community there during the same time (Participants in Vietnam Project 1965, SCPC).

The group arrived in Saigon in the oppressive heat of July and set up headquarters at the International Voluntary Service hostel. Lodging at the State Department–run IVS was no coincidence. The State Department encouraged the pacifists' first trip to Saigon because it hoped to enlist them as allies against Hanoi. State Department officials lined up contacts and meetings between the FOR delegation and government representatives and arranged trips to rural areas to demonstrate the helpfulness of Washington's aid programs there. The FOR delegates spent the next five days on a heavy schedule of meetings with American journalists, government and military officials in Saigon, and Buddhist and Catholic leaders.

One day they split into three groups and visited rural areas where they looked deeper into the web of war than they had first expected. Elsie Schomer went with a group to the province of Phuoc Long, flying there with an embassy official, Mr. Engel, on Air America. The provincial governor, Colonel Ma Sanh Nhon, greeted the group with expressions of gratitude to all Americans because, as he told them, he had received four years of military training with the United States Army, from 1955 to 1959, and had thereby risen far above, as he put it, his "humble origins." His American counterpart, military advisor Major Mitchell Sakey, tried hard, Schomer noted, "not to call the plays for Colonel Nhon." The two officers took the FOR group out to see a "pacified" hamlet. It was, in Schomer's words,

> a temporary camp . . . nothing but a few sheds in an enclosure, with no facilities for cooking or washing . . . with several hundred old men and women and children who had been removed from a rubber plantation a week before so that the S. Vietnam Army could destroy the plantation. This French-owned rubber plantation, and others like it, have been real strongholds for the Viet Cong—big enough to have supplies of gas and food and other facilities for a large group, the trees furnishing cover from air observation and ground observation, and yet the straight rows making them excellent positions from which to fire. (The French owners have knowingly permitted this use of their plantations—possibly because they dislike the S. Vietnam govt. and partly because the Viet Cong have threatened to destroy the plantations if they don't "cooperate.") The camp represented real misery . . . the only place I saw skin and eye diseases and the filth that goes with misery. The American soldiers who drove us there in a jeep (with another jeep behind us with soldiers with rifles ready to protect us from ambush) . . . remarked that something would have to be done soon . . . that they had become a sorry-looking sight in just a week without facilities. . . . We had lunch and visited the barracks of the American military advisors . . . simple, but adequate, with running water, plumbing, etc. (Schomer 1965, SCPC)

The camp that Schomer saw was part of Washington's "pacification" strategy. Borrowed from the British, who had honed the process in its colonial empire in Malaya, pacification in Vietnam meant rounding up villagers and herding them into camps that consisted of cleared grounds,

shelters, and some administrative buildings.[5] The complex was surrounded by barbed wire, and guards at the gates checked identification
papers of anyone entering or exiting. The villagers' homes and communities were burned, and American forces then considered that area a "free
fire zone," which could be bombed at will.[6] American policymakers justified destroying Vietnamese communities by arguing that it was the only
way to destroy support for anti-American military activities. Placing the
Vietnamese villagers in guarded camps would break their resistance and
leave the Vietnamese nationalists without homes. Bereft of their traditional fields, uprooted from their communities, guarded by foreigners,
the peasants appeared to Schomer not as the anticommunist bulwark of
which the military leaders boasted, but as a class of deliberately created
and maintained refugees.

The FOR's primary achievement on this trip, according to Alfred
Hassler, was "the contact we made with leaders of the Unified Buddhist
Church . . . who had emerged from their monasteries to lead their people's struggle for peace." In Saigon, Hassler began to hope for links to
Vietnamese religious organizations that could rally the public around a
political alternative to both the Saigon regime and the National Liberation Front. That meant working with the Buddhists, who appeared more
attractive to the FOR than did the Catholics because of their broader national appeal in Vietnam and because of their historic traditions of con-
templation and nonviolence.[7] The FOR's delegation struck up enduring
acquaintances in the Buddhist community during its first FOR trip to
Saigon. In a tin-roofed building at the Buddhist headquarters in Saigon,
while the monsoon rains poured down, they met with Thich Tri Quang, a
monk with piercing eyes who was Vietnam's most visible Buddhist leader
and, at that point, the best known Buddhist monk in the West. A fiery
speaker, introspective, intellectual, intense, and fiercely independent, he

5. The British military had first formally organized a "pacification" strategy in the Boer
War in South Africa in which thousands of civilians died of mistreatment and disease in
barbed wire concentration camps.

6. The U.S. Air Force produced a film about the program called "A Nation Builds
under Fire," which attempted to portray the camps in a positive light. The barbed wire surrounding the camps is clearly visible in the film, but the narration makes no mention of it.

7. Catholicism was a syncretic sect in Vietnam. Unlike Buddhism, it carried with it a
precise doctrine and Western organizational forms. Additionally, one was either a Catholic
or not, depending on one's family background, and one was either a northern or southern
Catholic, a distinction of some importance in Vietnamese politics. See Fitzgerald 1972.

had spent some time with the Viet Minh in the late 1940s. In the early 1950s, he returned to the pagodas in Hue to form a Buddhist movement that he led against the American-backed Ngo Dinh Diem in 1963. That protest culminated in Diem's ouster and assassination by Saigon military officers. Buddhist monasteries were well-known centers of opposition to the American-backed and largely Catholic Saigon regime. The American FOR delegates peppered the monk with queries about the Buddhist role in the politics of Vietnam. How far did their opposition go, the FOR delegates wondered. Which side were they on? Would they throw their weight with the National Liberation Front or did they stand opposed to both Saigon and the NLF? And, most important, what were monks, as contemplatives, doing on the "firing line of the war"?

Tri Quang replied by detailing the corruption brought to his country by foreign money and arms, and the divisions in his country created by American insistence on deceptively dividing Vietnam's choices between Western capitalism and Soviet communism. He turned the questioning around and pointed it at his American visitors. The FOR delegates were citizens of a country that had invaded his. How did they reconcile that reality with their religious ideals? Which side were they on? Did they believe in national self-determination, in independence, or would they follow their own government's imperial dictates? It was a striking moment for the visitors. "We had read a great deal about the war in Vietnam and its antecedents," Hassler confessed later, "but they had been written from a Western perspective, and we were conscious of it that day. We were not prepared to probe Tri Quang as he was prepared to probe us; consequently we were not able to respond as we could have wished" (1970, 8).

The day after meeting with Thich Tri Quang, the delegation met with Thich Nhat Hanh, a monk whose serenity was a welcome respite from Tri Quang's intense questions. Thich Nhat Hanh was a poet, peace organizer, and writer, and was the director of the Buddhist School of Youth for Social Service in Saigon. He had studied at Columbia University in New York in the early 1960s and then returned to South Vietnam after the 1963 coup in Saigon. Since then, he had organized a "coffeehouse group" of Catholics and Buddhists united by a commitment to ending the war. He spoke fluent English, a quality attractive to Americans of all political persuasions. To the FOR group, Nhat Hanh spoke of "the sufferings of his people, and especially of the peasants . . . and their longing for peace." He was kind when he spoke of American intentions in intervening in Vietnam, but he was unambiguous in condemning that intervention. "The right hand of your charity cannot undo the left hand of your bombing," he told the group (Hassler 1970, 7–13).

From contacts with the Buddhist community in South Vietnam, particularly Thich Nhat Hanh, Alfred Hassler adopted the concept of a "third force" solution to the war, a solution that called for a coalition of Buddhists, students, Catholics, and any others interested in a non-NLF government to replace the current Saigon government. This third force, Hassler hoped, would garner mass appeal in Vietnamese society, uniting peasants and intellectuals in principled nonviolent opposition to the war, the National Liberation Front, and the Saigon government.

Many in the U.S. antiwar movement initially sought alternatives to the National Liberation Front in South Vietnam, a quest they shared, for a time, with the Johnson administration. Washington was seldom satisfied with the Saigon government, and it periodically supported military coups there, but the new leaders were always drawn from within the same system that had produced the unsatisfactory regimes. For Hassler, there was no alternative within the military circle in Saigon. He hoped that a broad coalition of the religious and intellectual communities in Saigon could replace the current junta and negotiate a settlement to the war. The improbability of such a coalition would become apparent in the coming months, when Washington opposed it. Washington's rejection of a third force solution gave the Saigon government a free hand in dealing with its local opposition, a freedom it pursued with vigor.

Under pressure from third force advocates in South Vietnam, Saigon announced in April 1966 that elections would be held in six months. In response, and believing that American ambassador Henry Cabot Lodge, Jr., supported the elections, Thich Tri Quang toured the northern provinces of South Vietnam, calling on the Buddhists to prepare for political participation at the ballot box. The Saigon government quickly concluded that elections were too threatening to its position, and in May, General Nguyen Cao Ky dispatched a wave of fighter-bombers that attacked pagodas throughout those provinces. Thich Tri Quang pleaded with Washington to restrain Saigon, but Secretary of State Rusk replied that he could not pass judgment on Ky's use of force and that he hoped the Vietnamese would settle their "lesser differences" and concentrate on fighting the Viet Cong, according to a *New York Times* report on 17 May. General Ky handed the mopping up operation to Colonel Nguyen Ngoc

Loan, who, aided by American troops, proceeded to settle these "lesser differences" by laying siege to the Buddhist city of Hue.[8] The battles that followed left Thich Tri Quang near death. The Buddhists never fully re-covered, nor did Tri Quang, who forever blamed himself for leading his people into a trap. Many of the Hue university students arrested during this assault were still in prison nine years later when the Saigon govern-ment fell. "The most obvious reality in our country today," a bitter Quang wrote to Thich Nhat Hanh, "is that the Americans behave as colo-nialists" (Kahin 1986, 431). By the time of this crisis, historian George McTurnan Kahin concluded, the Buddhists had garnered so much popu-lar support that if the United States had not supported the generals in Saigon, the Buddhists' political demands "would have had to be met." After the crackdown on the Buddhists, there were only two options left for South Vietnamese: "supporting the NLF, or a Saigon regime shaped by and dependent upon the United States" (Kahin and Lewis 1968, 44).

The national press showered negative coverage on the FOR's visit to Saigon. The 12 July *New York Times* criticized the group's call for peace talks with the NLF and stressed instead the need to avoid "capitulation to the Communists." On 30 July *Time* magazine depicted the trip as a fad, beginning its story by observing flippantly, "Civil rights is old hat. Now, the area in which clergymen are seeking to prove the contemporary rele-vance of Christianity is foreign policy." Young Americans for Freedom's *Report on the Left* on 2 July 1965 reprinted FBI director J. Edgar Hoover's baseless charge that the FOR and its founder, A. J. Muste, were communist-inspired. The press had its own difficulty "seeing" women. On 12 July, the *New York Times* presented the group as entirely male and entirely clerical, leaving out of its coverage all the names and accounts of the female travelers, even though one of the three women was a minister and one of the men was not.

The FOR trip provoked Washington to sponsor its own official coun-tertrip. The Defense Department had in place a journalists' orientation program that took journalists on all-expenses-paid trips to South Viet-nam. Twenty groups of journalists had already traveled to Vietnam with this program, and immediately after the FOR group returned to the United States, the White House leaned on the Defense Department to

8. Correspondent Neil Sheehan said the pagoda headquarters in Hue looked like a "charnel house" (Kahin 1986, 429–30). Two years later, an Associated Press photographer caught Colonel Loan in the act of summarily executing a prisoner in the streets of Saigon.

use the program to send a group of religious editors to Vietnam. The Defense Department resisted, citing "the more serious situation in Vietnam, restrictions on journalists' group visits, the taxing of available transport during the build-up, and the difficulties involved in the security of the civilian visitor." The White House overruled Defense objections and ordered it to arrange the trip immediately. The Defense Department quickly complied, inviting four clergymen, at government expense, to a ten-day journalists' orientation program in Vietnam. They chose Ben Hartley, editor of the Presbyterian *Survey;* David White, editor of the *Jewish Digest;* Father Daniel Lyons, from "Our Sunday Visitor"; and Rev. Calvin Thielman of Montreat Presbyterian Church, described by the Defense Department as the "president's personal envoy (Butterfield to Jays 1965; Yarmolinsky to Assistant Secretary 1965, LBJL). The four men stayed in Saigon, their itinerary arranged entirely by American officials, who framed the military enterprise there as a fight against communism. Hartley, at least, was convinced by what he heard. "When the time came to return home," he told the *Christian Century* (22 Sept. 1965, 1123), "I wondered how anyone who has studied the problem in any depth could doubt the fundamental justice and basic rightness of our cause."

The second American group to travel to Hanoi came from an organization solidly rooted in the Old Left, the Du Bois Clubs. When W. E. B. Du Bois, the black American historian and opponent of racial discrimination, died in exile in Ghana in 1963, student Marxist discussion groups in the United States began calling themselves Du Bois Clubs in honor of the scholar. At the World Peace Conference in Helsinki in August 1965, North Vietnamese delegates invited some Du Bois members to Hanoi the following fall. The Du Bois travelers were Michael Myerson, the organization's international secretary, Jon Christopher Koch, program director of radio station WBAI-FM in New York, Harold Supriano of San Francisco, and Richard Ward, a freelance writer.

This first trip to North Vietnam directly from the United States was no simple matter for the Du Bois travelers or those who followed them. Flights from the United States to Hanoi were longer, more complicated, and far more arduous than were flights to Saigon, which were routed through California and Manila and generally took only a day or two. Flights to Hanoi were routed through Europe and across Asia, taking at least four days and usually more. After the flight across Europe and Asia, the final trip into Hanoi was uncertain and dangerous. American aircraft ruled the skies of North Vietnam and imposed "open windows" of only several hours daily for the air corridors into Hanoi. Flights to Hanoi from Beijing, Phnom Penh, and Vientiane were few, and they were canceled or turned back at the slightest sign of bombardment.

The Du Bois flight ended with a fifteen-hour prop flight from Beijing, touching down just before crossing the border into Vietnam to make a final check on the safety of the air corridor ahead. The plane flew into the Hanoi airport at dusk, and the Americans were met there by representatives of the Vietnam Youth Federation and by Nguyen Trung Hieu and Do Xuan Oanh, members of the Vietnamese Peace Committee whom they had met in Helsinki and whom future travelers to Hanoi would come to value as friends. They found life in Hanoi at once disrupted and yet astonishingly "normal." In Hanoi, Myerson wrote:

> city life was a paradox, military fortifications placed throughout in preparation for attack, and simultaneously a great effort was made to normalize existence. Everywhere, at the lakes, across bridges, at the university, government buildings and factories, antiaircraft fortifications were visible. At dawn and dusk, dozens of young people walked with rifles and camouflage to and from militia practice. At the same time, no curfew existed and there were no air-raid drills. (Myerson 1970, 133)

Myerson noted, with surprise, that one street in Hanoi was named for Alice Herz. The street stood in Hanoi as a public testimony, at the same time that American bombing in the North officially began, to individual acts of protest in America that told the Vietnamese that even American citizens could understand their plight. When Herz died, Oanh told Myerson, a nationwide silent vigil was held for her in Vietnam.

Vietnamese sentiment seemed profoundly nationalist and confident to the American visitors. Public morale appeared high, even heady. One student told Myerson that under colonialism illiteracy and hunger governed rural life, but now there was universal elementary education, and over a million adults attended evening school to learn to read and write. Under French rule, university students throughout Indochina studied only French law in preparation for lives as colonial bureaucrats. Now there were 20,000 scientific, technical, medical, and engineering students. For himself, the student told Myerson, life in Vietnam was marked by the fact of war, but it was much more than that, he said: hunger was a thing of the past, he hoped; they were making great strides against malaria and cholera; and through it all he hoped for peace and independence (Myerson 1970, 139).

The most vivid impressions of the journey came on the visitors' slow night trip out of Hanoi south to Thanh Hoa province, then undergoing continuous bombing raids. They began at dusk, riding in two jeeps without vehicle lights and camouflaged with fresh tree branches to avoid attention from the skies. It was a novel experience for the Americans. "If, after the war, there is an international night auto race for cars without lights," a Vietnamese poet smilingly told them in Hanoi, "the Vietnamese will surely win!" (Koch 1965, 9). Their night trip took them through Nam Dinh, the third largest city in the north, now battered under the steady bombing of the Seventh Fleet. They saw bombed hospital buildings, a schoolyard studded with craters, a pagoda in ruins, and a large textile plant reduced to rubble. It was the second wrecking of the textile plant. When the French army withdrew in 1954, it had carried off most of the textile equipment from the plant. That equipment had been laboriously replaced over the years, but the American air force had blasted the entire rebuilt structure in minutes. For blocks around the factory, rubble replaced the homes that once housed thousands of Vietnamese factory workers.

The sun set as they headed south of Nam Dinh and crossed the first of many bombed bridges, repaired by workers on trestles welding and bolting pieces in place under tiny lights. At some crossings, operators swung out pontoon bridges at dusk and hid them under overhanging trees at dawn. The famous Ham Rong bridge over the Song Chu River, one of Defense Secretary McNamara's primary targets, still carried a stream of freight cars. All night, in fact, freight trains rumbled along the pocked railroad that paralleled the highway south. There, too, crews labored through the night, rebuilding the railbed around the craters. Thanh Hoa lay on the coast of Vietnam, within easy striking distance from American aircraft carriers in the Gulf of Tonkin, providing American pilots with what they considered profitable training under limited combat conditions. In 1973, veteran pilots told *New York Times* reporter Seymour Hersh that they deliberately bombed North Vietnamese hospitals and NLF clinics in South Vietnam. "It wasn't something that was hush-hush," Allen Stevenson said, "we really didn't consider it that nasty an item."

In Thanh Hoa itself, the Americans saw the ruins of a five-hundred-bed tuberculosis hospital built in 1960 as a research and treatment center. The former director showed them around. On 8 July 1965, he told them, American planes had destroyed both the hospital and the staff living quarters a few kilometers away, killing forty people, including five doctors. The Americans asked if possibly the hospital buildings were mistaken for military barracks. The hospital had been there for five years, the director said, and the buildings had red crosses painted on their roofs. He believed that hospitals were prime targets. More than twenty throughout the country had now been destroyed, he said, including the Quynh Lap Leper Sanatorium on the seacoast. Fourteen separate raids had killed 120 patients there. The last raid fell on the funeral of the previous dead, killing several mourners and destroying the coffins. Because of the raids, medical workers were decentralizing the provincial hospitals and dispersing facilities into surrounding villages. Generators supplied electricity for the X-ray machines, and doctors operated at night with kerosene lanterns.

The bombing raids carried heavy physical costs, but Koch noted that they also drew communities together in common outrage:

> We visited one small dispensary for the victims of U.S. raids, where the doctor in charge was more bitter than most as he gave us case histories of his patients: a ten-year-old boy who had lost his leg above the knee when he was caught in his school yard by a strafing plane; a twenty-eight-year-old woman, seven months pregnant, caught on the highway during a raid, who had her back broken; a twenty-seven-year-old young man whose insides were torn out by bullets as he was working in the fields. The villagers do not forget these victims. Other North Vietnamese have seen targets destroyed which their whole community had participated in building. A dam in North Vietnam is the product of hundreds of people working with small shovels and baskets, and people are involved with it in a way that they can never be with a dam built by bulldozers and owned by a power company. There is a new nationalism in North Vietnam today that affects almost everyone. The North now produces almost 90 percent of its consumer goods, and although the quality is not high and the goods are frequently unattractive, the Vietnamese are proud of them. When a textile factory which produced the shirts they wear is destroyed, to many it is an almost personal affront. (Koch 1965, 12)

Koch observed that Vietnamese officials in Hanoi played down the cumulative casualty figures. He believed it was because Vietnam lacked even the air power to mount a credible deterrent to American bombers. Lying under virtually unhampered bombing made the country appear vulnerable—a weak, defenseless half of a country. From talking with the officials, Koch concluded that they wanted to assure their own citizenry that "despite the U.S. bombings our industrial and agricultural production is increasing and our defenses are stronger than ever." At the provincial and district levels, on the other hand, local officials could instantly provide precise information on the bombing's toll. An old peasant leader in one village gave Koch details of the previous month's destruction, down to the old bicycle it mangled. Vietnamese at all levels believed that their quick response in dispersing industrial and medical facilities and implementing warning systems kept fatalities low. During the early weeks of bombing, they were not yet skilled at "taking the necessary precautions," a provincial official told Koch, but after more than two thousand bombing sorties, in his area they reported "only" about two hundred people killed (Kock 1965, 11). The *Vietnam Courier* concluded that the war in South Vietnam, where chemical weapons were widely used in addition to the enormous tonnage of "conventional" bombs, inflicted higher human costs at that time (1965a, SCPC).

Despite the widespread destruction throughout the provinces south of Hanoi, Koch wanted to believe that it was accidental, damage unintentionally done while going about the business of war. For Americans, this distinction would matter in the years ahead. To the Vietnamese, the significance of the bombing lay not in whether hospitals were deliberately bombed, but in the fact that the country was being bombed at all. "It makes little difference to the Vietnamese whether or not such attacks are accidental," Koch concluded, "although they are convinced that they are thoroughly intentional. There is a parable attributed to Ho Chi Minh, which is frequently repeated to visitors in North Vietnam these days. "A bandit comes into your home, steals half your property, kills half your family, and then says, 'Let's negotiate.' Do you sit down at the table with him or kick him out first? This is the mood of Vietnam today" (Koch 1965, 12).

A few American pilots were making their way down from the skies to the soil of North Vietnam. In Thanh Hoa, the Americans were shown the contents of one downed pilot's survival kit. There was the compass, the maps, cooking utensils and rations. "And there was the poison capsule to be swallowed," Myerson wrote,

> presumably in order to escape torture. I wonder now how many, if any, American flyboys have died at the hands of DuPont Chemical and the USAF in order to avoid a punishment they would never have received. Also in the kit we found a U.S. Armed Forces phrasebook of what to say upon capture. Written in several languages by the Office of Naval Intelligence, the book was called *Pointee-Talkee*. Phrases every captured pilot should know, included in this bombardier's *Berlitz*, were: "Will you accept gold?"; "Where is the nearest telephone?"; and "Can you direct me to the nearest friendly guerrillas?", a question, I. F. Stone pointed out, the Pentagon has been asking wistfully about North Vietnam for several years. (Myerson 1970, 149)

Back in Hanoi, after requesting a meeting with prisoners of war, the Americans met Captain Robert Daughtrey from Texas, who had been shot down the previous month. Daughtrey's last bombing raid over Vietnam began at Korat Air Force Base in Thailand, he told Myerson, and his intended target was the Ham Rong Bridge in Thanh Hoa. His arms were both in casts from ejection injuries. After three operations on one arm, he said, he expected a full recovery. Captive only a month, Daughtrey appeared jaunty and confident. Myerson mentioned the bombing damage that planes like his had inflicted on the people and the land. Air force crews never discussed the purposes of the war, Daughtrey told them; that "could lead to a breakdown in military discipline." His job was a good one, he said, it had PX privileges, retirement benefits, and paid well, much better than the money he could wrest from a farm in Texas. He did not want to talk about the air war, and he had few other questions save for inquiries about the latest baseball standings in the United States, a question the American group could not help him with. When the group prepared to leave, they asked if there were any messages to pass on to his family. His only message was to his father, to return the air conditioners because he would not be needing them now.

When the Du Bois group returned to New York, the national media did not know what to do with their eyewitness accounts of bombing destruction. Their accounts confounded Pentagon claims of precision air strikes to which the national media gave respectful and affirming coverage. Of the ample press corps that turned out for the Du Bois group's press conference at the Overseas Press Club in New York on 15 September, only the *New York Times* and the *St. Louis Post-Dispatch* reported on the journey, and that on their back pages. The *Times* reported their accounts of bombing damage to schools, hospitals, and residential areas skeptically because on their short trip south of Hanoi they "actually witnessed" only one bombing raid—against a bridge.

The media's reluctance to cover these reports from North Vietnam, at the same time granting full coverage to the Pentagon's reports of "only steel and concrete" targets, could only encourage wider air strikes. The Pentagon enjoyed the privilege of keeping secret any information that it chose, disclosing to the press only what it wished to disclose. When eyewitness reports from North Vietnam were brought to the press, the Pentagon could count on the media ignoring most of them and reporting skeptically on the rest. Reports from Americans in North Vietnam should have posed a logical problem for the press; the reports coming from observers in North Vietnam, whether they came from different American groups, from journalists and visitors from Western and Eastern Europe and Asia, or from the North Vietnamese themselves, were consistent with one another.[9] Of the many reports of the nature of the bombing in North Vietnam, only the Pentagon's deviated from the others. A reasonable inference was that the diverse and consistent reports reflected reality and that the Pentagon was wrong. The press could not bring itself to draw this conclusion, embracing instead the claims of its government. The national media would not cover these travels to Hanoi in detail until it found a focus other than that of the air war, a focus that corresponded to the way that Washington began to frame these eyewitness reports, that is, the issue of the legality of the travel itself.

Travelers to Hanoi never encouraged officials there to rely on antiwar opposition in the United States to end the war. Instead, they pressed one point consistently: the antiwar movement in the United States should not be counted upon to change Washington's policy. From the beginning, activists pointed out that the movement was deep enough to endure in the United States, but the Pentagon was too large and the mass public too indifferent to produce predictable and tangible results. The Women Strike for Peace delegations made this point forcefully in Hanoi and Jakarta, and FOR delegates in Algiers that summer "repeated this several times" when they spoke with officials at the North Vietnamese embassy there. They even took copies of a Lou Harris poll that showed scant public support for the university teach-ins that spring (Gottlieb and Browne 1965, SCPC). Vietnamese officials listened as each new batch of visitors warned them not to expect the antiwar movement to change the military mind of the United States, and then told their visitors that they were well aware of this point. "Others have told us the same thing," was their usual response.

American antiwar activists who traveled to Hanoi hoped that their experiences and eyewitness reports would spur debate within the administration and the public over the course and conduct of the war. They discovered, one by one, that Washington was not interested—it was not talking to officials in Hanoi and did not care to listen to those who had. The national media was not interested either. Disappointed by their

9. British journalist James Cameron published a book of his dispatches in 1965 that read much like accounts of these activists. Agence France Press news reports also consistently carried the kinds of stories that American activists brought back. No journalist who traveled in North Vietnam published reports that supported the Pentagon's claims.

abrupt dismissal from the national media, travelers to Vietnam turned to the antiwar press in the United States. This press included new publications and established peace publications that began to devote much of their space to oppose this particular war. From their first issues in 1965 and 1962 respectively, *Viet-Report* and *Ramparts* carried extensive information from Southeast Asia and of antiwar actions. "*Viet-Report* is a wartime phenomenon," its editors wrote in the first issue in August 1965 and, the editors added in a rare burst of optimism, "we hope that each issue will be our last." *Fellowship* magazine, a publication of the Fellowship of Reconciliation, had an established national readership whose subscribers were numbered in every antiwar organization. *Liberation* magazine was founded in 1955 as a monthly periodical devoted to issues of national and international peace and justice and, along with *Fellowship*, it soon incorporated news from Vietnam and extensive coverage of American travelers there. Women Strike for Peace, the Women's International League for Peace and Freedom, the American Friends Service Committee, and numerous other antiwar groups published their own newsletters for thousands of their supporters. The explicitly antiwar press was small in 1965, but it was soon joined by other periodicals that opposed American military force in Vietnam; *The Nation*, *The Progressive*, and *Christian Century*, were established periodicals that regularly printed lengthy eyewitness reports from Vietnam.

Unlike the national media, the antiwar press was not primarily dependent on official sources for its information. In the early years of the war, the best media sources in the United States for information about Vietnam itself, and the historical context of the war, are the pages of this antiwar press. The national media focused on the United States, its purposes, its officials, and their interpretations. It did not treat the Vietnamese viewpoint as part of the "sphere of legitimate concerns," but rather helped to define the limits of acceptable debate by excluding from the public agenda those who violated or challenged the anticommunist consensus. Less than 10 percent of mainstream news coverage of the war even concerned itself with South Vietnam's political governance or its economy. Its coverage of North Vietnam was practically nil (Hallin 1986, 116–26).

Travelers to Vietnam reached out directly to the American public. They returned home with the energy and commitment to spend weeks and months on the road, addressing audiences ranging from a few people to thousands. The Women Strike for Peace delegation found that their outreach from their July trip was "greater than any previous project of Women Strike for Peace" (Herring 1965, SCPC). Members of that delegation addressed thousands of people in the next months, and the journey inspired others to go to Vietnam. The Du Bois delegates found invitations to address rallies and meetings piling up for them on their return. In the six months after his trip, for example, Michael Myerson spent most evenings and weekends addressing audiences at churches, universities, union halls, living rooms, and rallies across the nation. Even the Honolulu Junior Chamber of Commerce invited him for a week-long tour to address audiences in the islands.

Scant mainstream media coverage had an unintended effect—it meant scant government attention for most of 1965. The State Department ignored passport violations at first and, when a few reporters raised questions about them, discounted these trips to Hanoi as minor irritants. This state of benign dismissal did not long endure, but it lasted long enough to provide American citizens with a moment for action. Their success depended upon their own abilities, but also on the political opportunities offered them. And when Washington ignored their early efforts, it provided them with an opening, which they seized, to develop more enduring ties to Vietnamese officials, to strengthen their own networks, and to publish their reports, analyses, and calls for action in the growing literature of the early antiwar movement.

2

With the Other Side in
the North and South

In late 1965, Herbert Aptheker, a prolific historian of American race relations, and a member of the American Communist party, organized a small group to go to Hanoi. Despite the prohibition on travel to North Vietnam, Washington had virtually ignored earlier visits, and there was no indication that this journey would be treated differently than any of the others. The story of how Aptheker's group was formed and re-formed recalls the pattern of government harassment of the Old Left, reveals the strains that the war placed on the civil rights community during the 1960s, and discloses a potential direction for student activism that Students for a Democratic Society rejected.

Unlike the earlier travelers to Hanoi, Aptheker already had experience with passport controls. Only a year earlier, in 1964, he had won a Supreme Court case restoring his passport, which the State Department had seized, not because of his travel but because he was a Communist party member (*Passports* 1966, 47). In dividing the world into "free" and "communist" segments at the dawn of the Cold War era, the United States employed a two-track approach. The first limited the travel of all its citizens, and the second confined others, for political reasons, entirely within United States borders. All passports carried the warning that they were invalid for travel to selected countries. There was no clear logic to the changing composition of these lists. In 1952, the countries selected for the first banned list were Albania, Bulgaria, China, Czechoslovakia, Hungary, Poland, Rumania, and the Soviet Union. In 1955, the State Department dropped Czechoslovakia, Hungary, Poland, Rumania, and the Soviet Union from its list of prohibited countries and added North

Korea and North Vietnam (*Freedom to Travel* 1958, 16). In 1961, it added Cuba to the list.

These administration rulings were made and enforced without congressional legislation. Congress had never banned travel to particular countries; indeed, when President Kennedy proposed such legislation in 1963, it died in committee. Without specific legislation to enforce its passport restrictions, the government relied on a 1952 Immigration and Nationality Act that prohibited travel in or out of the United States without a valid passport. The State Department then wove a wall of regulations that restricted access to passports and provided grounds for their seizure, thereby confining selected individuals within United States borders. Not everyone gave up traditional traveling freedoms. By 1965, the Justice Department had collected files of more than six hundred citizens who had defied these passport regulations by traveling to segregated areas (*Passports* 1966, 39).

The Justice Department invalidated hundreds of passports for political reasons, but its prosecution of travel was highly selective. For example, it brought a criminal indictment against only one person out of the many who had visited Cuba—an African American reporter, William Worthy. A lower court eventually threw out that specific case, but the government relied on the threat of further selective criminal prosecutions with penalties of five years in prison and $5,000 fines to produce a chilling effect on travel to these areas. Government pressure on black Americans not to travel to communist countries or to develop international ties of solidarity with the decolonizing world was particularly intense (Horne 1985). Singer and actor Paul Robeson's passport was revoked in 1950 because of his "frank admission that he has been for years extremely active politically in behalf of independence of the colonial peoples of Africa" (Whitfield 1991, 195; Duberman 1988). Most black internationalists had their passports revoked, a move even most white liberals approved (DeConde 1992, Horne 1988, 1993).

Political pressure on black Americans not to speak out on international issues of colonialism in the Third World could be viewed as no more than a standard political tactic of applying pressure to some groups in order to carry out other policy goals. But it meant more than that. The voice of African Americans on those issues represented one of the most powerful moral arguments on international affairs coming out of the United States. When African Americans raised the issue of Vietnam, for example, their own experiences in a racist society was palpably present. In an early antiwar statement, Vincent Harding, black activist and historian, framed the two issues thus: "If the hooded terrorists of the southern night have no right to destroy someone they declare to be an enemy of *their* way of life, how can we be so comfortable in the face of our own forays of terror against the enemies of *our* way of life?" (Harding 1965, 581).

Washington forbade its citizens to visit some countries and could seize their passports if they did, but the government used another tactic to confine some Americans within its borders. A 1950 Subversive Activities Control Act provision made it unlawful for a member of a "communist-action organization" to apply for, be issued, or use a passport. Challenges to this law were unsuccessful until the Supreme Court ruled in *Aptheker v. Secretary of State* in 1964 that passport denials based on an applicant's political beliefs were unconstitutional. Writing for the majority, Justice Arthur Goldberg declared that "freedom of travel is a constitutional liberty closely related to rights of free speech and association" (*New Republic* 1966, 4).

With his court case behind him, Herbert Aptheker secured a passport that was hemmed in only by the ordinary travel restrictions that banned all travel to Albania, Bulgaria, China, Cuba, North Vietnam, and North Korea. In summer 1965 he attended the World Peace Congress in Helsinki, where the same delegates who invited the Du Bois representatives to North Vietnam asked him to come for a later visit. The proposed trip instantly raised the possibility that his newly issued passport could be quickly snatched back, but Aptheker agreed to go. He could select several others to accompany him, his Vietnamese contacts told him, but they wanted a diverse group. They knew that he was a member of the Communist party, and they asked him to invite people whose views and politics were different from his own (Aptheker 1966, 3).

Aptheker asked Staughton Lynd, a professor of American history at Yale, to join him. Lynd was a Quaker pacifist from a family of intellectuals. His parents, Helen and Robert Lynd, were the authors of *Middletown* and *Middletown in Transition,* two classic works on social and economic change in Muncie, Indiana. From 1961 to 1964, Lynd taught history at Spelman College in Atlanta, and he served as director of the Freedom Schools during the Mississippi Summer Project of 1964. A scholar of early American history, Lynd was familiar with historical accounts of Americans who had endeavored to promote peace during times of international tension and war. One such episode in particular had long impressed him; that of George Logan, a Philadelphia farmer and former member of Congress who, in 1798, traveled to Paris to meet with the government there during the height of the political hysteria over the XYZ Affair. Logan's goal was to elicit some concrete information from the French government that would end Federalist efforts to take the nation to war. His mission was successful, and the Federalists, including former president George Washington, loathed him for it. Outraged members of Congress attacked Logan's patriotism, called him a traitor, and passed an act forbidding such activities (Tolles 1950, 1953).[1]

The Logan Act survives to this day, making it punishable by fine and imprisonment for American citizens to discuss with foreign officials matters relating to "disputes or controversies with the United States." In historian Alexander DeConde's words, the Logan Act made it illegal for any citizen "to use his resources for peace in any quarrel that the United States had with another country, but it ignored those actions by private citizens that would stir up war" (1966). Scholars of constitutional law have long agreed that the Logan Act is too vague and allows too much prosecutory discretion to be enforceable in the courts (Vagts 1966; Kearney 1987).

George Logan's example inspired Lynd to try to turn this trip to Hanoi into a mission similar to Logan's, to find common grounds for negotiations between Washington and its current nemesis: North Vietnam. In 1965, the vast disparity between the respective military capabilities of the United States and Vietnam convinced many Americans, antiwar activists included, that an American triumph in Vietnam was ultimately inevitable. They aspired to lessen the projected carnage. In this vein, Lynd hoped to gain a better understanding of Hanoi's position, which he could convey to Washington in hopes of encouraging officials there to take steps that would lead to negotiations. Facilitating talks to end a brutal war seemed worth the risk of a seized passport, jail time, and a fine.

---

1. In its present form, the law reads as follows: "Any citizen of the United States, wherever he may be, who, without authority of the United States, directly or indirectly commences or carries on any correspondence or intercourse with any foreign government or any officer or agent thereof, with intent to influence the measures or conduct of any foreign government or of any officer or agent thereof, in relation to any disputes or controversies with the United States, or to defeat the measures of the United States, shall be fined not more than $5000 or imprisoned not more than three years, or both. This section shall not abridge the right of a citizen to apply, himself or his agent, to any foreign government or the agents thereof for redress of any injury which he may have sustained from such government or any of its agents for subject" (18 U.S.C. 953, 1982).

Aptheker asked Lynd to select the third person for the trip, and Lynd thought of Robert Moses, someone for whom Lynd had "infinite admiration." Moses was a twenty-nine-year-old black school teacher from New York who, in 1961, had gone to McComb, Mississippi, with the Student Nonviolent Coordinating Committee (SNCC) to register black voters there. Moses quickly became a movement legend because of his quiet persistence, his calm fearlessness in the face of local brutality, and his unwavering commitment to nonviolence. A. J. Muste, himself a legend in labor organizing and pacifist circles, called Moses "the spiritual leader of the Student Nonviolent Coordinating Committee" (Muste 1965, SCPC).

Moses readily agreed to go to Hanoi, but in the next few months rising concern within the civil rights movement over the effects of addressing foreign policy issues made him rethink the trip. In McComb during the summer of 1965, SNCC activists drew up a petition that linked the war in Vietnam and the civil rights movement and called on blacks to think hard about the military draft, which would send them "to kill other Colored people" (Jacob and Landau, 1966, 249). That same summer, Moses helped coordinate the Washington Action Project, which held workshops for people willing to renounce the war and cooperate on social reform (Burner 1994).

The McComb Petition and the summer workshops generated criticism from many older national black leaders, who had been warned by the White House that opposition to President Johnson's policy in Vietnam could diminish his commitment to civil rights legislation. This imposed a hard choice on civil rights figures, some of whom set out to make a separate peace with the president on the war. James Farmer, national director of the Congress on Racial Equality (CORE), led a successful move that summer to reverse a CORE convention resolution calling for the withdrawal of American troops in Vietnam. On 6 July, the *New York Times* quoted Farmer, who argued that, with the president committed to the war, CORE "should stay out of the peace movement" because it "ran the risk of losing the sympathies of many people if it became involved." In this light, the decision to go or not to go to Hanoi was not primarily a personal one for Robert Moses, as it could be for many white Americans who went. Under heavy pressure from the Civil Rights movement, he resigned from the trip in late November. SNCC was already in deep trouble over the war, Lynd said in an interview on 25 January 1993, and Moses "felt there was no way he could go. Even if he disavowed his role as a spokesman for SNCC, the trip would be associated with the organization."[2]

Lynd and Aptheker had planned to leave for Hanoi in the middle of December. The first week of December came and there was still no third person lined up for the trip. That weekend, Tom Hayden went to New Haven to visit Staughton and Alice Lynd, and on Saturday morning they took the Lynd children sledding. Standing at the top of a snowy hill, Staughton asked Tom if he wanted to go to Hanoi. Tom said he would.

Tom Hayden was best known at that time for putting together the Students for a Democratic Society manifesto, "The Port Huron Statement," in 1962. Once an organization of some promise for mobilizing young people, SDS was, in 1965, engaged in urban community projects. In April of that year, SDS had mobilized a march against the war in Washington D.C. The march was successful beyond their greatest expectations. After that success, however, SDS leaders disengaged from antiwar activity and instead concentrated on long-range organizing to change the way that public decisions were made in the United States, and so stop not this war, but "the seventh war from now." National SDS leaders proclaimed that single-issue protests were the province of "old and tired radicals." Real societal change, they said, required a concerted focus on the locus of power, rather than on specific policies and programs. Only the unimaginative could believe that "the only way to end the war is to organize people on the issue of the war." Despite SDS's conclusion, the issue of the war grew ever larger on campuses, where a willing and able grassroots constituency waited in vain for help and direction from national SDS leaders. Local SDS chapters were left stranded by the national office when they wrote to it for ideas and materials to use in mobilizing local opposition to the war, because the national SDS office placed a low priority on links with local offices. Traditional disarmament and pacifist groups, the same groups from which came travelers to Hanoi, filled the vacuum for local student organizations because they could be counted on to provide literature, speakers, and encouragement (Isserman 1992, 22–34).

In fall 1965, national SDS leaders had mulled over a proposal to begin a "Peace Brigade" project in North Vietnam, which would be made

2. Kenneth O'Reilly (1989, 242) notes that the FBI had already prepared a memo for the State Department, alleging a plan by civil rights activists and the Communist party to create social chaos so that communism could flourish in America.

up of American volunteers who would repair bombed-out hospitals, bridges, and roads. The plan grew out of the experiences of the Mississippi Freedom Summer volunteers. It was a daring idea with daunting obstacles, but it offered a striking possibility for the ties of international solidarity for which many people, disillusioned with great power conflicts, yearned.[3] Most SDS leaders discouraged the plan at the outset, and it was dropped because it seemed like something the "old" liberals would do (Booth to Sandperl and Baez 1965, SDS). When Hayden talked to other SDS leaders in December about Lynd's invitation to go to Hanoi, they discouraged the trip, but he decided to go anyway as an individual rather than as an SDS representative.[4]

Even before Lynd left for Hanoi, he was marked by suspicion at Yale University. A week before his departure, he was called into the provost's office for a talk with some members of the political science department, professors who "shuttled" between Yale and Washington contracts with the Central Intelligence Agency, and was "essentially told to keep my mouth shut while in Hanoi." The warning surprised Lynd, who was unaware that anyone at Yale even knew of the upcoming trip (Lynd 1993).[5] Planning for the trip involved a number of long distance calls, however, and the FBI was tapping SDS's phone lines and was aware of Lynd's

3. Other circles in the antiwar movement were discussing this idea, too. Ross Flanagan of A Quaker Action Group wrote a memo that discussed the prospect of sending Quakers to Vietnam as a "human deterrent in the war zone" (Boardman 1985, ix). In 1967, Noam Chomsky urged consideration of American volunteers going to North Vietnam as deterrents against further bombing. During the following years American peace activists continued to discuss a "peace brigade" to maintain a public presence in and around heavily bombed areas in North Vietnam. Nothing concrete came of these proposals, but the idea endured, and, twenty years later, continuous teams of Americans, derived from the same activist tradition, posted themselves in areas of Contra attacks in Nicaragua (Griffin-Nolan, 1991).

4. FBI file reports (taken from phone wiretaps) on SDS report that the "National Administration Committee of SDS did not want Hayden to go (to Hanoi) but Hayden disagreed and told Booth he was going anyway and would disassociate himself from SDS" (Isserman, 24).

5. In planning the course of the war, the Pentagon employed the consulting services of numerous experts at elite educational institutions. Some of their ideas were implemented, others eventually survived only as Pentagon lore. For example, Roger Fisher, a researcher at Harvard, proposed the Barrier Project, which called for an "air-seeded line of barbed wire, mines, and chemicals" along the seventeenth parallel. Fisher argued for the "political advantages" the barrier would provide in permanently dividing North and South Vietnam (*Pentagon Papers* 4:112, 160).

travel plans at least as soon as he talked them over with Hayden on the telephone (Isserman 1992, 24).

The trip to Hanoi coincided with a "bombing pause" over North Vietnam, which the White House referred to as a "peace offensive" lest the uninitiated should get the idea that it reflected a real diminution of warfare. In late November, in a memo to the president outlining the rationale for a bombing pause, Secretary of Defense McNamara had written that:

> It is my belief that there should be a three- or four-week pause . . . in the program of bombing the North before we either greatly increase our troop deployments to Vietnam or intensify our strikes against the North. The reasons for this belief are, first, that we must lay a foundation in the mind of the American public and in world opinion for such an enlarged phase of the war and, second, we should give North Vietnam a face-saving chance to stop the aggression (Pentagon Papers 1972, IV: 33).

Bombing pauses over North Vietnam soon appeared to be public relations efforts designed to pin the responsibility for renewed bombing on Hanoi. Washington would cease bombing for a few days or weeks while calling on Hanoi to end its support for the National Liberation Front in the South. While making these demands, Washington offered nothing in return, not even a permanent cessation of bombing. Bombing would later be "reluctantly" resumed due to Hanoi's "refusal" to respond. Hanoi officials maintained that the American bombing over North Vietnam defied the provisions of the Geneva Accords and had to end before a broader diplomatic solution could be reached (Porter 1975, 29).

Aptheker, Lynd, and Hayden left John F. Kennedy airport for London on the night of 19 December. From there they went to Prague, then on to Moscow, where a meeting with the Vietnamese ambassador, Lynd said later, indicated "certain limits" on their mission:

> My attitude at that point was one of compassion for these people being blown to bits and having jellied gasoline dropped on them. And I must have expressed that somehow through an interpreter—this was the big limitation on our trip. All of the Vietnamese political people spoke French but I did not speak French and neither did Herbert and neither did Tom. Through an interpreter [the ambassador] said, "Professor, you

don't understand. We're going to win." And I just couldn't believe my ears. What's he talking about? And then this tiny little man said, "Yes. You see, your country has only two choices. Either you leave right now, in which case we win, or you escalate your involvement and put more American troops in Vietnam and if you do that, with every soldier who steps onto Vietnam's soil, one more person will come to the National Liberation Front." Had I had the wit to take it all in, I would have realized right then and there, certain limits on what I was doing as a citizen diplomat because I was going on the assumption that these people were on their last legs, and to prevent them from being bombed into the stone age we had to stop this. That wasn't their attitude. Their attitude was that it wasn't yet the moment to make peace. The United States hadn't been whipped yet. (Lynd 1993)

From Moscow, the group flew on to Beijing and finally reached Hanoi on 28 December. While they were en route, the national press seized upon their trip and focused not on Aptheker, the sole communist, but on Lynd, a Quaker pacifist and intellectual. To the press, this group appeared, for various reasons, to be a group with which it could finally identify: all male, all white, part of the educated elite yet not elitist, persons of national stature, imbued with egalitarian ideals and knowledgeable about the world. On 28 December, *New York Times* reporter John Corry baptized Lynd as "perhaps the most articulate spokesman for the new American left." The media's problem then became how to frame this trip to Hanoi at a time when Vietnamese perspectives could not be covered seriously. Its solution was to frame the story as a contest over passports, disconnecting it from the war itself.

Reporters eagerly solicited the opinions of Washington officials on the legality of the trip, ensuring that the supply of quotes from them would keep the story going. The State Department confirmed crisply that the three passports had not been validated for travel to "Communist-controlled portions" of Vietnam and that they could be seized. The Justice Department told the *New York Times* on 28 December that "it was too soon to say" whether criminal charges would be brought, while making certain that the reporters understood perfectly the criminal penalties for violating the Logan Act. Former president Truman, himself an architect of the Cold War and a stout defender of it, demonstrated his belief that mere citizens had no business questioning their government on matters of foreign policy by direct information seeking, and his ignorance of legal opinion on the Logan Act. He called the trip "a publicity stunt.

They made a trip to get themselves into the penitentiary," he blustered to a *Times* reporter on 29 December, while on his morning walk outside the Carlyle Hotel in New York. "They have no business over there. What's the Logan Act for? They haven't got any sense." In Hanoi, the three heard all of these stories from the Voice of America and from American news correspondents who phoned them there with the latest "threat" from Washington. Aptheker (1966, 27) responded that Truman, himself proud of being from the "Show Me" state, should understand that Americans would want to see for themselves.

In Hanoi, the three spent much of their time as the Du Bois group had, meeting with officials, leaders of youth groups, women's groups, trade unions, Catholics, Protestants, and intellectuals, including those who had been in Jakarta in July with the Women Strike for Peace delegation. They went wherever they wished in Hanoi, hampered in talking to people on the street only by their own inability to speak French well or Vietnamese at all. They came to know their interpreters well, particularly Do Xuan Oanh, secretary of the Peace Committee. Oanh was a poet, fluent in English, who had recently translated Mark Twain's *Adventures of Huckleberry Finn* into Vietnamese. Their interpreters were at first reluctant to talk much about themselves, but as they accompanied the Americans from one event to another, bits and pieces of their lives emerged. Oanh, age forty-three, was born into a fishing family along the coast. When he was young, he went with his stepfather to work in the French-owned mines. Later he joined the Viet Minh and when he was assigned to guard French prisoners of war, he began learning their language. After the French left in 1954, he began studying English and then went to work for the Vietnam Peace Committee as an interpreter. He wrote poetry and composed songs about Vietnamese nationalism and rural life. Oanh's nationalism seemed passionately personal—he had scant interest in ideological constructs (Hayden 1966).

Their impressions of Hanoi were similar to those of the Du Bois groups. Hanoi was a city fortified for air attacks. Individual cement-and-dirt bomb shelters lined streets everywhere. Many Vietnamese were fully armed as they went about their work, but there was a concerted effort to "normalize" daily existence. There were flower stalls on the streets, cafés filled with young couples and older people, and, Aptheker noticed, bookstores filled with avid readers. Among the most popular foreign books were those by American authors: William Faulkner, O. Henry, Mark Twain, Jack London. He could never stock enough books by Hemingway, a bookseller told Aptheker regretfully. The Voice of America floated in unimpeded on the radio, bringing in even Bob Dylan singing "Blowin' in the Wind." Most children had been evacuated from the city, and their absence was a constant and silent reminder of the war, but in most respects daily life went on. "There is no national emergency which can fully erase the fact that shopping must be done, the fields tended, and young couples married," Lynd and Hayden (1966, 57) wrote. Having expected to find the city gripped in a siege mentality, they found themselves instead caught in "an emotional shock . . . as we entered this little world forbidden to Americans, so unknown to our people and so exposed to our military power. Hanoi itself, though fully prepared for battle, did not appear agitated or mobilized. Only an occasional soldier was visible, and infrequently a truck full of armed men or supplies would rumble down the pavement" (Lynd and Hayden 1966, 58).

The memorials to Alice Herz that had impressed the Du Bois group in August were now combined with memorials to Norman Morrison, who had followed Herz in self-immolation that fall. Morrison, a thirty-two year old father of three and a clerk at the Stony Run Friends' meeting in Baltimore (where Alice and Staughton Lynd had been married), was deeply troubled over the air war and frustrated by the inability of American citizens to stop it. On the morning of 2 November 1965, he read an account in *I. F. Stone's Weekly* of a French priest in Vietnam whose parishioners had been bombed by American pilots. "I have seen my faithful burned up in napalm," the priest cried. The same newspaper carried an appeal to Americans to write their legislators protesting the war. Morrison had written his representatives repeatedly, but still the war widened. Late that afternoon, he left a note for his wife: "Know that I love thee, but I must act for the children of the priest's village." Carrying his eighteen-month-old daughter, Emily, he walked to the river entrance of the Pentagon, where he put his daughter down, doused his clothes with kerosene, and struck a match. Emily was unharmed but her father died in the flames (Hendrickson 1996).

"Wherever one goes in the Democratic Republic of Vietnam," wrote Aptheker (1966, 54), "one sees the image of Norman Morrison. Photographs and drawings of him adorn buildings, schools, churches, factories; streets have been named for him; and among the first questions asked American visitors are those concerning Morrison, his wife, Anne, and their children." The Revolutionary Museum in Hanoi had an exhibit of photographs of protest against the American involvement in Vietnam from countries around the world. One wall of the exhibit room held large pictures of Norman Morrison and Alice Herz. Vietnamese poets wrote poems and dedicated their works to Morrison and his family. Aptheker copied the English translation of a widely circulated poem, written by poet To Huu, from the visual perspective of Morrison himself:

Look this way
For this one moment, look at me
Not just a man with a child in his arm. I am Today itself,
And this, my Emily, is all our tomorrows.
Here I stand, summoning the great heart of America
To rekindle on the horizon
The beacon of justice.

(Aptheker 1966, 57)

Herz and Morrison had chosen forms of protest foreign to American tradition and firmly within Buddhist experience. As symbolic actions, their protest placed them unequivocally on the side of the Vietnamese civilians under the bombs. Self-immolation also called attention to the fiery military tactics of napalm bombing. To the Vietnamese, Lynd believed, Morrison "represented an American who had some glimmer of what they were experiencing. They were being burned alive and their children were being burned alive" (Lynd 1993).

The news of Alice Herz's and Norman Morrison's action spread rapidly through Vietnam because the form of their sacrifice reinforced the belief of many Vietnamese that American citizens could sympathize with their struggle. The *Vietnam Courier* and Radio Hanoi, for example, consistently denounced the American role in the war in harsh terms, using words that translated, for example, as "aggressor," "war crimes," "criminal acts," but they did not usually rail against the United States as a nation or its people. They railed against specific leaders, especially Johnson, McNamara, and Rusk. At the same time, they depicted many other Americans in positive terms. Hanoi's newspapers and radio carried reports, often taken directly from United States media sources, of international sentiment and protest against the war, and they derived from these accounts the larger depiction of Americans as potential allies. These reports also bolstered a Vietnamese sense that the world was not arrayed against their country. The fact that Vietnam was small and impoverished was ameliorated by the fact that, with respect to the pursuit of military policies in Vietnam, the United States became ever more isolated in the world community.

Herz and Morrison represented something to American officials as well. Morrison burned himself in front of the Pentagon, and the act shocked Secretary of Defense McNamara, who was sitting inside. He later wrote somberly that he was all too well aware of Morrison's death "within forty feet of my Pentagon window." McNamara's account of that day includes a meticulously rendered quotation from Anne Morrison, who said at the time that Norman's death was "an outcry against the killing that was destroying the lives of so many Vietnamese and American youth." McNamara wrote later that he reacted to Morrison's death by "bottling up my emotions and avoiding talking about them with anyone—even my family. I knew Mary and our three children shared many of Morrison's feelings about the war as did the wives and children of several of my cabinet colleagues. And I believed I understood and shared some of his thoughts. . . . The episode created tension at home that only deepened as dissent and criticism of the war continued to grow" (McNamara 1995, 216).

Going to Hanoi to meet their government's "enemies," Lynd said, offered Americans like himself the opportunity to confront their own stereotypes. One day, when he went to visit an agriculture implement factory in Hanoi, Lynd noticed news pictures and posters of war protests in the United States hanging in one section. He recognized himself in one, speaking from the back of a pick-up truck at an antiwar rally. After the tour, the group gathered in a small room with white tablecloths and small dishes of hard candy on a few tables, and the manager launched into a welcoming speech "that I thought I'd heard about six thousand times before," Lynd said.

> I sat with my head down, sort of doodling on my paper and bored, waiting for the speech to be over. The manager said, "although we have a very serious difference with the government of the United States, we admire the American people and their declaration of independence written by Abraham Lincoln." And at first I had a superior feeling but then I thought to myself, I haven't a clue as to *his* history. He, at least, has a name and a document—he's ahead of me. But the next words he said were, "but just now, the word 'American' has become difficult for us to say." And there was this pause and I was sitting there playing with my hard candy waiting for something to happen, and finally I looked up and there was this 'inscrutable' Oriental weeping. And that was the end of my notions about inscrutable Orientals. (Lynd 1993).

A belief shared by many Americans at the time was that the Vietnamese civilians who supported the struggle for independence were inspired primarily by ideological fervor. Some activists, those who wished to revolutionize American society in short order, regarded this support as a positive attribute and hoped to find a kinship in Vietnam on this level. Others, those who advocated reform of American institutions, saw ideological fervor in a less positive light and went to Hanoi hoping to transcend it. In either case, they all discovered a state of affairs in Vietnam different from one governed primarily by a response to the ideologies of the Cold War. The Vietnamese that Americans met in Hanoi were generally uninterested in theoretical discussions of the precise paths revolutions or socialism should take. They focused instead, on the meaning of this particular conflict at this particular time, and of its significance in their own history and future. Vietnam's long wars against colonialism had shaped their own lives, their culture, and their economy in precise ways—but that encounter with colonialism, they insisted, was particular to Vietnam. Particular historical forces, not abstract ideological ones, would shape their future. On this trip, for example, Tom Hayden frequently pressed his hosts for their theoretical positions on patterns of global revolution, but he emerged from the conversations with little satisfaction. At one point he persistently questioned Nguyen Trung Hieu, one of the interpreters, about his beliefs on the issue of "socialism in one country." What was the correct action if revolutionaries in another country, India, for example, called upon a future independent Vietnam for help? The somewhat baffled interpreter said he didn't know. "We will worry about that when the time comes," he finally told Hayden (Lynd and Hayden 1966, 64). A further encounter with three National Liberation Front soldiers who were on a speaking tour in North Vietnam engendered a similar response. When probed for the origins of the ideological fervor that Hayden supposed had propelled them into the NLF, they responded with accounts of personal experiences with French colonialism that had served as their propelling impulse. Oanh told Hayden later that his emphasis on theoretical issues in these conversations presumed too much ideological "sophistication" on the part of the Vietnamese (Lynd and Hayden 1966, 171).

The books that the three travelers wrote upon their return convey the relative emphases on ideology with which they had gone to Hanoi. Lynd and Hayden teamed up to write *The Other Side,* the book most associated with the journey, and Aptheker wrote *Mission to Hanoi.* The title *The Other Side* conveys the authors' intention to help Americans see the war from Hanoi's perspective. Nonetheless, the book presented the war very much from an American viewpoint: the perspective of Americans caught up in theoretical and domestic issues that concerned Americans more than the Vietnamese. Lynd and Hayden's discussion of the war in Vietnam repeatedly fell into a detailed examination of the relative merits of various theories of war and revolution, a discussion informed primarily by the American Cold War, American anticommunism, and the theoretical hair-splitting that the New Left associated with the Old Left. These digressive debates seemed to have been of little interest to the Vietnamese, who preferred discussions of the concrete reality of the war, its impact on their country and political struggle, and its place in their own history. *The Other Side* itself divides up Vietnam and the Vietnamese in ways reminiscent of Washington's own mythical divisions. Chapter headings are, for example, "In Hanoi: The People"; "In Hanoi: The System"; "Varieties of Revolutionary Experience (Prague, Moscow, Peking)"; and "Revolution and Violence." But Lynd and Hayden wrote that they had gone to Hanoi because "it seemed unendurable to stand by and do nothing" (4), and the book is a testimony to the "unendurability" of doing nothing.

Aptheker's book, *Mission to Hanoi*, written by an active communist, is less rhetorical than *The Other Side*. Aptheker began by clearly stating his own position and then focusing on the war and its impact on Vietnam and on himself while he was there. His book is filled with photos he took on the trip and unabashedly human vignettes of his encounters with the Vietnamese. Aptheker conveyed a clearer sense of "the other side," and of the Americans as well, in many vivid descriptions like the one of his encounter with an elderly Catholic priest in Nam Dinh who said he could not forget, as he daily prepared the sacraments that, during the French occupation, Christianity itself came in national and racial hierarchies. The French, he said "had two Christs" during the colonial era, "one for the Vietnamese and one for the French." The aged Vietnamese priest asked Aptheker why his own country, so far away, came to bomb the priest's city. Standing inside the bombing zone, Aptheker hardly knew what to say. Then, suddenly, American planes were sighted in the distance, and he knew he would have to leave quickly. "My hosts come and tell me we must leave," he wrote. "There is an alert; they are forty miles away and we are not sure but it is not safe. I beg to be allowed to remain, but they will have none of it and I must leave. We say goodbye—the old priest and this American Communist deep in the heart of crucified Vietnam. I ask the Father's pardon for leaving so quickly—and to myself, I ask the Father's pardon for a million other things, too" (Aptheker 1966, 49).

Soon after arriving in Hanoi, Lynd had asked Do Xuan Oanh if they could meet with some American prisoners of war to carry some messages back to their families. The meeting was not easily arranged. Their hosts were willing but army officials flatly refused. It took Oanh and the Peace Committee days of patient negotiations before an agreement was finally reached: only one prisoner and only a short visit. Army officials made it clear they were unhappy with the meeting. They placed the American pilot at a table noticeably lower than all the others in the room and refused to change the seating arrangement despite Lynd's forceful objections. The seating arrangement was symptomatic of a deeper discomfort on all sides. Allied with an "enemy" in the eyes of the American pilot, but talking with the "American criminal" in the eyes of their Vietnamese hosts, Lynd and Hayden wrote, "was nearly insufferable." Beyond this, they knew that in several days they would be going home while the pilot "would still pace a small cell, hoping, as he told us, that 'this ends as soon as possible.'" The pilot was similarly uneasy, his phrases as cautious as their own. He knew vaguely who they were, talked warmly about his family, whom he missed dearly, especially his children, because "this is the age when they are really forming their opinions" (Lynd and Hayden 1966, 104).

The pilot told the three Americans that he and his fellow POWs had heard that the NLF had recently released two American prisoners in South Vietnam. The prisoners in Hanoi wanted to go home, too, and they hoped that other early releases would follow. The released prisoners to whom they referred were Green Beret sergeant George E. Smith and Specialist Fifth Class Claude McClure, who had been prisoners of the NLF in South Vietnam for over two years. A month earlier, at Thanksgiving, the NLF had released the two, as the NLF statement put it, "to replace Morrison and Alice Herz, the two who had given their lives for the cause of peace in Vietnam" (Lynd and Hayden 1966, 107). What the POWs in Hanoi had not heard was that Smith and McClure were now under house arrest by order of the United States Army. Soon after his release, at a press conference, Smith had said he was treated well in captivity and that he wanted to help other Americans understand the truth about the war in Vietnam. Both Smith and McClure were then placed under house arrest and were being held in Okinawa charged with "aiding and abetting" the enemy. Lynd reluctantly told the American prisoner of war in Hanoi what he had heard of the story from news accounts. After being held for four months and threatened with a court martial, Smith and McClure were both abruptly granted honorable discharges and released on

15 April 1966. Smith wrote a book, *P.O.W.: Two Years With the Vietcong* about his ordeal and later was a witness at the Winter Soldier Investigation. He told the investigation that, according to his Army superiors, one of his "offenses" was telling the press that while in captivity he had received Red Cross parcels.

Hearing of Smith's and McClure's fate must have been instructive for the first American prisoners of war in Hanoi. It was a warning that, in addition to the strain of life as prisoners, they had to walk a fine line while in captivity or risk punishment by their own government when they were released. While captive, a reasonable cooperation with their captors offered some measure of mental and physical well-being. But this tactic held the risk of court-martial or a curbed career upon release. Even meeting with American visitors in Hanoi made them suspect in Washington. Another message was equally clear—upon release, the safest course for their reputation and military futures was to be militantly anti-Vietnamese and supportive of the war's continuation.

Before leaving Hanoi, Aptheker, Lynd, and Hayden spent over an hour with Premier Pham Van Dong. The premier reiterated the points he had made to Women Strike for Peace, points that nationalist Vietnamese, North and South, insisted upon in each meeting with American activists: Washington must withdraw foreign troops from Vietnam and end the bombing. As long as there was no apparent commitment to withdrawing foreign troops from Vietnamese soil, Premier Pham Van Dong told his American visitors, real negotiations could not begin. The United States was on the wrong side of history, the premier believed. It was still seeking the prerogatives of colonial overlordship in an era when colonial empires were breaking up. Furthermore, the premier told his guests, the Christmas "bombing pause," which Johnson presented as a beneficent gift from Washington, was accompanied by continued and heavy overflights of airspace in the North and increased American air strikes and ground warfare in the South (Lynd 1966a, 1966d).

Hanoi officials believed that the way Johnson announced and conducted the bombing pause indicated that it was little more than a public relations ploy. In December, immediately preceding the "peace offensive," they reminded Lynd, the United States had authorized "hot pursuit" into Cambodia, conceded that it was using toxic chemicals on South Vietnam's rice fields, sent four thousand new American troops to Pleiku, launched hundreds of B-52 sorties in South Vietnam, and convened a gathering of the U.S. Army's chief of staff, the chairman of the Joint

Chiefs of Staff, and the secretaries of the army and the air force. In their experience, they told Lynd, such gatherings preceded fresh escalations. "What is the reason for the peace offensive?" Premier Pham Van Dong asked the three Americans, and then he answered his own question, sounding as though he had been privy to memoranda flowing between the Defense Department and the White House. "To win public opinion, particularly American public opinion. Only by so doing can President Johnson escalate the war." Indeed, a classified National Security Office memorandum the following month stated that the purpose of the December pause was to demonstrate to the American public "that we have explored fully every alternative but that the aggressor has left us no choice." Extending the bombing pause, the memo went on, was "a matter of our desiring to place full responsibility on Hanoi and the Viet Cong for the renewal of hostilities" (Rostow 1966b, LBJL).

The three Americans left Hanoi on 6 January, returning as they had come, by way of Beijing, Moscow, Prague, and London. Press reports of the "illegality" of their trip preceded them. In Beijing, they were met at the airport by a member of the Chinese Peace Committee, who carried a copy of the *New York Times* under one arm, and told them, smiling broadly, "there's been a great deal of interest in your trip!" The State Department alerted American consulates along their "likely" return route to stamp the travelers' passports valid only for return to the United States, but they did not stop in at any consular offices and returned to the United States with their passports intact. The links between Washington's foreign policy and domestic goals, links that had dogged the composition of the group, were highlighted when the *New York Times* reported on 29 December that the president planned to cut nine million dollars of federal aid to New York City schools, "thus freeing more money for the Vietnam war."

Comedian Bob Hope had been in Saigon entertaining American troops while the three were in Hanoi. On the flight across the Atlantic back to New York, Aptheker read *Newsweek*'s breezy account of the comic's effort to bring some Americana to Vietnam. Hope's "best" jokes, the magazine said, came on the aircraft carrier *Ticonderoga*, when he conflated racial tensions within the United States with the war in Vietnam. "They roared," *Newsweek* reported on 10 January, "when he called the United States bombing raids of North Viet Nam 'the best slum clearance project they ever had.'" While Hope's troupe, including the latest Miss U.S.A., was on the carrier, a returning navy plane missed a recovery cable and plunged into the sea in flames. "This really brought the war home," a shaken troupe member said. A year later Hope acknowledged that "a few" performers had turned down his invitation to join his Christmas tour in Vietnam. But by then, as the *New York Times* reported on 22 December 1966, he had a new act lined up—the "Korean Kittens," a female trio in high heels direct from Seoul, South Korea—to entertain American men in South Vietnam.

Back in the United States, Lynd requested a meeting with the Senate Foreign Relations Committee, headed by J. William Fulbright, an emerging critic of the war. Fulbright rejected his request, referring the group to the State Department. But the State Department had little use for them either; it was preparing to seize their passports at an opportune moment. Johnson's "peace offensive" had won the desired praise for its restraint. In addition, with the war in Vietnam billed as a war for democratic freedoms, prosecuting people whose "crime" was international travel had to be managed carefully because it undermined America's own claim to freedom. The passports of the three travelers were not seized at Kennedy International Airport when they returned on 9 January, though customs agents confiscated some of Hayden's books and tape recordings to determine whether they were "subversive."

Lynd used the media's preoccupation with the legality of the trip to publicize, as far as possible, his talks with Premier Pham Van Dong, in an effort to move the media's focus to the state of negotiations with Vietnam. "The trip has been the subject of wide publicity and has elicited a number of questions at daily press briefings as well as substantial public mail and inquiries from a dozen or more Congressmen," noted a State Department memo (Schwartz 1966, LBJL) in late January. Media reports revolved around Premier Pham Van Dong's statement to Lynd that, despite Washington's claims, it had not contacted his government directly during the "peace offensive." When Lynd made this information public upon his return, noting that he himself had easily contacted an NLF representative in Prague, who even spoke English, by "simply picking up the telephone" from his home in New Haven, Vice President Humphrey expressed concern. "I am disturbed over the attached story as marked," he wrote on 10 January to presidential advisor McGeorge Bundy, enclosing a news clipping of Lynd's comments. "I make no case for Lynd, as you know. I do, however, feel that his comments about our lack of direct approach to Hanoi will have some effect on the people's attitude toward the President's peace offensive. What are the facts?" (Humphrey to Bundy

1966, LBJL). Bundy dismissed Lynd's account. "As I am quite sure you have learned from Dean Rusk," he replied to the vice president the next day, "Lynd is quite uninformed. The President has asked that we hold the full facts very closely, but at your convenience I will be glad to fill you in" (Bundy to Humphrey 1966, LBJL).

Throughout the "peace offensive," the White House insisted that direct contacts with Hanoi had been made, but it refused to release any information about them. On 6 February, after the bombing over North Vietnam resumed, the *New York Times* reported that Henry Byroade, American Ambassador to Burma, had been the link to Hanoi. Byroade's meeting with his contact in Rangoon had been "brief," the source noted. Byroade later confirmed that his "contact," delivered to a Vietnamese office in Rangoon on 21 January, over a week after the three travelers had returned from Hanoi, consisted of nothing new—only a written summation of Washington's position. President Johnson ordered the bombing resumed on 31 January.[6]

In February 1966, with the "peace offensive" over and the bombing resumed, the State Department set out to confiscate the three passports. Lynd was in London at the time as a panelist on a British Broadcasting Corporation program about the war in Vietnam. When he returned to New York, officials at the airport canceled his passport and ordered Aptheker and Hayden to surrender theirs. The State Department decided to make examples of previous travelers to Hanoi, as well, and revoked the passports of the Du Bois travelers. Clarke and Gordon's trip to Hanoi in May had been little noted in the media, and they kept their passports for a while, at least.

The Justice Department then petitioned the Subversive Activities Control Board to order the Du Bois clubs to register as a "Communist-front organization." The courts had consistently rejected as unconstitutional the 1953 law requiring such registrations. But Attorney General Nicholas Katzenbach told the *Times* on 5 March that he had learned that when the unenforceable law was invoked against an organization, "membership falls off and the organization collapses." Two days later, the San Francisco headquarters of the Du Bois clubs was dynamited and de-

---

6. The State Department's recently declassified listing of contacts made during the "Thirty-seven Day Pause" lists diplomatic contacts ranging from Lester Pearson of Canada to "Haile Selassi" of Ethiopia, but no direct contacts with any Vietnamese official (Reston 1966b, LBJL). See also Kraslow and Loory, 1968.

stroyed. That year, the Control Board met more than sixty times, and its main target was the Du Bois clubs (Schultze 1967, LBJL).

Lynd immediately filed suit to recover his right to travel. While the passport cases wound their way through the courts, the plaintiffs could not leave the United States. Secretary of State Rusk determined to further tighten travel restrictions. He stripped Abba Schwartz, who headed the State Department's Bureau of Security and Consular Affairs, of his passport duties. Schwartz was an advocate of liberalized travel regulations and a thorn in the side of Rusk's efforts to deny passports on political grounds. Rusk handed passport regulation to Schwartz's subordinate, Frances Knight, who had long protested Schwartz's "dangerous" policy of granting passports to "suspected Communists." Schwartz resigned, but the president's press secretary, Bill Moyers, said it did not really matter who was in control of passport issuance. The administration's "progressive" policies remained in place, he told the *New York Times* on 11 March, pointing to the recent and "liberal" decision to grant scientists a special dispensation to visit these countries forbidden to all other citizens.

Indeed, the State Department had again rearranged passport restrictions. On 29 December, after it had publicly threatened to revoke the passports of the Hanoi three, the State Department abruptly lifted travel restrictions on "physicians and medical scientists to visit Communist China, Cuba, Albania, North Korea, and North Vietnam." Persons in these approved categories had to apply individually for visa dispensations, and the State Department still reserved the right to refuse any application without explanation. The medical community had urged this course, Secretary of State Rusk told the *Times* on 30 December, because it could help attack diseases that "were no respecter of frontiers." Problems in the field of health and medicine transcended national borders, the Secretary insightfully offered, and were "not problems which ought to be governed by the political process but ought to be governed by the elementary interest of man in his health."

Lynd eventually got his passport back, but not his profession. Yale's president, Kingman Brewster, Jr., had initially called Lynd's trip "a conscientious effort" and said that "the long-run charge which this university bears from its own tradition makes it unthinkable that we should penalize a faculty member for this political position" (*Nation* 1966). In Hanoi, however, Lynd was asked to address a Cultural Congress, and his address there, Lynd believed, marked his exit from Yale. Hanoi released a transcript of the Congress, including Lynd's speech, in which he called the

American air war "inhuman, unlawful and anti-democratic." President Brewster condemned the speech when he heard of it, calling it "naïve" and "irresponsible." Lynd had given "aid and comfort" to the enemy, Brewster told the student editors of Yale's *Daily News,* and went on to assert that Lynd had "done a disservice to the causes of freedom of dissent, freedom of travel, and conscientious pacifism." Lynd's characterization of the war was one that many Americans soon came to accept, and more scathing denunciations of the war were uttered shortly within the halls of Congress and in the pages of the nation's newspapers. But Yale denied him tenure and Lynd set out on a new job search, applying to a total of five other universities. In each case, the faculty voted to hire him, but the administration vetoed the faculty decision. By 1972, Lynd gave up searching for a university position and turned his energies to labor advocacy.[7]

The three travelers addressed numerous audiences throughout the country over the course of the following months. Reports that the three wrote upon their return reached an even wider audience. Detailed accounts of their Hanoi trip appeared in *Liberation* in February and in May. *Viet-Report* devoted much of its January and February issues to reports from Lynd and Hayden, along with transcripts of conversations that the three had with Vietnamese officials. The magazines printed, in their entirety, Hanoi's Four Points, a basis for a peace settlement modeled on the Geneva Accords, along with a fourteen-point "rebuttal" that the Johnson Administration had unveiled. Some traditional religious periodicals also covered the trip and the travel issues it raised, but they were reluctant to open up their pages entirely. Aptheker had brought back from Hanoi an appeal from the Catholic and Protestant churches there, with a request that it be published in the United States. He sent the appeal to *Commonweal* and *Christian Century,* the leading lay Catholic and Protestant periodicals. American churches were not ready for international ecumenism to go this far. Both periodicals refused to publish the Vietnamese appeal, so Aptheker included the appeal in an appendix to his own book.

The flurry of passport confiscations in early 1966 ended American citizen travel to Hanoi for most of the coming year. Some of the travelers whose passports were confiscated contested the seizures in court, and

---

7. The five institutions were Chicago State College, Roosevelt University, Northern Illinois University, University of Illinois, Chicago Circle Campus and Loyola University. Herbert Aptheker never had, before the trip, and never had subsequently, a permanent position at any university.

court rulings handed down over the course of the next two years steadily eroded the administration's attempts to control citizen travel. Eventually the courts agreed that the government could not prohibit travel; it could only seize a passport that had been carried into a forbidden country. If travelers left their passports behind when they went to North Vietnam, they faced no prosecution nor could their passport be seized. These rulings were poorly covered and explained in the media, and many activists continued to believe for some time that the government could seize passports and bring criminal prosecution because an individual had traveled to Hanoi.

Government statements encouraged this perception by continuing to raise that threat even after it had acceded to the court decisions. By depicting travelers to North Vietnam as criminals, and seizing their passports, the State Department encouraged the media to focus on domestic legal issues rather than on the air war in North Vietnam. The national media did not require much coaxing in this area; it generally was more comfortable framing these travels as passport violations, a convenient approach that removed journalists from the uncomfortable prospect of alienating their government sources.

At the same time the government was seizing passports that had been in Hanoi or that belonged to Americans who had been in Hanoi, it continued sponsoring and paying the expenses of other groups to go to South Vietnam. For over a year, the State Department had been bringing Vietnamese student groups to the United States to tour campuses, hoping to counter the effects of the university teach-ins. The *New York Times* reported on 19 March that one Vietnamese student group consisted of "five North Vietnamese students who had defected," but the National Student Association (NSA) had found these five "unconvincing and disappointing," so in spring 1966, the State Department sent delegates from the NSA to South Vietnam to visit "social and economic development programs" run by the U.S. government.

The National Student Association delegation, led by its president, Philip Sherburne, a student at the University of Oregon, left for Saigon at the end of March 1966. "Though the war in Vietnam is the most exhaustively reported in history," Sherburne told the *Times*, "we know little of the views of South Vietnamese students on the great issues of the war itself. We plan to find out what those views are and we plan to communicate them to American students when we return." The delegation spent two weeks in South Vietnam, conferring with scores of student representatives. Rather than confining their visits to "social and economic development programs" in Vietnam run by Washington, as the State Department wanted them to do, the group also sought out leaders of the Buddhist community and students who were then involved in a widespread and eventually fiery clash with Saigon and American troops.

The report they brought back was not polemical—the NSA was, before 1968, considered the most "moderate" of the major student organizations, and in early 1966 it was only mildly critical of Washington's tactics in Vietnam. The report was reflective, bleak, and discouraging, however. No matter how well-intentioned American policymakers were, the delegates concluded, American policies had "hopelessly alienated" most of the South Vietnamese civilian population, created suspicions about American intentions, and failed even to achieve its nonmilitary goals. "Anti-American sentiment is deeply felt by many student and religious leaders," the report concluded, because of "extensive American control over Vietnamese affairs and the destructive impact of the presence of large numbers of American troops." Many Vietnamese students believed that negotiating with the Ky regime was "really meaningless as the Ky regime has been merely an American creation from the outset." The NSA's report from Saigon circulated that spring and summer at its 301 affiliated colleges and universities and served as a basis for the NSA's reappraisal of its foreign policy platform at its August Congress at the University of Illinois (People's Peace Treaty 1971, SCPC).

With travel to Hanoi rendered more difficult by Washington's passport restrictions, activists turned to other geographical arenas. In April 1966, one group went to Saigon in a highly publicized protest action, and later in the year another group went to Cambodia on a fact-finding mission on the bombing campaign there. The April journey was organized by the Committee for Non-Violent Action (CNVA), a pacifist group organized in 1957 by people with long histories in labor struggles, peace organizations, and civil rights reform, people who could feel the heavy atmospheric testing of nuclear bombs "in their bones" (Katz 1974, 3). The first CNVA action in 1958 sent a small sailing vessel, *The Golden Rule*, into the testing zone around the Enewetak atoll in the Pacific Ocean to protest nuclear bomb testing there. U.S. Coast Guard officials seized the vessel and imprisoned the crew (Bigelow, 1959). In 1960, a group of CNVA marchers completed a "San Francisco to Moscow Walk" to publicize issues of nuclear disarmament (Lyttle, "San Francisco," SCPC; Gottlieb "Peace Walk," SCPC). After the Cuban Missile Crisis,

the CNVA organized a "Quebec to Guantanamo Walk for Peace" in summer 1963. When the marchers passed through Albany, Georgia, police
chief Laurie Pritchett threw the group in prison. They finally set sail from
Miami in a boat christened *Spirit of Freedom,* but the Coast Guard
boarded the boat, impounded it, and filed charges against the crew in a
court case aptly named *The United States of America v. The Spirit of Freedom* (Deming 1964, 1966).

In early 1966, the revered A. J. Muste was chair of the CNVA.
Muste, a white-haired man with a long reputation as a careful listener and
consensus builder, was eighty-one years old, but this inveterate and lively
activist was not prepared to slow down. With other CNVA members, he
planned to carry protest against the war to Saigon itself, and he invited
Martin Luther King, Jr., to go along. King declined, pleading other re-
sponsibilities (Muste 1966, SCPC). Muste's record as an activist was as
long as his arrest record: for leading labor strikes in the twenties and thir-
ties, for failure to take shelter during practice air-raid drills in New York
city in the 1950s, for "trespassing" at an Atlas missile base in Nebraska,
for refusing to pay war taxes. Ever since 1948, Muste had sent the IRS, in
lieu of his tax return, a copy of Thoreau's essay "On Civil Disobedience,"
a copy of the Gospels, and a letter in which he outlined his reasons for refusing to contribute to American armaments. The IRS never prosecuted
Muste because, as the agency noted, "Taxpayer has no funds. He has voluntarily lived for years at a subsistence level" (Robinson 1981, 94). A
charter member of the American Civil Liberties Union and involved in
the most significant labor struggles of the 1920s and 1930s, Muste was
now also the executive secretary of the Fellowship of Reconciliation and a
leader in the War Resisters League, the Church Peace Mission, and the
New American Forum for Socialist Education. Social critic Paul Goodman called him "the keenest political analyst in America" (Robinson
1981; Dubovsky 1988).

According to the 29 April publication of the New York Workshop in
Nonviolence (*WIN*), the other CNVA members bound for Saigon were
veteran activists in civil rights and peace issues. Barbara Deming, a writer
and editor for *Liberation* magazine, had gone on the San Francisco-to-
Moscow walk in 1960 and had been imprisoned in Albany and Birmingham for civil rights protests. William Davidon, a prolific writer and activist
on issues of nuclear testing and arms control, was chair of the Physics Department at Haverford College. Bradford Lyttle, after serving a prison
term for "noncooperation" with the draft in 1954, had been involved in

most of the major direct nonviolent actions for peace. Karl Meyer was editor of the *Catholic Worker* and a veteran of numerous direct action projects, and Sherry Thurber, the youngest member, was a student at Sarah Lawrence College who had worked on Southern Christian Leadership Conference voter registration projects in Alabama and with CORE in Georgia.

After the State Department seized passports of travelers to Hanoi, the CNVA team feared at first that they could not get passports to go to South Vietnam. Bradford Lyttle said that he "hopelessly looked at the passport form that asked where I was going and why; since I don't want to lie to the government, I simply left that blank. I altered the 'oath of allegiance' to the effect that I would defend the Constitution of the United States nonviolently." To their surprise, their passports came through in several days. The next problem lay in getting a visa to South Vietnam. "If you're going to South Vietnam to protest the presence of American troops," Lyttle thought, "the South Vietnamese government isn't going to cotton to this" (Lyttle 1966b, 11). They then discovered that Saigon did not yet require prior visas of Americans but rather issued them to bearers of American passports at the Tan Son Nhut airport outside of Saigon.

CNVA's journey to Saigon was undertaken "to know more at first hand about conditions in Vietnam and surrounding countries"; to protest this war that Muste called "profoundly immoral and inhumane" on the territory where it was fought; and to protest the American involvement directly to the Americans there. "By standing on that very spot where our country's power is striking blindly and brutally, and so sharing a little of the risk taken daily by the many who are suffering there, our words and actions will gain a little resonance," Barbara Deming wrote as she planned the trip. William Davidon linked their efforts to a larger international effort. "During the past months," he wrote, "thoughtful and responsible men and women throughout the world have joined in condemning the war with its devastation and demoralization." He noted that Buddhist and Catholic leaders in Vietnam, U.S. senators, the Secretary General of the United Nations, lawyers, doctors, Nobel Prize winners, mothers, ministers, students, and others had joined together in opposing the war and went on to observe that "one of the healthier parts of our own tradition is that individuals and voluntary non-governmental groups take the initiative to meet pressing needs." Even if their efforts did not yield their objectives, he said, "There is still, we believe, intrinsic value in the at-

tempt itself." And Sherry Thurber wrote, "At least the people of Vietnam
will know that, though thousands of Americans have poured into their
country to make war, some came who wished to stand nonviolently for
peace" (Reports from Saigon 1966, SCPC). Muste wrote in *WIN* on 29
April 1966:

> We go not because we are anti-American, [but as] human beings who
> are antiwar and pro-mankind. It is frequently said that in wartime criti-
> cism has to cease, opposition must be stifled, and all energies concen-
> trated on waging the war and achieving military victory. We categorically
> reject this contention. It is precisely in wartime when the stakes are so
> high, when the dangers of national hysteria are so great . . . that free-
> dom to think, to speak and to oppose has to be cherished and practiced.
> Otherwise nations will be trapped in what the great Jewish philosopher,
> Martin Buber, described as "the speechlessness of slaughter."

In early April 1966, Muste's group flew to Tokyo, where they met
with members of Japanese peace organizations, who provided them with
names of individuals and groups in Saigon who could help them there.[8]
On 15 April they landed at Tan Son Nhut Air Force Base, just north of
Saigon, one day after a mortar attack on the base had killed nine Americans. They thought the base might be closed for at least a day after this
direct attack, but it was not. Bradford Lyttle's reaction to this "normalcy
in time of war" resembled that of the American travelers to Hanoi. "To
our surprise, we went in on schedule. . . . War goes on, people are killed,
there are attacks within the city limits; and yet life continues for the people there. The destruction and the bodies are simply cleared away, and
business is normal" (Lyttle 1966b, 11).

The group passed easily through customs at the airport and managed
to book a suite in the Caravelle Hotel in Saigon, where many of the news
agencies were headquartered. From Friday until the following Tuesday,
they met United States Agency for International Development officials,
American correspondents, Buddhist monks, Catholic priests, and Vietnamese students who had known little but war. One of them told the
group bitterly, "You must realize that we are a special generation in Vietnam; we've known war all our lives; we understand perhaps better than
anyone else in the world what war is. We want to tell other young people

---

8. American and Japanese peace activists developed strong ties during this time, both
in activism against the war and in antidraft activities (Haven, 1987).

around the world but we can't—we have to remain silent. Why is it that Johnson sends ambassadors all over the world talking about peace, but if we in South Vietnam mention peace we are labeled as Communists and put in jail?" (Thurber 1966, 19).

One woman asked Thurber if her government realized that "with every bomb that is dropped on a village there are more enemies made for America? If this war continues," the woman went on, "America will have no friends left anywhere in Vietnam." This sentiment turned up time and again as the group met with members of the Vietnamese community embroiled in that spring groundswell for a negotiated peace in Vietnam. The Catholics that the CNVA group met in Saigon belied the widespread image in America of the Catholic community in Vietnam as solidly opposed to the National Liberation Front and to Hanoi. Priests, too, were drawing up petitions and circulating them for signatures calling upon the government to negotiate with the NLF. There was a certain "wistful quality," Thurber noted, to the carefully outlined "alternative future," which students, religious figures, and political leaders sketched of a neutralist government that could negotiate with the NLF toward an ultimate goal of national reunification. One point on which all of these groups were agreed was that none of their plans for a negotiated settlement and a neutralist government could be implemented as long as American troops remained in Vietnam (Reports from Saigon 1966, SCPC).

The CNVA group scheduled a press conference in their Caravelle suite at ten o'clock on Wednesday morning, just before their planned picketing of the American Embassy. But at nine-thirty, Saigon police officers barred the press from the hotel, and the hotel management, with some visible chagrin, canceled their press conference, saying they did not have a permit for it. When the group persisted, police officials drove them to City Hall to meet with Major Nguyen Van Truong of the Saigon Security Forces. The Vietnamese major, accompanied by an American who remained silent throughout the entire exchange, took their passports and suggested they move the venue of the press conference to the Saigon council chambers. It could provide them with better security, he told them.

While the major set up the conference, another American, who refused to divulge his name, questioned them at length about their objectives in Vietnam and warned them not to travel outside Saigon for their own security. At five o'clock their passports were returned, and they were permitted to proceed with the press conference, which the police had moved to the Saigon council chambers. The police were there in large numbers, as was the press, whose numbers had steadily swelled as the day's events unfolded. The police also allowed about fifty self-described students into the council chambers. Soon after the CNVA activists began taking questions from the press, these "students" began to harangue the activists, pounding on tables and throwing eggs, tomatoes, and even a light bulb at them. An American news correspondent at the press conference told Lyttle that he recognized several of the "students" as security agents who had recently broken up Buddhist demonstrations.

The police finally moved the "students" out of the room, herded the activists into automobiles for their own "protection," and drove them back to the Caravelle. There, the nervous manager told them they could not eat in the hotel's restaurant and had to leave early the next morning. At five in the morning, the police arrived with jeeps to "take them to the Embassy," but by this time, the activists preferred to do without police protection. They set out on foot for the embassy, followed by four jeeps loaded with Saigon police. Near the embassy, the police ordered them into a paddy wagon. Preceded by jeeps with whistles and sirens blowing, they whizzed past the embassy and on to the airport. En route, the activists slipped the antiwar pamphlets that they had intended to distribute at the embassy through cracks in the paddy wagon, leaving a trail of leaflets streaming behind them. At Tan Son Nhut airport, they were placed aboard a Pan American World Airways jetliner bound for Hong Kong (Lyttle 1966a, 1966b).

Barbara Deming worried most about A. J. Muste, the eighty-one-year-old activist, she said in a 1967 memorial piece about Muste in *WIN:*

> As it turned out, they (the police) were gentle with us, but up to the last moment of course one was never sure that the next official to handle us would be gentle. When they had put us finally in a kind of detention room out at the airport . . . I looked across the room at A. J. to see how he was doing. It was a broiling hot day and we had spent sometime just sitting in the paddywagon out under the full sun, and that hadn't been easy for him. I looked across at him and he looked back with a smile, and with that sudden lighting up of his eyes which many of you will remember, and he said, "It's a good life!" He had done what he thought had to be done (that trip was above all his idea); and he had done it as well as he knew how; and then—he was able to be happy. What more could he do, until the next time?

Muste later said he did not worry about his own safety during the trip. He had been subjected to far worse treatment over the years at the hands of American police officers, he said, beginning when he led the 1919 textile-mill strike in Lawrence, Massachusetts.

The CNVA team stopped in Tokyo on the way home to meet with Japanese peace activists and report on their experiences in Vietnam. "I shall never forget A. J. standing on one leg at a time to take off his shoes on entering our Japanese Meeting House," noted DeWitt Barnett (1966, SCPC), an American Quaker living in Japan. "I know some people a lot younger than 81 who find it difficult to stand stork-like to take their shoes off!"

CNVA's expulsion from Saigon was front page news in the United States, and the press turned out to meet the group in New York. After a twelve-thousand-mile journey, *New York Post* reporter Pete Hamil noted on 25 April, "Muste's tweed coat was wrinkled and the grey suit gone baggy and he needed a shoe shine. . . . But the handshake was firm, the voice was sure and he looked at you with eyes made clear by the almost forgotten practice of virtue."

Saigon students sent letters to the team in the weeks and months following their trip. The letters showed a sense of excitement over the possibilities opened up by international activism. "You are foreigners who proclaimed deep aspirations of our whole people," one of them noted, "but we dare not ask more of you because we also know each people must . . . find for themselves a good way for their own country. . . . We are sure we will succeed especially with the help of those who have goodwill like you." In a letter published in *Liberation* magazine that July, another student said:

> Your actions brought a new strength to our struggle. I have even heard a saying from a cyclo-driver. He said to his friend: "I must stay here to witness the demonstration of six American Pacifists. This is a fact that I haven't ever seen in my life!" The most important thing is that you are Americans. I suppose if you were French or German the problem perhaps should not be mentioned seriously like this. At first it was a great surprise for me when seeing you, hearing your speaking, realizing your will. But I found that there is something in every people's heart, whether East or West, American or Vietnamese, that is THE THIRST FOR PEACE. And perhaps we have met one another at this point.

Contacts with Buddhists in South Vietnam resulted in an important eastward exchange across the Pacific. Thich Nhat Hanh, the Buddhist monk whom antiwar groups had come to know in Saigon, came, at their invitation, to the United States in May 1966, shortly after Muste's group

visited Saigon and after the Buddhist spring uprising in South Vietnam
had been crushed by American-backed Saigon forces. A writer, poet, religious leader, teacher, philosopher, and scholar, Hanh came to serve as an
"interpreter" of Vietnamese culture and life: a bit of Vietnam in America.
For those who continued to believe in it, he embodied the concept of a
third force for peace in Vietnam, and for all, he embodied the international struggle for freedom and peace. He was the perfect Vietnamese
speaker for many antiwar activists—committed to nonviolence and to social change, thoughtful, earnest, speaking impeccable English. The Fellowship of Reconcilation sponsored his stay in the United States, where
the slight, fervent bonze traveled tirelessly across the country for the next
two years, speaking to countless audiences, repeatedly moving his listeners to tears. He was, the *New Yorker* noted on 25 June, a voice describing
"the aspirations and the agony of the voiceless masses of the Vietnamese
people."

Nhat Hanh's books sold well in Vietnam and in the West. *Vietnam:
Lotus in a Sea of Fire,* written for American readers in 1967, was published
in eight languages. His writings reflected "engaged Buddhism," combin-
ing the quest for political peace with inner peace, and his poetry expressed
heartfelt connections between personal peace and peace on earth:

> Yesterday six Vietcong came through my village.
> Because of this my village was bombed—completely destroyed.
> Every soul was killed.
> When I come back to the village now, the day after,
> There is nothing to see but clouds of dust and the river, still flowing.
> I feel I am like that bird which dies for the sake of its mate,
> Dripping blood from its broken beak, and crying out:
> Beware! turn around to face your real enemies—
> Ambition, violence, hatred, greed.
> Men cannot be our enemies—even men called "Vietcong."
> If we kill men, what brothers will we have left?
> With whom shall we live then?
>
>   (Hanh 1967b)

Shortly before Nhat Hanh came to the United States in 1966, he had
sent an open letter to Martin Luther King, Jr., which appeared in *Liberation*'s December issue. The letter explained the philosophy behind the
self-immolation of Buddhist nuns and monks, and appealed to King not
to remain silent in the face of "the indescribable suffering of the Viet-

namese people." A warm personal friendship developed between the two leaders. King was so moved by Nhat Hanh's work in Vietnam and his teachings of peace that he nominated him for the 1967 Nobel Peace Prize, saying that he knew "of no one more worthy of the Nobel Peace Prize than this gentle monk from Vietnam" (Hanh 1991).

By mid-1966 the war clearly had spread into Cambodia and Laos. American planes had been bombing Cambodian border areas since 1961, and in May 1965 Cambodia's Prince Norodom Sihanouk had broken relations with the United States, saying they could not be restored until Washington acknowledged Cambodia's borders and her neutrality, ceased its attacks, and paid indemnities for damaged property. The bombings continued. Washington shrugged aside Cambodia's protests, declaring either that its maps of Asia showed that the areas in question were in South Vietnam and could therefore be bombed at will, or charging that Cambodia was harboring "Viet Cong" and therefore deserved bombing.

Awareness that the United States was bombing Vietnam's neighbors, combined with the fact that travel to North Vietnam was sharply attacked in Washington, turned the attention of activists to Cambodia. The issue came into focus in February 1966, when *Ramparts,* a magazine written for the Catholic laity, published an article by Donald Duncan, a highly decorated master sergeant in the Special Forces, or Green Berets, as they came to be called. After ten years in the army, Duncan had just turned down a commission to the rank of captain, left the service, and published an account of his years in Vietnam. His account detailed the role of the Special Forces in training and infiltrating groups into North Vietnam, Laos, and Cambodia, and in teaching torture methods to South Vietnamese forces, to whom they then turned over their prisoners. "We were continuously told," Duncan wrote, "you don't have to kill them yourself—let your indigenous counterpart do that" (Duncan 1966, 12).

After *Ramparts* published Duncan's article, Dagmar Wilson of Women Strike for Peace proposed a fact-finding delegation to Cambodia to inspect the border area and report back. Cambodia was not an off-limits region for American travel, so there would be no passport difficulties there. Duncan's credentials for such a trip were impeccable and he agreed to go. Wilson helped organize a group called "Americans Want to Know," chaired by herself and Ossie Davis. The five-person delegation to Cambodia included Duncan, Floyd McKissick, the new director of CORE, author Kay Boyle, Rabbi Israel Dresner of Temple Sharon

Shalom in Springfield, New Jersey, and Russell Johnson, New England's AFSC Peace Education Secretary (Wilson Files, SCPC).

The group reached Phnom Penh on 27 July and toured border areas for the next two weeks. Prince Sihanouk had previously pledged them his full cooperation, had guaranteed them access to all border areas, and had drawn up an itinerary for them. But the group wanted to spend more time on the border than the preplanned itinerary called for, and, after a three-hour session with the Cambodian liaison team, their suggested alternatives were accepted. "This last minute itinerary change underlies why we believe that nothing was staged for our benefit," Johnson wrote in September's *Liberation* magazine.

The group flew over border areas that the Pentagon claimed were "Vietcong sanctuaries," and Duncan searched the terrain for residual evidence of truck or military personnel movements. He found nothing. They traveled overland along the Laotian border, where they stopped trucks and checked their cargoes, finding, among other things, beer, California abalone, and prunes headed for Saigon. But they also found large open areas in the forest marked by shattered trees and water-logged bomb craters. While they were there, two American helicopters attacked the nearby Cambodian village of Thloc Trach. When they reached the village, they found burning homes and the body of a woman machine-gunned as she fled from her house. The tree under which she lay was riddled with bullets, showing how deliberately the helicopter gunner had aimed. Thatch roofs still smoldered, as men, women, and children stood by bewildered and weeping. The following day, as three members of the International Control Commission (ICC) stood among the ruins of Thloc Trach, American planes returned, sending the ICC members scrambling for cover. Duncan and McKissick returned to the village a day later and discovered that there had been yet another bombing raid; two more people were killed and the last homes were destroyed. In their days along the Cambodian border, the group found few signs of Vietnamese activity, but plenty of evidence that the Americans had been there. The terrain was pock-marked by bombs, and they also saw many Cambodians who had been wounded by strafing and napalm. Duncan identified the military evidence they found in the forest as "trademark U.S.A: American bombs, American rockets, American napalm" (Johnson 1966, 15).

In Phnom Penh, Prince Sihanouk stressed to the group his willingness to restore normalized relations with the United States, offering to drop his prior insistence on indemnification. He confided to them his more serious concern: growing along the border were groups of "Khmer Serei," ethnic Cambodian guerrillas trained in sabotage in U.S. Army camps by Americans who transported them to the Thai-Cambodian border, where they then blew up bridges, laid mines, and raided Cambodian militia posts. "We were convinced," Kay Boyle said, "that the prince was trying desperately to keep his country out of the tragic Southeast Asian conflict" (Boyle 1966, 19). From their observations they concluded that small groups of Vietnamese did move across the border—the Cambodians freely acknowledged that—but that the Vietnamese presence in Cambodia left no military or political marks in Cambodia itself; it was the repeated American bombing that was polarizing political forces there.

As head of a small country caught up in the anticommunist theology of Washington, Prince Sihanouk had developed his own understanding of the "three branches of government" concept that Americans revered. There were three American governments that he had to contend with, he told Americans Want to Know. There was the White House, he said, "not so bad," but "there is secondly, the CIA, and third, the military." His dealings with Washington convinced him that these three "governments" were not always aware of what each other was doing. The White House, he told Johnson, was sending him signals that it wanted to improve relations—presidential special envoy Averell Harriman had recently "invited himself" to Phnom Penh to talk with the prince—but simultaneously the U.S. military bombed his country, and the CIA had tried to assassinate him in 1959; now it was sabotaging his country, and the State Department kept insisting that some Cambodian areas were really inside Vietnam (Johnson 1966, 14–15).

The prince used the independent confirmation by Americans Want to Know of the bombing inside Cambodia to renew his public call for Washington to cease raiding Cambodian territory. He repeated his condemnations of the bombing, his offer to drop demands for compensation, and his wish for better relations with Washington. These claims were duly noted in the American media, which reported on Sihanouk's protestations of American bombing invasions with far less skepticism than it usually accorded governments that contradicted Washington assertions. The *New York Times* on 17 August 1966, carried the Americans Want to Know reports from Cambodia as though they were factually defensible. On 17 August, less than a week after the group returned to New York, the State Department acknowledged that Thloc Trach was indeed inside Cambodia and that its maps in Saigon were "wrong."

From 1966 to early 1968, the State Department continued to seize passports and travel cases piled up on court dockets. A year after Lynd's trip, in January 1967, the Supreme Court ruled unanimously, in a case involving nine travelers to Cuba, that visits to forbidden lands were not subject to criminal prosecution. However, the ruling left intact the State Department's authority to deny and seize passports for political reasons. Finally, on 20 December 1967, two years after Lynd's trip, the United States Court of Appeals in Washington handed down its decision in that case, ruling that federal statutes granted the government control of the travel of the passport but not of the citizen. The government could only prohibit travelers from taking their passports into banned zones. It could not stop travelers themselves from going. Nor could it seize passports if travelers left them behind while in the banned area. At the same time, the Court upheld the State Department's right to deny passports to individuals if they refused to promise that they would not carry them at some future unspecified time to banned countries. After two years of legal rulings, travel rights remained in a confused tangle of prescriptions over a document that began as a badge of privilege for the wealthy and was not even required for ordinary traveling folk until the First World War.

Washington's efforts to curry public favor by financing groups to tour South Vietnam while it denied Americans passports for travel to Hanoi failed. The "radicalization" that government-funded trips to South Vietnam produced in the moderate National Student Association pointed to narrowing differences between the composition, orientation, and conclusions of citizen groups that went to Vietnam. Whether they went to the South or to the North, their experiences there moved them toward similar assessments about the war: that not only Washington's tactics but also its goals in Vietnam were misguided and inhumane. Washington's attempted prosecution of those who went to North Vietnam emboldened the Saigon government to expel American activists who traveled there. With expulsion from Saigon a reality, travel to Hanoi, despite threatened passport confiscations, offered some activists their only possibility of visiting Vietnam.

Early contacts between Americans and Vietnamese resulted in exchanges that went beyond matters of war. They reinforced the strong spirit of religious ecumenism already in place in the postwar world. Thich Nhat Hanh's sojourn in the West came at a time when the attention of the religious community in the West was turning toward Asia, and his writings on "engaged Buddhism" formed part of a bridge between the spiritual heritage of the East and that of the West. Long after the war was over, his addresses to Western audiences enlarged their understanding of religious experience and helped to bring Eastern concepts and religious interpretation into mainstream Catholic and Protestant thought.

The first citizen groups who traveled to Vietnam came from across the spectrum of domestic activism and reform. But as the war continued into 1966 and 1967, some groups were less represented in these travels. Those whose aim was to "revolutionize" American society in short order showed little sustained interest in trips to Hanoi and the spirit of internationalism those trips could create, except insofar as those activities served the purpose of fomenting domestic change. Their focus was on America itself and on their visions of ushering in a radically altered system of governance at home. Students for a Democratic Society was not interested in developing a dialogue with North Vietnam. The organization did not develop internationalist ties. Those groups and individuals who viewed the war as a pressing issue in and of itself, however, continued to go in greater numbers. Their domestic goal was reform, not revolution, and encompassed domestic issues of racism and poverty as well as international problems created by war. They yearned for a sense of universal community. Their immediate goal was to end the destruction of the war while continuing to work for alternative methods of resolving international conflicts, methods that placed the needs and interests of all peoples on a equal plane. They believed in the agency of citizens in shaping foreign and domestic policy, in the influence of information, in the power of words. Indeed, words were the only weapons they had in the struggle to end the American occupation of Vietnam.

3

Bringing Back the News

In March 1965, when President Johnson had first ordered ground troops to South Vietnam, he and his advisors had assumed that Vietnamese resistance would soon be broken. By late 1966, that assumption was shattered. In October 1966, Secretary of Defense Robert McNamara wrote to the president, "I see no reasonable way to bring the war to an end soon." This despite the fact that the military situation was better than he had expected; the numbers of American troops fighting the Vietnamese National Liberation Front steadily increased and the bombing runs over North Vietnam had gone from 4,000 per month to 12,000. "The one thing demonstrably going for us in Vietnam," McNamara added, "has been the large number of enemy killed-in-action resulting from the big military operations" (*Pentagon Papers* 1972, 4:348).

Still, the secretary went on, morale among the Vietnamese resisters, both North and South, was high, and their recruitment more than kept up with casualties. Heavy bombing in North Vietnam yielded small gains. It was an agrarian country; there was not enough industry, not enough infrastructure to bomb. "There is agreement in the intelligence community on these facts," he noted. The secretary bluntly laid out "the discouraging truth"; it was the American-backed Saigon troops who remained disappointingly unmotivated. There were now 325,000 American troops in Vietnam, and he recommended increasing their numbers to 470,000. Compared to expectations a year earlier, "we find ourselves . . . no better, and if anything worse off," he observed. The secretary concluded that the solution to this military disappointment lay in ever more American troops, more bombing, more "pacification." The cost of maintaining an occupation army in Vietnam was no immediate constraint, although the

68

monetary price of maintaining expensively equipped American forces 6,000 miles from home steadily increased. That same year that McNamara concluded that American military gains in Vietnam were meager, the Central Intelligence Agency estimated that it was costing the United States $9.60 to inflict one dollar's worth of damage on North Vietnam (*Pentagon Papers* 1972, 136, 348–54).

McNamara's report was secret at the time, as were other intelligence findings that reached similar conclusions. In public, officials maintained a more optimistic posture and vigorously denied eyewitness reports from Vietnam by American activists that confirmed the Pentagon's pessimistic and secret reports. Vociferous and aggressive official denials rendered American traveler reports from North Vietnam suspect in the eyes of the media and the general public. The strength of the denials even made American activists hesitant, on occasion, to believe their own eyes while in North Vietnam. It was relatively easy for Washington officials to accuse Americans in North Vietnam of being blinded by "propaganda," of suffering a surfeit of sympathy for the communists, of failing to appreciate American values of honor and patriotism, and of lying about what they saw, and to have that assessment unchallenged by the American media. Despite this, Americans continued to go to North and South Vietnam, and they continued to bring back reports from the other side.

After the State Department seized and revoked passports for travel to North Vietnam and levied threats of criminal charges against the next travelers, it came as no surprise that the next American to organize a trip to Hanoi despite these strictures was David Dellinger, who appeared to have a dynamic spirit of resistance to injustice bred in his bone. Born to New Englanders with flawless credentials, descended from Benjamin Franklin's nephew, a summa cum laude economics graduate of Yale University, Dellinger was a veteran activist and unwavering pacifist. His life's work encompassed two traditionally characteristic strands of American social activism: attention to international issues of justice and peace and a struggle for domestic racial and economic justice. He was first imprisoned during World War II for refusing to register for the draft. As a seminary student at the time, he was exempt from conscription, but he objected to the unfairness of the exemption system and to the draft itself. Sentenced to prison for a year and a day, he spent part of that time in solitary confinement for sitting in the black prisoners' section for the segregated Sunday night movies. After the end of the war, he organized numerous nuclear testing protests and civil rights actions (Dellinger 1993).

In fall 1966, Dellinger went to South and North Vietnam. It was his first trip to Southeast Asia, and it marked the steady commitment to improved relations between the United States and Vietnam that he continued long after the war was over. Dellinger went first to Saigon to meet with Buddhists, students, intellectuals, and members of the Ky government there. Even as he arrived at the Saigon airport, he caught a sense that reflected the pessimism of the bleak report that McNamara was then pulling together. Striking up a conversation with some young Vietnamese men at Tan Son Nhut airport, Dellinger discovered that they were students leaving to study in the United States, leaving on the same planes that carried young American men into the country and into the war. Did they feel some hesitation about leaving their country to study elsewhere while Americans were coming in, some of them to a certain death? "As a human being, yes," one of the students replied. "But you must remember that it is the United States which insists on continuing the war" (Dellinger 1986, 65). If students with solid connections to the Saigon government, westernized and English-speaking, believed that the war was an American war, others felt it even more keenly. The anguish over a war for which Vietnamese increasingly blamed the United States reverberated throughout Dellinger's visit to Saigon. A government official there told Dellinger, "We have had war since 1939. My hair has become gray. War, always war, and everyone suffers . . . the United States is insistent on continuing the war" (Dellinger 1986, 65).

From Saigon, Dellinger flew to Phnom Penh to catch one of two International Control Commission planes that made biweekly flights to Hanoi. Just before he reached Phnom Penh, however, one ICC plane disappeared in the air corridor to Hanoi. The plane was never found. All air travel between Hanoi and other areas of Southeast Asia was suspended temporarily, and Dellinger's route to Hanoi instantly became more complicated. After some effort, he was able to patch together an itinerary from Phnom Penh to Moscow, then on to Beijing, and finally down to Hanoi from the north (Dellinger 1992).

When the pacifist finally arrived in Hanoi, he was skeptical about Vietnamese references to the "deliberate bombing" of residential areas and hospitals. "Something, perhaps my own type of Americanism, rose up inside me and I tried to deny that Americans would knowingly bomb and strafe civilians, at least as part of deliberate government policy," he wrote (Dellinger 1966, 6). The center of Hanoi itself had not yet been bombed. The accounts he heard from Vietnamese of fuel tanks or bombs dropping on their homes, Dellinger hoped, could be explained as isolated events. A Polish diplomat in Hanoi told him that, from within his embassy, he had caught on tape the explosion of American bombs in the embassy district. It created a sensation in Warsaw, he told the American visitor (Dellinger 1986, 71). The Vietnamese expected the city itself to be battered eventually, but Dellinger reminded himself that "even the Nazis did not bomb Paris during World War II." While he remained inside Hanoi, he continued to hope that the bombing of civilian areas in North Vietnam could be explained as "accidents" incurred during bombing intended to be as limited and precisely aimed at "steel and concrete" as his president assured his nation that it was (Dellinger 1986, 73).

Trips outside Hanoi convinced Dellinger that the bombing was neither limited nor precise. His hosts were not eager to take him outside Hanoi into the most heavily bombed regions. "They were always scared that Americans would be killed over there," Dellinger said, "and at first didn't want me to go. But they finally arranged (the trip) and then I could see why they hadn't wanted me to when I was lying in a ditch by the road and the planes came over and made it look like daylight with their flares. The whole sky was illuminated and bombs were falling around me" (Dellinger 1992).

The city of Phu Ly, thirty-five miles south of Hanoi and once a bustling town of over ten thousand residents, had not a building left standing. The original targets appeared to have been a railroad terminal and a bridge. Survivors told him that after the heaviest attacks, planes returned at intervals of twenty to thirty minutes to strafe anything that moved. In Nam Dinh, 60 miles southwest of Hanoi, entire blocks of residential housing were leveled. Even the dikes and brick retaining wall that kept back the Black River from the city of Nam Dinh were bombed. In Thanh Hoa, about 110 miles south of Hanoi, Dellinger saw block after block of rubble. In the ruins were a Franciscan Seminary, a Buddhist pagoda, and the general hospital. Outside the city limits, he saw the ruins of the six-hundred-bed Thanh Hoa tuberculosis sanitorium, which had been struck directly five times. Huge red crosses identifying it as a hospital had been painted on its roof. There was no conceivable military target for miles around. "I didn't expect that the U.S. aggressor was so barbarous," one bereft mother there told him bitterly (Dellinger 1966, 10).

In smaller villages Dellinger saw more destruction, and there he concluded that the bombing campaign had the unintended effect of stiffening resistance, a conclusion with which the CIA's then-secret reports concurred. A young villager told him that "when the planes come bombing and strafing our native land we feel a great indignation. We are making every effort to shoot them down in order to avenge our young people who have been cut down by the American aggressors." She could carry twice her weight in ammunition to the antiaircraft gunners, she told him. "At night when the planes come," she went on, "I volunteer to cook rice. During the day I go to the fields and gather vegetables for the army. They come, we open fire; they go, we continue picking vegetables. . . . Bombing is continuous but we never feel tired" (Dellinger 1966, 11–12).

A student, Vu Thi Minh, told him how her brother Vu Dinh Tanh, twenty years old and a poet, had written a poem for Norman Morrison when he heard of his death on the Pentagon steps. When the planes strafed Nam Dinh, they killed Vu Dinh Tanh. Her youngest brother then joined the army "to avenge his brother." Her sister, now at the Polytechnic College, planned to join the army when she graduated. "We are determined to take arms against the American planes," she said. "We are determined to fight until final victory." A seventy-one-year- old woman from the village of Kieu Dai lost her arm during an attack on her village. More than thirty villagers were killed. "The pain in my heart is as big as the pain in my body," she told Dellinger. "If we speak of indignation and hatred, we have no words to describe them. The people now working in the fields do not do anything to the Americans, why do they come here to kill us? . . . The more we hate the Americans the more we unite with each other. We will keep up this hatred forever. We can never live under the same sky as the American aggressors. I am very old, but I am thinking very much about the children" (Dellinger 1966, 13).

Village memorials constructed to honor the dead often listed only their names, but sometimes they served as the voice of the survivors. In the village of Phuxa, where a raid killed twenty-four people, Dellinger's hosts translated the memorial for him:

> In Hatred against the U.S. Pirates
> Who Killed Our Countrymen
> of Phuxa Village
> Nhat Tan Commune
> On August 13, 1966.

The other side carried an exhortation:

> Firmly Hold the Plow
> Firmly Hold the Rifle
> Be Determined to Fight and Win
> Over the American Aggressors
> In Order to Avenge Our Fellow Countrymen
> of Phuxa, Nhat Tan.
>
> (Dellinger 1966, 13)

Hatred for "U.S. pirates" did not generally extend to himself or to the American public, Dellinger said. The inhabitants of Phuxa blamed President Johnson. Whenever Johnson uttered a speech assuring the world of his love for little children and his devotion to world peace, one Vietnamese writer told Dellinger, they had come, through experience, to expect heightened bombing. "We are as offended by Johnson's hypocrisy as by his cruelty," the writer said. "You have no idea how angry Johnson makes us with his 'carrot' of a million dollars for economic aid," a doctor told Dellinger. "He is as cynical as he is barbarous. Why, do you realize that some days the planes come dropping bombs and killing our children, and then the next day they may drop toys and candy and leaflets urging us to surrender?" (Dellinger 1966, 8).[1] Like American antiwar activists, the Vietnamese had already labeled this "Johnson's war," leaving them some political space for American and Vietnamese people to build their own relationship. One of the war's harshest critics told Dellinger, "on your return I hope that you can help the American people to understand the truth and if you don't mind, I send my regards both to the peace movement in your country and also to your wife and to my brothers and sisters in your family. As for me, I have no alternative but to go on fighting" (Dellinger 1966, 6).

Dellinger's observations convinced him that Vietnamese numbers on damage and deaths were not overstated; in fact, their figures were often several bombings behind. For example, the mayor of Nam Dinh told Dellinger that 13 percent of the city had been destroyed. After touring the area, Dellinger observed that the destruction appeared to be significantly greater than that, and he asked the mayor about her figures. It

---

1. For one account of the propaganda war that dropped toys, soap, dolls, combs, and tons of leaflets on Vietnam during the bombing campaign there, see Chandler, 1981.

turned out that the official figures were current only as of two weeks ear-lier. The seven separate raids of the preceding week were not yet calcu-lated (Dellinger 1966, 10).

Dellinger's report from his two-week sojourn in North Vietnam em-phasized the human cost of the bombing there and offered some conclu-sions about its extent and physical damage. Civilian casualties represented a large share of total casualties in North Vietnam, he concluded. A CIA secret report written that fall had reached the same conclusion, estimating that 80 percent of the bombing casualties were civilian. Dellinger's report that morale among civilians was high was also borne out by the CIA's re-port, which stated that "the bombing had not succeeded in materially lowering morale among the people, despite some war weariness." Dellinger pointed out that whole hamlets were sometimes wiped out to destroy a bridge that was at most thirty feet long, but the streams were quickly spanned again. The massive bombing destroyed comparatively small amounts of infrastructure; there was little industry in North Viet-nam to destroy, and much of that was quickly rebuilt. The CIA's report of the bombing campaign in 1966 carried the same conclusions: "Hundreds of bridges were knocked down, but virtually all of them had been quickly repaired, replaced, or bypassed. . . . There was no evidence of a serious transport problem due to equipment shortages" (*Pentagon Papers* 1972, 4:136). Dellinger also pointed out something that the Pentagon studies ignored: "Though the bridges could be quickly restored, at least to a rough but serviceable state, the people could not" (Dellinger 1966, 14).

"Apart from the widespread destruction of villages, cities and towns," Dellinger said, he could see "no way to explain away the universal use of fragmentation bombs" in North Vietnam. Fragmentation bombs were large "mother bombs" (in the jargon of the Pentagon), which were filled with 300 smaller bombs the size of baseballs. Each of these was filled with 150 steel pellets. Fragmentation bombs did relatively little damage to steel and concrete, but they wreaked carnage among humans. The pattern of bombing, villagers told Dellinger, was for American pilots first to drop heavy explosive bombs and then follow up a few minutes later with the fragmentation bombs, which would kill or maim those trying to flee the area or help the wounded.[2] When Dellinger examined some of the spent bombs, he discovered timing devices that allowed them to eject their

2. For similar descriptions of bombing patterns from an American journalist who flew with the planes, see Frank Harvey 1966.

murderous barrage over time. Doctors in Vietnam told him they had the utmost difficulty extracting the pellets because they were hard to locate except through X rays, and X-ray machines were scarce in North Vietnam. Later, American ingenuity replaced the steel pellets with fiberglass ones. X rays could not pick up fiberglass, and the pellets became even more difficult and painful to remove (Young 1991, 130).

Upon his return to Washington, Dellinger asked a Pentagon spokesman to explain the purpose of fragmentation bombing in the North, because the president continually asserted that targets in Vietnam were only "steel and concrete." Fragmentation bombing "cuts down the activities of the guerrillas," the nonplussed officer told him, though there were no guerrillas in North Vietnam. The widespread use of fragmentation bombs in North Vietnam shattered any illusions Dellinger might have carried that the air war there sought to spare civilians. "The best defense my American pride could muster was to say the American people would not knowingly tolerate such practices. . . . When the American people found out the nature and effects of the bombings, they would put an end to them," he wrote hopefully. Bring in American journalists to report "the facts" to the American people, he urged Vietnamese officials. When Americans saw pictures of things he had seen—the civilians killed, the children now without arms or legs, the baby born with shrapnel in her cheek after her mother was hit by bombs in Haiphong—they would rethink the war and consider the cost. Perhaps they would even put themselves, however fleetingly, in the position of the Other. "What would Americans think if they were living peacefully and suddenly another country came and started killing them?" asked a young woman whose two small brothers were killed in a field as they tended buffalo (Dellinger 1966, 9).

Throughout the year, American bombing in North Vietnam rendered civilian flights into Hanoi ever more difficult. There was only one flight weekly from Beijing, and three International Control Commission flights every fortnight from Vientiane. The planes from Beijing and Vientiane were canceled at the slightest sign of bombing. It was a time of maximum difficulty both in legally leaving the United States and in safely entering Hanoi.

Facilities for travelers in North Vietnam remained few and sparse. Only Hanoi and Haiphong had hotels left that could even modestly accommodate foreigners. Hotels in Nam Dinh and Nam Binh were destroyed. American visitors in rural areas often stayed in village hostels, but these were vulnerable to attack, and the Vietnamese host groups were fearful of having American visitors killed while in their care. They usually arranged for a physician to accompany groups on trips outside Hanoi, but physician services were urgently needed in Vietnam's own hospitals. American visitors rarely spoke Vietnamese or even French, so Vietnamese translators, also scarce, were needed to accompany them. Only a few visitors could be conveniently hosted at any given time, but Vietnam's Foreign Ministry was inundated with cables requesting permission to visit. In late December 1966, one official showed a *New York Times* reporter a stack of cables nearly six inches high, from all over the world, each cable asking to allow an individual or a group to visit Hanoi.

Christmas seasons began, in 1966, to produce a pattern of greater-than-normal bombing intensity followed by a bombing "pause." Washington officials called for bombing pauses at the holiday season because it lent the bombing itself an aura of civility. Massive bombing was the symbol of the entire war effort, and at a time of "peace on earth," suspending bombing for a few days or weeks allowed American officials at all levels to enjoy their Christmas cheer without the immediate unpleasantness of warfare. In North Vietnam, these bombing pauses made it safer for visitors to fly into Hanoi and to travel the countryside during the limited duration of the actual halt, which was preceded and followed by ever more vigorous bombing to "make up" for the bombing halt. Travel outside Hanoi immediately before and after bombing halts was generally even more dangerous than usual.

Dellinger's reports of extensive civilian bombing destruction in Vietnam were followed by others until they could no longer be ignored. The Christmas season of 1966 marked the season when these reports reached a critical mass sufficiently weighty to breach the administration's wall of denial. That Christmas season, four Americans from the civil rights and antiwar movements went to Vietnam at an invitation from the Vietnamese Women's Union. The four were Barbara Deming, who had been deported with the Muste group from Saigon in April, Grace Mora Newman, Patricia Griffith, and Diane Nash. Newman was an antiwar activist from the Bronx whose brother, Dennis, was one of three soldiers at Fort Hood who were facing three-year prison sentences for refusing army orders to go to South Vietnam (Alice Lynd 1968). Griffith was active in Women Strike for Peace at Ithaca, New York, and Diane Nash was a Student Nonviolent Coordinating Committee activist who had helped to desegregate lunch counters in Nashville and continue CORE's Freedom Ride when its bus was fire-bombed in Birmingham in 1961.

The women flew into Hanoi on 22 December from Vientiane after several delays caused by heavy pre-Christmas bombing around Hanoi. They reached the Hanoi airport at night. The city was darkened to avoid being a target. It was hard to believe, Deming said, that the city had once held over a million people. As soon as the plane touched down, the runway lights were shut off and they taxied up to the ramp in darkness. The flight attendant switched on a flashlight to help the few passengers disembark and enter the dimly lit terminal. Members of the Vietnamese Women's Union met them there and took them to the Thong Nhat Hotel, which had been called the Metropole when the French ruled Vietnam. There were other guests at the hotel when they arrived: a group from the Japanese antiwar organization Beheiren; a labor union delegation from Moscow; a Cuban camera crew; and four West Germans, including Martin Niemoeller, who had arrived early to meet a later American group (Deming 1985).

Each morning, the visitors got up at four o'clock and went out in the darkness to visit surrounding villages. In an area of Vietnam fast becoming the bomb depository of the American Seventh Fleet, they talked over tea to villagers who had witnessed what seemed to them endless bombing raids, who had lost friends and family, and who described it all in numbing detail. There was plenty about the war that disturbed the Americans, but the fragmentation bombs disturbed them the most. From the long incisions in many of the patients in the hospitals, they could see how diligently doctors tried to remove the steel pellets. At one school, fragmentation pellets were still embedded in books destroyed in the raid. They visited hospitals, schools, and factories where bombs fell, and everywhere villagers gathered around these American visitors to talk of their experiences. These encounters with villagers were the most remarkable thing that Deming remembered from the trip. The victims would tell of the moment of horror, describing in detail the day the bombs fell into their lives. They would break down sometimes, Deming said, and sometimes would stop to regain composure, but they were determined to finish the stories for their visitors and for themselves. It seemed to be a rite of renewal, Deming observed, an effort to put their lives back together by making themselves face over and over the moments that had shattered their lives, even drawing courage from these encounters with visitors from America.

Before leaving Hanoi, the group visited two American prisoners, both first lieutenants, who gave them letters from themselves and from other pilots for their families in the United States. The men urged the Americans to do everything they could do to end the war. Regardless of the outcome, they said, "most of the men here want to go home." They also spent an hour with President Ho Chi Minh, who waved away his interpreter and spoke to them in English. If the Americans say they will leave tomorrow, he told them, the Vietnamese will send them off "with music and with bouquets around their necks." If they would not leave, the Vietnamese would continue resisting, he believed, because each generation of Vietnamese had grown stronger in its rejection of foreign domination. As the women stood to leave, the aged leader reached into a vase by his chair and handed each of them a rose (WIN 1967).

Despite President Johnson's declared bombing halt during the Christmas season, American reconnaissance aircraft continued to fly over Hanoi. There was no respite from air-raid warnings. Two days after Christmas, early in the morning, the women found themselves with seven other international guests—German, Italian, Soviet, Cuban—in the hotel's concrete bomb shelter, while outside, the hotel employees, both men and women, stood at the entrance with rifles at the ready, prepared to fire at low-flying jets. After introductions all around, they discovered that Americans made up the majority in this darkened bomb shelter in Hanoi. Harrison Salisbury, a *New York Times* assistant managing editor, had flown in three days earlier. He was beginning to send out reports from Hanoi that confirmed all that prior travelers reported.

Salisbury's dispatches on the air war in Vietnam appeared first on Christmas Day 1966 in the *New York Times* under a banner across the top of the paper: "Today is Christmas Day! Remember the Neediest!" Salisbury was a veteran journalist from behind the lines, having reported from Siberia, Bulgaria, Rumania, and Mongolia during the height of the Cold War. He had won the Pulitzer Prize in 1955 for his reporting on the Kremlin, but he noted that the *Times* frequently censored his reports from Moscow between 1949 and 1954, and he grew accustomed to being labeled a "communist sympathizer" for being insufficiently harsh toward the Soviet Union. At the beginning of 1966 he had applied for a visa to visit North Vietnam, but he received no response until early December, after Anne Morrison, widow of Norman Morrison, wrote a letter to Hanoi on his behalf. "After I reached Hanoi and learned of the sanctity in which Morrison's memory was held," Salisbury wrote, "I came to feel that Mrs. Morrison's letter, simple and direct, had probably been my best credential in getting the visa" (Salisbury 1967, 8).

Salisbury's Christmas dispatches described in spare detail extensive bombing damage in and around Hanoi. Deep craters and rubble in residential areas, which he saw, convinced him that American bombs were falling heavily on civilian areas. "Contrary to the impression given by United States communiqués," he wrote in his *Times* 25 December report, "on-the-spot inspection indicates that American bombing has been inflicting considerable civilian casualties in Hanoi and its environs for some time past." At one residential site, an agitated young medical worker, who had treated the wounded during a bombing attack the week before, showed him a dirty leaflet dropped by the American planes during the attack. It warned people not to live near a military target. Where, asked the angry young man, was the military target? Salisbury turned away unable to answer. When he visited Nam Dinh, he had no answer either to equally angry questions about why that city, twenty miles inland, was a favorite target of the Seventh Fleet. There were few conceivable military targets left there. Block after block of city streets had been smashed into rubble and it was now largely evacuated.

Salisbury concluded that the bombing targets of American pilots were often beyond their capabilities for precision strikes. For example, the Pentagon listed the Van Dien truck park in Nam Dinh as a "major" military target of a strike on 13 and 14 December. The Pentagon claimed it contained 184 buildings and that two thirds of those buildings were damaged or destroyed in December attacks (*Pentagon Papers* 1972, 4:135). Such destruction must have seemed, in Washington, like an impressive strike at Vietnam's infrastructure. But Salisbury saw that the truck park comprised only six modest loading sheds. The bombers had destroyed these sheds, but the planes continued their bombing swath past them through the surrounding residential area, culminating in the complete destruction of a school ten blocks away. A foreign journalist told him that there had been only a dozen or so old vehicles parked in the truck park when it was hit. For this kind of target, Salisbury wondered, was it worth sending in two-million-dollar planes, jeopardizing American pilots, killing civilians there, and destroying the surrounding areas?

Salisbury noted that when Americans bombed rail lines, they often chose to do so at places where they ran through small towns and villages, destroying them as well. Even the diplomatic zone in Hanoi, including the Chinese, Polish, and Rumanian embassies and the Canadian Mission to the International Control Commission, had been hit. One of the Canadians told Salisbury that he had sent some of the bomb fragments found in his building back to American officials in Saigon with a note saying, "Look here, chaps, this is going a bit far" (Salisbury 1967, 211).

Salisbury could follow the stir that his dispatches created in Washington by listening to the Voice of America in Hanoi. If Washington officials hoped the transmission would make an impression in Vietnam, their hopes were fully realized—they would never jam the Voice of America, one official in Hanoi told Salisbury wryly. "We like our people to hear the V.O.A. They can see what lies the Americans tell. For instance, it was very amusing for the people of Hanoi to hear the V.O.A. deny there had been any raids on their city on December 13 and 14" (Salisbury 1967, 48).

The Defense Department responded to Salisbury's dispatches by insisting that "all possible care is taken to avoid all damage to civilian areas." Still, after many denials, officials finally admitted that their bombs had hit the embassy area in Hanoi. On 31 December, President Johnson, with evident agitation, called a press conference to insist that the bombing was directed only against legitimate military targets and that every effort was made to avoid civilian casualties (*Pentagon Papers* 1972, 4:135).

After the *New York Times* printed Salisbury's dispatches, official rhetoric justifying the bombing changed. The administration now admitted that bombs fell on civilian areas, but framed that as an inevitable part of war. On 28 December, the *Times* quoted former president Eisenhower, leaving the Walter Reed Army Medical Center, as he summed up the new strategy. He tipped his hat to reporters who inquired about his reaction to Salisbury's dispatches and asked with a smile, "Is there any place in the world where there are not civilians?" And on 29 December the *Times* reported that some American pilots claimed to be perplexed about all these claims of civilian bombing. "I found [Salisbury's] story about Nam Dinh simply unbelievable," said Robert Mandeville, commanding officer of a naval attack squadron in the Gulf of Tonkin. "He's describing what he's seen on the ground," the commander went on, "I guess we're looking at it from two different points of view."

Press reaction in Europe to Salisbury's reports was sharply critical of Washington. Salisbury's reports were new for the American media and public, but European correspondents had long been reporting the same stories in their outlets. On 28 December, London's *Daily Express* said that the earlier refusal of the administration to admit the bombings "damages still further its already tarnished reputation as a source of truth." The same day, *Le Monde*, which had its own reporter in Hanoi, editorialized, "Not a day passes anymore but that the most moderate American press catches the President or his collaborators in the flagrant act of lying." The London *Daily Mail* was more charitable to the American president. It was the Hanoi government itself that was responsible for the casualties because of its "little concern for the safety of its own civilians. Such unconcern," the editorial went on, revealing the editor's own cultural insights, "would at any rate be consonant with both the Oriental and the Communist character." Also on 28 December, the official Vatican newspaper, *L'Osservatore Romano,* praised Salisbury's dispatches as "a service to truth," and called for Catholics to rally around Pope Paul's efforts for peace "without any possible partiality or reticence." The editorial was seen as a pointed reprimand to New York's conservative Cardinal Spellman, who had spent that Christmas with American troops in South Vietnam. The *New York Times* on 25 December quoted Spellman defending the American war there as a "fight for ideals and principles we account worthy of preservation." The cardinal told the troops at a midnight mass at Cam Ranh Bay that "war, in fact, has brought out the noblest instincts and the best traits of human courage and endurance in the annals of history." The following day, the paper quoted the cardinal telling the American soldiers that the war in Vietnam was "a war for civilization."

American travelers to Hanoi had repeatedly reported the same things that Salisbury now did. Their reports had been coming out for over a year now. The reports were consistent with each other and with reports from international journalists. But the American mainstream press began paying some attention only when Salisbury's reports came out. Even so, Salisbury's dispatches were battered by a media still skeptical of any perspective other than that of Washington. The Defense Department fed stories to the *Times*'s competitor, the *Washington Post,* which called Salisbury's dispatches a communist propaganda pamphlet and said that his trip handed Hanoi a new weapon as diabolically conceived as "the Vietcong's poison-tipped bamboo spikes." The facts of Salisbury's dispatches were never seriously challenged, and the *Times* at first stood by his reports, but under constant battering from the Defense Department and the White House about Salisbury's and the paper's lack of patriotism in running the stories from North Vietnam, the *Times* backed down. It even ran editorials questioning its own wisdom in printing Salisbury's reports (Catledge 1971, 293).

Historian Daniel Hallin noted that Salisbury was heavily criticized by

Washington officials and by many of his colleagues because his reports from Hanoi came at a time when "television painted an almost perfectly one-dimensional image of the North Vietnamese and the Vietcong as cruel, ruthless, and fanatical—clearly beyond the bounds of Legitimate Controversy" (Hallin 1986, 147). For example, Salisbury's critics, who had never been to North Vietnam, said the fact that Salisbury used Hanoi's official casualty figures completely discredited his reports of bombing targets and damage there. As other visitors had pointed out before in published accounts, the Vietnamese tendency was more to downplay the figures than to pad them. They were always "several bombings behind," as Dellinger put it. If anything, the figures as Salisbury reported them were too low. The media scorn heaped on the official damage figures compiled in Hanoi came from its acceptance of Washington's depiction of the North Vietnamese as little more than devious fanatics who lived to lie, and this approach served the administration's interests perfectly. As Hallin put it, Salisbury applied the same journalistic standards to his reports from Vietnam that he did to reports emanating from the State Department. He "treated the North Vietnamese as though they belonged to the Sphere of Legitimate Controversy, summarizing their views as a Washington reporter might summarize those of American officials" (1986, 148). Later that year, a jury of newspaper editors awarded Salisbury the Pulitzer Prize for his dispatches from Hanoi, but the Pulitzer advisory board, composed largely of newspaper publishers, vetoed the award. "They made no bones about it," *Times* editor Turner Catledge said later, "they supported the war so they voted against Salisbury" (1971, 293).

Travelers' reports from North Vietnam drew heightened attention from around the world to the air war there as 1966 turned into 1967. Pope Paul's repeated and urgent call for an end to the bombing worried President Johnson because, by singling out the bombing as an issue, it counteracted the public relations gloss of the bombing pause. The president told Secretary of State Dean Rusk to "get together with the Pope and tell him he wants only even-handed peace pleas at Christmas time" (Rostow 1966, LBJL). Pope Paul was not sufficiently responsive to Dean Rusk's entreaties to be even-handed about the bombing, so the president determined to keep future Christmastime calls for peace at bay in his own way. In mid-December 1967, he arranged a trip to Thailand, Vietnam, and Australia, and then flew far out of his homeward way to meet with the pope just before Christmas. Pope Paul was apparently not eager for the visit. Throughout the president's Asian tour his staff made repeated requests for an audience with the pope, but there was no clearance from the Vatican for a presidential visit. Despite this lack of response, when Air Force One left Australia for Washington, it flew directly toward Rome. Not until the plane crossed into air space over Turkey, demonstrating the president's determination to see the pope this Christmas, did the president's entourage receive papal clearance for an official visit. Johnson emerged from his brief stopover at the Vatican telling reporters that he had urged Pope Paul to direct efforts toward American prisoners of war in Hanoi. Washington would cease bombing North Vietnam anytime, he had told the pope, if only Hanoi would "guarantee" some movement toward peace. This was the news from the Vatican on Vietnam on Christmas Eve 1967 (Johnson 1967, 2:1186).

European criticism of the war accelerated until, according to the *Pentagon Papers*, "as window-dressing, the U.S. asked United Nations secretary general U Thant to take whatever steps were necessary to get talks started" (1972, 4:136) The secretary general took his task seriously. On the last day of 1966 he said at a press conference that the first step toward negotiations must be an "unconditional" bombing halt. "This evoked little enthusiasm and some annoyance in the Johnson administration," the *Pentagon Papers* recorded, and went on to observe that "1966 drew to a close on a sour note for the President."

To others, the outcome looked more optimistic. Rumors spread that U Thant's efforts were paying off, and the timing seemed auspicious for A. J. Muste (1967) when he received, in late December 1966, an invitation to visit Hanoi. He had wanted to visit North Vietnam and, with the secretary general of the United Nations pushing negotiations, the war, he hoped, would soon be over. He inquired at the State Department about having his passport validated for travel to North Vietnam, but officials told him that he did not qualify. Additionally, the eighty-one-year-old activist was scheduled to appear at a court hearing on 3 January 1967 for his recent arrest after entering the Army Induction Center on Whitehall Street in New York City in protest of the bombing in Vietnam. Muste's lawyer secured a postponement in the trial, and the veteran activist, with three international colleagues, set off on the arduous trip to Hanoi. "I let the State Department know I was going," he told reporters with a smile. "I do not expect any trouble." With him went sixty-seven-year-old Rabbi Abraham L. Feinberg of Toronto, an American citizen and activist in the Canadian peace movement, and Ambrose Reeves, also sixty-seven, and assistant bishop of the diocese of Chichester, England. Reeves was no stranger to issues of national boundaries and exclusions—he had been expelled from South Africa for his active opposition to apartheid. His primary concern on this trip, he told *New York Times* reporters on 29 December, was race relations that were being "embittered" across the world by "white America's war against non-white Vietnamese." The State Department also refused to validate Feinberg's passport for travel to North Vietnam. "Up to now," Feinberg said after he decided to make the trip anyway, "I could never quite bring myself to violate the law" (Feinberg 1968, 59). The fourth member of the group was Pastor Martin Niemoeller, World War I submarine commander turned evangelical theologian, imprisoned in Germay during World War II for his antiwar activities, and currently president of the World Council of Churches. To those who believed that the antiwar movement was by, and for, the young and that the older generation was "washed up," this trip was one of many contrary examples. The average age of these four men was seventy-three.

Muste's group arrived in Hanoi on 9 January 1966 after a two-week journey marked by delays and detours. Their week-long stay extinguished their hopes of a timely end to the war. Their hosts did not expect a quick conclusion, and the bombing destruction they saw horrified the men. They went to a garden marketing village four miles from downtown Hanoi that had been struck several months before. The attack came during the day, when many of the villagers were inside eating their noonday meal. There were not many people killed, Feinberg wrote, "only" 24 out of a population of 345, but for the survivors all the world lay in those deaths (Feinberg 1967, 21).

The villagers, who were mostly Catholic, had already replaced the bombed church's tiled roof, though the windows were still shattered. A new brick kindergarten stood where the old one had been. All of the other buildings had been rebuilt except for one that was left as a memorial to the dead. An entire family had perished there. The surviving villagers had constructed a small room of concrete and tile on the site and filled it with vestiges of the bombing: twisted shards of fragmentation bombs with United States markings on them, the personal effects of those who died—a teacup, a comb, a wedding dress, an undelivered letter, prayer books, pieces of a tiny plaster image of the Virgin Mary with her head blown off. The bomb canister was stamped with the information that it had been manufactured in the United States in July 1966. In August, only a month later, it reached the outskirts of Hanoi (Feinberg 1967).

The productivity, efficiency, and ingenuity for which Americans prided themselves in the years after World War II came to the Vietnamese through American weapons. People told American visitors that they were continually amazed at the methods by which Americans made their already difficult-to-extract pellets ever more difficult, how they could make napalm even deadlier. Every villager who examined a fallen bomb canister, stamped with its date of manufacture in the United States, was impressed by the speed with which these bombs were made in America, transported six thousand miles, organized, loaded, and dropped on them within weeks (Berrigan 1968, 68).

"Nothing could blunt the sharp pang of shame that assailed me," Rabbi Feinberg wrote, because the bombs "had been dropped by a plane built for bombing and dispatched for bombing by the United States, to which I have always been proud to claim loyalty and affection as a native-born citizen" (Feinberg 1967, 21). In the hospital lay two paralyzed girls, their spines pierced by the pellets like those that had killed their infant sister. "It was more than a person could bear," Muste told David Dellinger later, "I just couldn't take it" (Dellinger 1967). The scenes he saw, Feinberg added, were scenes that "no decent and concerned human being can casually abide." He was not surprised to find that "capturing an American pilot was the crowning ambition of every young person in Vietnam" (Feinberg 1968, 102).

Muste asked to meet with American prisoners, and permission was reluctantly granted. The group met two pilots, a captain from Florida and a lieutenant from Kansas, at a "nondescript" iron-barred villa near their hotel in Hanoi. Their hosts made no effort to conceal its location. Both pilots talked of their last flights from Thailand and their ejections over the skies of North Vietnam, one of them losing consciousness immediately and awakening in the hospital, the other hiding in the forest, fearful of capture, but having been treated "darn well." Muste and Feinberg feared that the pilots would give them the cold shoulder, but they both talked readily and seemed at ease. "We did not probe the mind of either prisoner about the war," Feinberg said, but "they were eager to talk and did so without prohibition." On of them admitted deep confusion: "I never thought or read much about politics. . . . I never could understand what the war was about. . . . It was my patriotic duty to serve and I did it," adding pensively that now that he knew "the enemy" personally, it was difficult to think of them as the enemy. "They put up a tree and gave us little presents last Christmas," he said. Back at the hotel, the Americans compared notes and observations of the prisoners—were they brainwashed? The question seemed important in light of the Pentagon's charges that captured American pilots who expressed regret at bombing Vietnam must be brainwashed. Feinberg concluded that they seemed to be as normal as men could be expected to act after near-death experiences and over eight months of captivity (Feinberg 1968, 218).

Before leaving Hanoi, they met for several hours with Premier Pham Van Dong and President Ho Chi Minh. Here they could do away with the interpreter—the president spoke to them in English, which, he said chuckling, he had learned as a cook in Soho and Harlem and as a sailor on boats putting into port in New York when he was a young man. He seemed especially pleased to meet with these American men so close in age to himself. He was now seventy-seven years old, he told them, and he thanked them for coming so far to visit his people, in view of their ages. He remarked on the variety of their experiences: "Here we are of many religions. You are Presbyterian, Anglican, Jew; over there (pointing to Oanh who accompanied them) is a Buddhist; I am a Communist. Yet we can meet and talk together in brotherhood." Their amiable chat about their own lives turned serious when the president turned in his chair to face the foreigners directly and said with deliberate precision that he had something to say that he hoped they would publicize. "Mr. Johnson has said that he would meet anyone, anywhere, anytime to talk about peace. I invite him to come here as our guest, sitting where you are. Let Mr. Johnson come with his wife and daughter, his secretary, his doctor and his cook. Let him not come with a gun on his hip or with generals and admirals. As an old revolutionary, I pledge my honor that Mr. Johnson will have complete security" (Feinberg 1967, 21).

After this invitation, the president left the room, returning shortly with presents for his guests: three walking sticks made of contrasting stripes of ebony and ivory, topped by exquisitely carved dragon's heads for handles, fitting gifts for these elderly men on their long journey. At that point Feinberg "summoned up courage" and, "as a matter of obligation," told his hosts not to expect too much of the peace movement in the United States. It was supported by many "prestigious" voices, he said, "but it is a weak minority" and the president wields "enormous power in foreign relations." Furthermore, he went on, "Americans pride themselves on having never been defeated in war. They believe they should be able to defeat a small and poor country like Vietnam." Premier Pham Van Dong agreed with him. "I have no illusion," he said, "other friends have told me what you have just said" (Feinberg 1967, 21; Joint Statement 1967, SCPC).

When he returned home, Feinberg requested a meeting with American officials about his discussions with Ho Chi Minh, but the State Department turned him down. He tried other approaches, finally even contacting the British embassy in Toronto, which cabled Washington recommending that someone there talk to Feinberg. William Richard Smyser, who worked in the Far Eastern Affairs Division of the State Department, then went up to Toronto, but Feinberg found him less interested in news from Hanoi than in trying to impress Feinberg with information that he claimed to have on Ho Chi Minh. In a series of rambling remarks, the State Department representative told Feinberg that Ho had "a colorful reputation as a lover" and that he was "fond of girls." Shortly after Smyser met with Feinberg, the American consulate in Toronto seized his passport.

The trip to Hanoi was to be A. J. Muste's last journey in a long life devoted to building what he called "the beloved community." He died in his sleep of a heart attack on 11 February, just two weeks after returning from Hanoi, and after a full week of committee meetings, speeches, radio and television appearances, and work on two articles on his trip. "It was typical of A. J. that he worked at least twelve hours a day right up to the end," David Dellinger said, "and allotted only a few minutes for dying. His life was in order" (1967). "We all took him for granted and thought he would be around forever," I. F. Stone said in the 19 March *Mobilizer*, the newsletter of the Mobilization to End the War in Vietnam. The newsletter finished its tribute to Muste by invoking his life and spirit: "In lieu of flowers, friends are requested to get out and work for peace, for human rights, for a better world."

As antiwar activists returned from Hanoi fanned out across the country telling groups of citizens what they had heard and seen there, they sometimes found a studied resistance to their testimony. When Barbara Deming (1985) spoke at universities about her trip to North Vietnam, she noted that many students were unwilling to believe her reports. At one college students argued heatedly that the Vietnamese had created all the civilian bomb damage themselves—the craters, the destroyed buildings, the blasted bridges, the flattened villages—with bulldozers. U.S.

Army photographs proved it, they insisted (Deming 1985, 172). This belief fit in perfectly with the media's dismissal of Hanoi's figures on casualties. It rendered American actions plausible, and interpreted the Vietnamese as abnormal, even psychotic. The alternative image, that Americans in Vietnam were destroying villages, bombing hospitals, and dropping napalm on civilians was repressed. Carl Gerstacker, chairman of Dow Chemical Company, drew on these cultural presuppositions to explain to NBC's *Today* host, Hugh Downs, why Dow continued to supply the Pentagon with napalm for use in Vietnam. *The New Republic* quoted the chairman on 26 July as saying that napalm was a "good discriminate, strategic weapon, and if we are indiscriminately and unnecessarily hurting civilian people, this is being done by these half million of our young people who are representative of our whole society, and I just can't believe that of them."

Throughout 1967, diplomatic exchanges between Hanoi and Washington remained stymied. Hanoi steadfastly repeated its position that the Geneva Accords had established a principle of no foreign troops on Vietnamese soil, and called for Americans to end the bombing and withdraw its troops before substantive negotiations could commence. President Johnson believed in negotiating from strength, and waited for a definitive improvement in his military situation before opening talks. Into this impasse stepped a few individuals outside of the antiwar movement who believed at first that they had the active encouragement of the White House to contact Hanoi officials. All of these efforts, carefully planned and undertaken with what the participants at first believed was the full cooperation of the White House, came to naught. On one occasion, during the December 1966 initiative known as "Operation Marigold," in which the White House used Polish diplomats as intermediaries, the Pentagon stepped up bombing in North Vietnam immediately after a date for preliminary talks was established, dampening Hanoi's interest. When that stepped-up bombing damaged even the Polish embassy there, Polish enthusiasm for continuing an intermediary role quickly waned. Another initiative shortly thereafter came to a frustrating end when the two Americans involved, Harry Ashmore and William Baggs, discovered that the administration, while seeming to be working with them in drafting a letter to Hanoi, sent a different letter to Hanoi, which, when they later read it, appeared to them to be "designed to be rejected."[3]

---

3. For more on this and other initiatives, see Kraslow and Loory 1968, Porter 1975, Cooper 1970, and Reston "Marigold," LBJL. For a more complete account. see Ashmore

The hopeful negotiators felt a keen sense of betrayal and were more willing to talk to reporters about these failures than the White House wished. David Kraslow and Stuart Loory's book, *The Secret Search for Peace in Vietnam*, was based on extensive interviews with a wide variety of individuals and officials who had been involved in some aspect of these quasi-official initiatives. Kraslow and Loory were able to reconstruct the total picture of different initiatives that had been only partially clear to many participants. The White House soon caught wind of their endeavors because of the nature of their questions to lower level officials, and it responded by "suggesting" that such officials "duck appointments with these reporters without stating that they have been instructed to do so." If officials continued talking to the reporters, Benjamin Read, executive secretary in the State Department warned, the book "will spell trouble for the administration" (Rostow 1968b, LBJL).

In February 1967, the Fellowship of Reconciliation sent Alfred Hassler to Saigon again, to see how it might help the Buddhists after the debacle of the previous year. He found a much less promising reception than his delegation had received in 1965; Thich Nhat Hanh had left Vietnam, the Buddhist movement was largely destroyed, and Thich Tri Quang, in isolation in a Saigon pagoda, had vowed to speak to no Americans until the war was over. After repeated requests, he agreed to meet briefly with Hassler, but his bitterness toward the American government was intense, and Hassler was "not much encouraged" about the possibility of future work together.

Hassler even had difficulty securing an invitation to visit the Buddhist School of Youth for Social Services outside Saigon, a school that Thich Nhat Hanh had founded and FOR had supported since 1965. The students at the school were less hopeful and less committed to nonviolence than they had been in 1965, when he had last seen them. Hassler, noting with some sympathy their lessened commitment to nonviolence in the face of their own bitter experience, observed that "one must not discount the possibility that some of these young people will be driven by sheer frustration into going to the NLF." Indeed, talking with people from across the political spectrum in Saigon gave Hassler the feeling that he "was living in an Alice in Wonderland situation. The Armed Forces Radio and the local press, like our own back home, are fill of stories of the clobbering that our troops are giving to the NLF and the North Vietnamese

---

and Baggs, 1968; Miller 1980, 472–77; Ashmore 1994; and Ashmore, "Oral History Notes," LBJL.

and clearly are sure that we now have the upper hand. The students ridicule this notion . . . and say that the sympathies of the people in Vietnam are going more and more to the NLF" (Hassler 1967d, SCPC).

Americans working with voluntary humanitarian organizations in Saigon confirmed these observations. Paul Longacre, director of the Mennonite Central Committee, which sponsored agricultural projects in rural South Vietnam, remarked to Hassler that, based on his years of observations of rural and urban life in South Vietnam, American military "victories" were increasingly confined to areas immediately around major cities and that "travel in the country was more dangerous now than ever. . . . The VC in some ways range more widely than before and are exceedingly well-disciplined and effective." In Saigon itself, the American presence appeared to Hassler to be

> both overwhelming and curiously insignificant. Visually it is inescapable. Not only the men in the armed forces, seen everywhere in the streets looking grim and competent in their battle dress, and like giants next to the Vietnamese, but their vehicles—jeeps, trucks, ambulances, etc. are everywhere in the crowded Saigon traffic. They have taken over many hotels and other buildings and, like the embassy, each one is guarded, often with barbed wire entanglements. . . . Many stands on the street markets reflect the black market in PX goods, Lux, canned foods . . . on the other stands there will be bottles of liquor; on still others American pocketbooks and girlie magazines. But on the other hand, curiously, the life of Vietnam gives the impression of going on around all this, with the Vietnamese themselves not paying very much attention to it directly. (Hassler 1967c, SCPC)

Hassler believed that the forces of national self-determination were as pervasive in South Vietnam as other Americans were finding it in the North; even the Buddhists had grown hesitant of working with American pacifists during this time of war. Both the Buddhist School of Youth for Social Service and groups of students at the university were more wary than ever of alignment with any American groups, however well-intentioned they might have been.

The greatest disappointment of Hassler's trip came when he returned to the United States. In one of the last student meetings in Saigon that Hassler attended, the students were discussing favorably the efficacy of mass self-immolation against the war. Hassler had argued against it, volunteering his own belief that developing links with American student groups would be more productive. A year earlier, the students had met with the National Student Association delegates, and they decided to send a letter to them through Hassler, asking for some form of solidarity and partnership against the war. Hassler brought back the letter, written and signed by seventy faculty and student leaders in Saigon and addressed to the hundred-plus National Student Association members who recently had sent an open letter to President Johnson protesting the war. The letter, along with the students' names and college affiliations, had appeared earlier in the 30 December *New York Times*. When he returned to the United States, Hassler sent copies of the Saigon students' letter by registered mail to each of the NSA student leaders who had signed the letter to President Johnson. He got not a single response. That spring, Hassler went to the NSA national meeting to encourage the students to respond. The students explained that they were "moved" by it, but they felt they could not afford any public exposure in working with the Saigon students because they "did not wish to damage the credibility of their moderate position." They had just come from a meeting with Secretary of State Dean Rusk, and they thought "they were having an effect on him." The following month, one of the Vietnamese students who had sent the unanswered letter, Phan Thi Mai, burned herself to death on the steps of the Tu Nhgiem pagoda in Saigon (Hassler 1970, 197–204).

Travelers' reports of widespread fragmentation bombing and civilian bombing in Vietnam in 1967 raised high the issue of war crimes—an international issue of the utmost sensitivity in Washington. Only twenty years earlier, the Nuremberg Trials had divided World War II into a good side and an evil one, and America at that time stood four-square on the "good" side of war, so firmly that the issue of President Truman's use of atomic bombs in Asia was consigned for a long time to near-oblivion. To have the issue of war crimes in Asia raised only twenty years later in the context of this war without foreseeable end was irksome indeed. British philosopher and mathematician Bertrand Russell raised it anyway. Russell, already ninety-five years old, charged that evidence garnered in Vietnam warranted hearings on the issue. He planned a War Crimes Tribunal and organized, through the Bertrand Russell Peace Foundation, more than thirty international observers to go to Vietnam to accumulate evidence and testimony. Some of these observers were Americans, among them three Student Nonviolent Coordinating Committee members: Julius Lester, Charlie Cobb, and Conrad Lynn. John Gerassi, former editor of *Time* and professor of journalism at New York University, and Carol

Brightman, editor of *Viet-Report* also spent the month of February traveling throughout Nam Binh and Thanh Hoa provinces collecting testimony for the commission (Gerassi 1967b).

The twenty-seven-member tribunal convened in Stockholm in May 1967, pointedly calling itself an investigative, not a judicial, body. "It is true," said Jean-Paul Sartre when he convened the tribunal, "we are only a jury. We have neither the power to condemn, nor the power to acquit, anyone. Therefore, no prosecution. We, the jury, at the end of the session will have to pronounce on the charges: are they well-founded or not? But the judges are everywhere. They are the people of the world, and particularly the American people. It is for them that we are working" (Julin 1967).

The tribunal met in two sessions, ending on 1 December 1967. It held that the United States had violated the Hague Conventions of 1907 and the Geneva Conventions, with particular respect to its use of weapons and products prohibited by them, namely napalm, phosphorus, defoliation sprays, fragmentation bombs, and the turning over of prisoners to the South Vietnamese Army knowing that some of them would be summarily executed (Duffet 1968).

The issue of war crimes in Vietnam had been raised before. Bernard Fall wrote in *Ramparts* as early as December 1965 that he believed the time had already come when Americans were "no longer . . . able to see the Vietnamese as people against whom crimes can be committed." Reports of war horrors were beginning to appear in national periodicals and newspapers. Sometimes, stunned families published letters sent by GI family members detailing massive and wanton destruction by American soldiers.[4] In January 1967, *Ladies Home Journal* and *Redbook* published articles that implicitly criticized the wide aerial bombing in Vietnam and the civilian casualties it created. Still, discussing the war in terms of war crimes made many people, even antiwar activists, uneasy. The War Crimes Tribunal was one-sided, some said; shouldn't the crimes of the Vietnamese be considered? There was no one there to defend the United States; others objected, although the tribunal had invited Washington to send a delegation. Washington preferred to ignore the whole thing, hoping it would go away. "I'm not going to play games with a ninety-four-year-old Englishman," Secretary of State Dean Rusk said with evident irritation when a *Times* reporter pressed him on the subject.

---

4. See, for example, a letter published in the *Akron (Ohio) Beacon-Journal* in June 1967 and reprinted as "We Burned Every Hut" in *The Progressive*, July 1967, 21–22.

The White House and the State Department were keenly interested in the proceedings, although they publicly ignored them. President Johnson instructed Walt Rostow to deliver a private protest to the Swedish government regarding its decision to allow the tribunal to be held in Stockholm. Rostow reported back with evident relish that he had "delivered the message loud and clear" so that "the Swedes are properly churned up on the Russell business." The White House asked the FBI, the American embassy in Stockholm, and the United States Information Agency to send in regular reports on the proceedings, with particular regard to how the international press received them. The Western press opted to focus on the internal dynamics of the tribunal committee and on the evident reluctance of other journalists to cover the story. Scant and superficial press coverage of the War Crimes Tribunal pleased the White House. The president may be "a little cheered," Walt Rostow wrote to Johnson at his Texas ranch, by the way that the press covered "the shenanigans in Stockholm" (Rostow 1967c, LBJL).

The Russell War Crimes Tribunal generated more superficial criticism than seasoned analysis in the media, but the question of war crimes came up over and over in the next few years because too many Americans felt in their bones that something was wrong with the war. As books by former GIs, policymakers, and analysts tumbled off the presses, documenting in stunning detail the air war, the conduct of the ground war, and official deceptions and coverups, "war crimes" became a phrase that entered the arena of legitimate controversy.[5] The issue was ultimately raised by an eminently centrist figure with no hint of prior antiwar sentiment: Telford Taylor, the chief United States prosecutor at the Nuremberg Trials and later professor of law at Columbia University. In 1971 Taylor told TV talk show host Dick Cavett that if the standards established during the Nuremberg Trials were applied to General Westmoreland, the American general could well be convicted of war crimes.[6] Shortly after Taylor's remarks, the *New York Review of Books* carried a lead article by reporter Neil Sheehan on 28 March 1971 reviewing thirty-three recently published books on Vietnam, including congressional reports and hearings. Sheehan wrote that "if you credit as factual only a fraction of the information

5. See, for example, "What Every Vietnam Vet Knows," *The New Republic,* 19 Dec. 1970; Harvey, 1967; and *In the Name of America,* 1968.

6. Taylor made his remarks on ABC's "Dick Cavett Show," broadcast on 9 Jan. 1971. For press coverage of the show, see the *New York Times,* 9 Jan. 1971. Taylor followed up his remarks by writing *Nuremberg and Vietnam: An American Tragedy* in 1971.

assembled here about what happened in Vietnam, and if you apply the laws of war to American conduct there, than the leaders of the United States for the past six years at least, including the incumbent President, Richard Milhous Nixon, may well be guilty of war crimes."

As the courts appeared increasingly unlikely in 1967 to uphold criminal penalties for travel to international areas or even to allow the federal government to ban it for political reasons, the White House stepped up its efforts to find other grounds for prosecuting travelers to Hanoi. Sometime before October, the Johnson Administration directed the Central Intelligence Agency to study the "international connections of the U.S. peace groups" (DeBenedetti 1983, 31). The CIA's report, which is still heavily censored, focused largely on what it called a "small group of dedicated men"—James Bevel, Nick Egleson, Tom Hayden, and David Dellinger—as being behind the travel to Hanoi (Rostow 1967e, LBJL). Of these, only Dellinger could have been, even then, considered a leading figure in fostering international connections in the antiwar community. In assuming that only men would be found in these activities, the report ignored almost entirely the role that many women were playing in travel to Hanoi.

The report is deeply flawed in other respects, primarily because of the methods the analysts used. They appear to have been searching for tightly guarded secrets, for deep plots, for conspiracies, and they ignored the information open and available in the antiwar press and even in the national press. Consequently, the CIA's chronology of citizen travel to Hanoi is incorrect and vastly incomplete. It focuses on minor figures, ignores major actors, and provides significantly inaccurate details. White House officials could have easily gathered far better information by clipping and filing news accounts from the national media and by reading magazines like *Ramparts*, *Viet-Report*, *WIN*, and *Liberation*, whose editors were eager to distribute their publications as widely as possible. The irony is that travelers to Hanoi repeatedly requested interviews with the White House, which usually turned them down, turning instead to the CIA to try to find out clandestinely what it could have had openly.[7]

The CIA concluded, after all its work, that there was "no significant

7. When the Treasury Department seized a bank account that had been used for donations of money for humanitarian aid to North Vietnam, for example, the organizers published the new address for those wishing to mail contributions to the fund in the 31 January 1968 issue of *WIN*.

evidence that would prove Communist control or direction of the US peace movement or its leaders." (Rostow 1967e, 15). The president could hardly have been mollified by this news. Citizen travel to Hanoi rankled him, and he wanted to stop it. At a lunch with some cabinet members after reading the CIA's report in early November, Johnson burst out that he was "not going to let the Communists take this government and they're doing it right now. . . . I've got my belly full of seeing these people put on a Communist plane and shipped all over this country. I want someone to carefully look at who leaves this country, where they go, why they are going, and if they're going to Hanoi, how are we going to keep them from getting back into this country" (Jones 1967, LBJL).

The president's CIA director, Richard Helms, was not hopeful about stopping them. He told the president gloomily that "under the laws today you cannot prosecute anybody for anything" (Jones 1967, LBJL).

Throughout all of this, Women Strike for Peace continued organizing group travel to Southeast Asia. Americans Want to Know had been a WSP project, as had been the group that met up with Harrison Salisbury in a bomb shelter in Hanoi. In September 1967, WSP members Mary Clarke, Dagmar Wilson, and Ruth Krause went to Hanoi and toured surrounding provinces. Their observations matched those of previous groups: morale seemed high, in spite of bombing; destruction lay everywhere; educational and medical facilities were dispersed throughout North Vietnam; and, except for Hanoi and Haiphong, urban life had practically disappeared. Premier Pham Van Dong met with the WSP activists for several hours and specified three conditions for negotiations: cessation of the bombing without preconditions, withdrawal of American troops, and recognition of the National Liberation Front as a legitimate negotiating force. The United States did not have to implement these provisions before any talks began, the premier told them, but it had to demonstrate evidence of accepting these provisions in principle. The details could be worked out later in agreements.

The United States had never sat down with its Vietnamese opponents to discuss war issues, but Washington was beginning to narrow the avenues of negotiations to the basic points upon which Hanoi and the NLF insisted. The president could still adamantly insist that the United States would never withdraw, but by mid-1967, the option of withdrawal began to stand out. Public figures, along with antiwar activists, began to frame their positions on Vietnam around particular conditions of withdrawal, usually framed as an "honorable" peace. In June, sixteen of the most notable doves in the Senate, including Frank Church, Robert Kennedy, George McGovern, and J. William Fulbright, published an open letter to President Johnson in the *New York Times* on 17 May expressing hopes for "negotiations for an honorable settlement of the war." The signers hedged this position by rejecting a "unilateral" withdrawal from South Vietnam. It was now politically permissible to discuss a withdrawal, as long as a çase could be made that Hanoi reciprocate in some way. The senators directed their letter to Hanoi as well as to the White House, saying that it would be "tragic" if there were any misconception in Hanoi about the "nature of the dissent in this country." The signers may have hoped that their letter would be a signal to Hanoi, but they hardly imagined that it would be literally dropped on that country. When Mary Clarke was inspecting the bombed-out debris of the Sacre Coeur Catholic Church in Ninh Binh Province in North Vietnam on 9 September 1967, she saw leaflets that had been dropped by American pilots along with their bombs. The leaflets were Defense Department translations into Vietnamese of the Church letter, complete with the names of all sixteen signers.

The Church letter linked the signers' position on a unilateral withdrawal to concerns about the impact of the antiwar movement on Hanoi. The administration constantly fretted that Hanoi counted on domestic opposition to the war to weaken American "resolve." This fear fit in with growing perplexity in the United States about how that powerful country could lose a war against a poor and small country that was, by any calculation, no military match for the Pentagon's arsenal. If America's unmatched military might was defeated, the cause must come from within that nation itself. Only America could defeat America, as Richard Nixon later put it. Following this line of thought easily led to the charge that to be openly against the war and for a unilateral American withdrawal was akin to treason.

Travelers to Hanoi were concerned about Hanoi's understanding of the nature of dissent in the United States too, but for another reason— they knew the antiwar movement was not popular among the American public and that it enjoyed neither the resources or the automatic respect still commanded by the American government. They hoped that antiwar protest would help end the war, but it would be misleading, they thought, for Hanoi to expect that the marches they read about in wire releases would influence Washington's military decisions. On the same trip to Hanoi during which she found the Church letter among the debris of the Catholic Church, Mary Clarke brought up the issue to North Vietnam's foreign minister, Nguyen Duy Trinh. Clarke told the minister that many Americans believed that the North Vietnamese were counting on the American peace movement to end the war. If this belief were true, it was not a realistic assessment, she went on. Trinh responded by observing that it was heartening that so many Americans opposed the war because it demonstrated that even people who were not Vietnamese could understand their struggle. Still, he added, the Vietnamese were counting only on their own resources to reunite Vietnam (Clarke 1967, SCPC).

Citizen contacts with Vietnamese had always depended on the freedom to travel, and Washington officials went as far as the courts would allow to take away that freedom. By late 1967, the State Department had seized the passports of twenty-seven citizens after they traveled to North Vietnam, including all the WSP travelers. Other prospective travelers were denied passports, effectively banning all international travel for them. As long as these conditions continued, citizen contacts with Vietnamese were difficult to plan and sustain. They threw a chill over potential plans to travel even to Europe to meet with Vietnamese. Under these conditions, for example, Martin Luther King, Jr., turned down requests from activists to go to Vietnam and Paris to meet with Vietnamese officials because he was convinced that the United States would revoke his passport if he met with Vietnamese leaders in either place (Hoover 1967, LBJL).

International travel by black Americans exercised the State Department more than did travel by white activists. In late 1967, Stokely Carmichael went on a trip to a number of Asian countries including North Vietnam. The trip, which the media publicized liberally, outraged many white Americans who appeared to view white citizen protest with considerably more equanimity than they viewed black protest. The White House received far more mail protesting Carmichael's trip to Hanoi than it got regarding any other trip to that country. The letters that poured into the White House about Carmichael's trip to North Vietnam fill two thick name files that excoriate Carmichael with venomous and explicit racial epithets, baiting the administration with questions about whether Democrats were up to dealing with "traitors" like Carmichael. The letters often go on to excoriate Martin Luther King, Jr., as well, though he had never been to Vietnam (WHCF n.d., LBJL). The State Department responded by proposing legislation mandating criminal penalties of one year in prison and $1,000 in fines for anyone traveling to "unauthorized" areas. When Undersecretary of State Nicholas Katzenbach announced the proposed criminal legislation for travel to Hanoi, he told the *Times* on 12

December that it was "obviously related to travel by Stokely Carmichael and others, to places such as North Vietnam. All his public statements and pronouncements have been under scrutiny for some time by the Department of Justice." The State Department had no grounds for prosecuting Carmichael for treason or sedition but, as *New York Times* legal correspondent Fred Graham put it on 12 December, "a lot of people are peeved at the government for not doing something about him." When Carmichael returned to New York, he was greeted by U.S. federal marshals, who subjected him to a rough body search at the airport and seized his passport.

The State Department continued to seize passports held by American citizens even after the U.S. Court of Appeals in Washington, D.C., ruled on 20 December 1967 that only passports actually carried into the forbidden zones could be confiscated. Even if citizens said plainly that they intended to go to a forbidden country, the court ruled, the State Department was bound to give them passports. Nor could a passport be seized later merely because the holder had entered a forbidden zone. Only those passports which had been carried into a prohibited country could be taken. No further penalties were legal.

Despite these rulings, most travelers simply gave up their passports when demanded and then filed suit to reclaim them. But after one traveler refused to hand over his passport, the charade ended. When, in February 1968, State Department agents turned up in the Manhattan law offices of Conrad Lynn, a black lawyer who had gone to Hanoi for the War Crimes Tribunal, he refused to turn over his passport, citing the earlier court ruling. He had not used his passport in Vietnam, he said, and he demanded a State Department hearing. When questioned by a *Times* reporter on 6 February, a State Department official confirmed that Lynn's interpretation of the court decision was correct, but defended the government's action by saying that the State Department might, sometime, appeal the court's ruling. Lynn's passport was the last one the government tried to seize in these cases. On 27 March 1968, the State Department announced that it would not appeal the court ruling and that, in accordance with that ruling, it would not seize any more passports as long as they were not taken into forbidden zones (Watson 1968, LBJL).

Four days after the State Department announcement, President Johnson, alarmed by the Tet Offensive, announced that bombing in North Vietnam would continue between the seventeenth and twentieth parallels, but it would be halted unconditionally north of there. Every

American who had ever been to North Vietnam knew that officials there were adamant that an end to the bombing without preconditions was, for Hanoi, the first step toward fulfilling the spirit of the Geneva Accords, the necessary condition under which negotiations could begin. The partial bombing halt was not the unconditional and complete halt that North Vietnam had called for, but it represented a surety of the administration's intentions, and Hanoi took it in good faith as a certifiable "winding down" to which it could respond.[8] The president's simultaneous announcement of a token increase in U.S. troop deployments, rather than the large increases that General Westmoreland requested, limited Washington's military commitment, and, for the first time, pointed to a change in ground strategy that could include an American withdrawal. Vietnamization had yet to be named, but it had already begun (*Pentagon Papers* 4:599).

President Johnson's change in strategy at the end of March rested on two considerations, one domestic and one foreign. His principal civilian advisors were convinced that sending more troops to Vietnam would not produce a military victory there, and he held a deeply felt conviction that he needed to restore unity to an America torn by opposition to the war. The solution, then, must be political, not military. The most promising means to that end were the ones that American travelers to Vietnam had begun calling for three years earlier—an end to the bombing of North Vietnam and withdrawal of foreign troops. The president took unmistakable first steps in this direction. His convictions even propelled him to designate publicly the United States representatives for the proposed talks. It was the first time the president had prefaced calls for talks with such concrete steps, and Hanoi responded with a promptness that surprised him. Four days later, the White House announced agreed-upon dates for the first meeting between American and North Vietnamese representatives, which took place on 13 May in Paris. On 31 October, just before the fall elections in the United States, President Johnson ordered a full bombing halt in North Vietnam, that is, north of the seventeenth parallel (Pentagon Papers 4:603).

Richard Nixon's election in 1968 brought in a new set of American

8. Rather than ending the bombing, the president shifted it to other areas of Southeast Asia. A White House cable sent to diplomatic posts abroad just before the announcement stated that "air power now used north of 20th can probably be used in Laos (where no policy change planned) and in SVN" (*Pentagon Papers* 4:595).

officials with their own fresh determination not to "lose" Vietnam while ending the war. That determination included resuming the bombing in North Vietnam while slowly withdrawing American troops. For the next years, the Paris negotiations between the Americans and the Vietnamese went through rounds of deadlock, progress, and setbacks, but that is another story. What is significant is that when Washington refused to talk to officials in Hanoi during the great American build-up in Vietnam, the Vietnamese sent their diplomatic messages directly through American citizens who had initiated the first contacts between themselves and Vietnamese officials in a sustained climate of openness and accessibility. The secrecy in official foreign policy-making that marked Washington's diplomatic endeavors was not replicated in Hanoi or with the American activists. Hanoi had no secret strategies, no wish even for "secret" talks—only for talks. Washington officials would slowly come to learn over the years of negotiations in Paris that the North Vietnamese officials said the same things in these private talks that they said in public. "What really infuriated Kissinger," Walter Isaacson concluded, "was not that the North Vietnamese were devious, but the opposite: that they said the same things in the private, secret talks that they were saying in public—indeed, they stubbornly seemed to mean what they said" (1992, 245). The message that American citizens in Hanoi received was exactly that which Hanoi took to the negotiating table in Paris: the bombing must end, foreign troops must leave. Talks could begin and would continue as long as perceptible progress on these two elemental points continued.

Those two points endured throughout the war because they appealed to many people, whether or not they were Vietnamese. The call for foreign troop withdrawals fit in with the worldwide movement toward decolonization; its roots in the Geneva Accords appealed to the sentiment for international law to replace the colonial divisions of the world. The bombing was difficult to defend in any case. One did not have to be radical to endorse these points. The pope endorsed them, the United Nations secretary general did, even New York Mets pitcher Tom Seaver was quoted in the *Times* on 11 October 1969 as saying that "if the Mets could win the World Series, then we can get out of Vietnam. I think it's perfectly ridiculous what we're doing about the Vietnam situation. It's absurd." Even Americans who considered themselves supporters of their government's foreign policy could ask that their "boys" be brought home.

For many American activists at that time who examined the history of the conflict in Vietnam, the calls for an American troop withdrawal and an end to the bombing had the virtues of being in accord with ideals of national self-determination and in tune with concepts of fair play in international relations. Beyond that, they were clear proposals that anyone could grasp. The first meeting between American activists and Vietnamese officials in Jakarta in July 1965 had yielded the first agreement between American citizens and Vietnamese on these points, which were consistently carried back to the U.S. antiwar press by subsequent groups, endorsed by the larger American and international antiwar movement, and gradually accepted by the American public and eventually by a reluctant White House. Washington officials could refuse to talk to Hanoi and to many Americans who traveled there, but eventually the calls to end the bombing and withdraw troops became so loud and clear that Washington could not help but listen. American citizen travelers to Hanoi were vital in conveying to the larger antiwar coalition the picture from "the other side" by building a framework of agreement on common negotiating points for the diverse groups who made up the American antiwar movement and who argued over many other things.

With direct talks with Vietnamese officials underway, the Johnson administration moved to cut off private contacts with citizen activists who had information from Hanoi. A week after announcing that peace talks were being scheduled, the president sent a memo to Secretary of State Dean Rusk:

> I wish to have you lay it down as a flat rule in the Department of State that we shall have no further contacts with private persons going to Hanoi or otherwise engaging in contacts with representatives of the government of North Vietnam or the NLF. I am convinced that no matter how we restrict those contacts, they result in a posture of quasi-negotiation which misleads Hanoi and undercuts our position at home. (Rostow 1968a, LBJL)

Despite the president's order, it would prove impossible to cut off the influence of the citizens who continued to go to Hanoi. The courts backed the freedom to travel. With official talks scheduled between Hanoi and Washington, citizen activists turned their attention to other matters: organizing humanitarian aid for North and South Vietnam, establishing reliable mail service between American prisoners in Hanoi and their families in the United States, and working for early releases of American POWs in North Vietnam. Through all this, they strove to keep the concrete realities of the war before the public at home.

4

Humanitarian Aid

As reports streamed home of the destructive impact of the air and ground war, antiwar groups began to organize humanitarian and medical aid for North Vietnam and for National Liberation Front areas in the south. Penicillin, anti-malarial drugs, syringes, prosthetics, and medical equipment constituted most of these shipments. This form of citizen aid offered an avenue for transforming the energy of the antiwar movement into a constructive force that moved beyond mass street protests. Washington responded by forbidding humanitarian aid to all save United States–controlled areas, or by regulating it obstructively. Still, Americans who had traveled to Hanoi organized donations of medical supplies to Vietnam by air and sea, their efforts spurred by the continuing reports of the air war's destruction there.

Two concerns about the air war were shared by Americans with varying stances on the war: the bombs themselves and the chemicals rained upon the land. Bombs aroused concern because the imprecision of the large bombs inflicted large-scale civilian damage, and the precision of the smaller ones did the same. Senator Edward Brooke wrote to President Johnson in mid-1967 about this aspect of the bombing campaign: "It has been my understanding that bombing delivery has become increasingly precise since my combat experience in the Second World War," the senator wrote. "I have been told repeatedly that bombs dropped by modern aircraft fall within a hundred feet or so of the target. . . . This seemed to me to be the implication of Secretary Brown's remarks last March when he said, 'Our fighter pilots are not considered qualified until they can put a series of bombs within 140 feet of a target.'"

In light of this assurance, Brooke went on, he had been inclined to discount "charges of visitors to the area that U.S. weapons are frequently landing far from their presumed targets and producing undue collateral damage." But he had gone to South Vietnam himself, the senator went on, and what he had seen and heard there made him skeptical of official claims and more inclined to believe the visitors. In South Vietnam, "experienced personnel" told him that bombs often were more than a thousand feet off the aim point, that pilots dropped their weapons on the smoke left by previous strikes without any idea of how close the bombs were to their targets and, if they broke through cloud cover well off their intended approach, they "unloaded" their ordnance anyway. His own trip to South Vietnam left him more willing to believe the consistent pattern of reports that returning activists brought from Hanoi. "One person who recently returned from Hanoi," the senator wrote to the president, "described, in terms more credible than I had previously heard, an almost random pattern of bomb strikes in that vicinity" (Rostow 1967b, LBJL).

The second concern, that of the vast quantities of chemicals that the air war rained upon the land and people in Vietnam, evoked images that tapped into growing fears about America's own fate. Americans woke to the impact of toxins on their own soil when Rachel Carson published *Silent Spring* in 1962, and they began to restrict their use and disposal at home. At the same time, the United States military poured massive quantities of pesticides and herbicides on Vietnam. Visitors to Vietnam pointed out this contradiction, and some scientists quickly took up the issue. Two American biologists, Arthur Galston and Jean Mayer, published articles in *Scientist and Citizen Magazine* in 1967 charging that United States defoliation of forests and fields hit Vietnamese civilians the hardest. The wide use of herbicides in Vietnam was a tactical failure, the two scientists went on, but the Pentagon still had plans to spray, and destroy, a million acres of forest and half a million acres of cropland. The spraying was so enormous, the article pointed out, that American chemical companies could not keep up with military demand for the herbicides. Pentagon officials denied the scientists' conclusions but did not deny their figures. Using herbicides could not be considered a tactical failure, officials said, when "you consider the possible saving of countless American lives" (Panzer 1967, LBJL).

The Pentagon provided no official estimates of the civilian casualties of the war. There were official figures on almost everything else: how many hamlets were "pacified," how many were not, how many "enemy" bodies were counted, how many tons of rice were harvested, what the cost of the war was ($332,000 for each enemy soldier killed in 1967). Despite all the intelligence gathering, the Defense Department insisted that it was impossible to find out how many civilians were killed and wounded in Vietnam. On 17 August 1966, General Westmoreland told the *New York Times* that, to date, there had been 137 civilians killed inadvertently through United States military operations in South Vietnam. When this offering was greeted with unmitigated skepticism, a Defense Department spokesman added that Westmoreland's figure "bore only a random relationship to the total number of civilian casualties."

If there was no effort to count the casualties, there were figures on the burgeoning numbers of refugees. The "pacification" strategy used in the ground war in the south of Vietnam created masses of refugees—one million by the end of 1965 alone. The program rounded up villagers, destroyed their homes, and herded them into "strategic hamlets," which the Vietnamese called concentration camps. These hamlets were surrounded by barbed wire and required passes for those leaving and entering (Hess 1993). Humanitarian aid for refugees who resided in these camps was considered "legitimate" humanitarian aid by Washington officials, and American relief organizations directed the bulk of their efforts at them.

Providing relief for the official refugees raised troubling questions for American humanitarian organizations. Were they contributing to the refugee solution, or providing the needed "cushion" so that the American military could complacently uproot more villages? In 1969, Don Luce, director of the International Voluntary Service in South Vietnam, said that American troops built their military strategy partly around the services of relief organizations. He was first made aware of this when a military commander radioed in from his patrol to the area where Luce was working to ask if anyone there could take in fifty refugees. Assured that they could be accommodated readily, the commander said that, in that case, his troops would just burn the whole hamlet and bring in three hundred and fifty refugees (Luce 1968). "The greatest need in the Vietnamese refugee problem is to quit making refugees," one weary relief administrator wrote (Krabill 1966, AFSC).

Washington welcomed private humanitarian aid to the refugees in South Vietnam who were under United States control. Humanitarian aid to those under the American bombs in North Vietnam or in National Liberation Front areas in the south fell into another category entirely, and it became the most direct form of citizen protest of the Vietnam war. Carrying on a war with popular support requires that the line between one's own and one's enemy be firm and unwavering. Humanitarian aid to those civilians who were bombed by American pilots became the ultimate test of this line. The Johnson and Nixon administrations held that humanitarian aid to any North Vietnamese fell within the category of "trading with the enemy," and required that it be done only under the watchful eye of the Treasury Department, which usually refused to issue export permits for it.

Washington wanted Americans to stay out of North Vietnam; their reports about the bombing campaign raised questions that undermined the administration's military claims. At the same time, Washington allowed organizations to send all manner of humanitarian aid to Saigon and U.S.-controlled areas without supervision. As the war widened in 1966 and 1967, some antiwar groups organized donations of money and medical and relief supplies for NLF areas in the south and for North Vietnam. These efforts met steady government obstruction. Still, it was a difficult issue for Washington to prosecute because humanitarian aid itself was rooted in ideas and practices upon which Americans of all political persuasions prided themselves.

Humanitarian aid to North Vietnam and to areas of the National Liberation Front was an issue that at first divided many organizations and groups opposed to the war. The line dividing the enemy and one's own government was a safe line behind which many activists felt more secure, reasoning that the United States might be wrong in Vietnam, but the "communists" were wrong too, and not to be identified with in any form. Humanitarian aid that crossed the line to civilians on the enemy side could be given a traitorous twist. If they sent bandages and medicines, might those goods be used for combatants? If they sent money, some activists asked, would the Vietnamese not use it to buy bullets? That their own tax monies went to buy American bombs usually went unquestioned. In the heat of the war, sending humanitarian aid to civilians on the other side could never be as politically safe as lobbying legislators or marching in street demonstrations. The American Friends Service Committee, for example, had always considered that its mission was to "minister impartially to civilians on all sides who suffered from war, without respect to their race, religion, politics, or national origins" (Indochina Humanitarian Program, AFSC), but it was faced now with suffering civilians on a "side" that its own country's troops were fighting.

Initial reluctance by Americans to offer humanitarian aid to Hanoi was matched by Hanoi's reluctance to accept it. That reluctance came from several sources, one of which was a fear that international medical aid would project an image of a people battered by war and dependent on others. In 1966, the American Friends Service Committee printed and distributed *Peace in Vietnam*, a pamphlet critical of American policy in Southeast Asia. The pamphlet was intended for distribution within the United States, and its cover depicted Vietnamese people weeping over a war that left them bereft of home and family. When AFSC representative Joseph Elder gave the pamphlet to a Vietnamese translator in Hanoi in 1969, she pointedly objected to the cover, saying that it conveyed a limited image of the Vietnamese, an image of them as helpless victims. Their successes in building a country despite the war's ravages should define them, she believed, not images of them as helpless below the bombs (Elder 1969c).

A related reluctance to define the Vietnamese-American relationship by charity stemmed from a determination to be as self-reliant as possible in all aspects of the war effort. This determination existed at all levels, and many visitors to Vietnam noted it. In 1967, when the AFSC offered North Vietnam technical training in prosthetics for war casualties, the Vietnamese quickly told them that perhaps the Americans could learn something about rehabilitation from programs in North Vietnam. When an American doctor was captured by the NLF in Hue during the Tet offensive in 1968, she repeatedly offered her services in caring for the ill and wounded among them, but was decisively rebuffed. They had their own medical personnel and did not need outside help, they insisted. Even the Du Bois delegates had offered, seriously or not, to stay in Hanoi in 1965 and help with the war effort from there, but their offer was unequivocally rejected.

Other obstacles to humanitarian aid programs arose because an American embargo against North Vietnam had been in force for years, so American materials no longer matched what was already in place in North Vietnam. The Vietnamese preferred money to American-made equipment so that they could buy materials that were compatible with equipment they already had. In addition to these impediments, the Vietnamese mistrusted many Western international organizations, a mistrust arising out of the role they believed some of them had played in destroying the Geneva Accords and bolstering the American military presence in South Vietnam. They were skeptical of the International Red Cross, for example, viewing it as a mouthpiece for Western interests. Thus at the beginning of the war there was mutual suspicion on the issue of humanitarian aid from Americans to Vietnamese.

Most antiwar organizations were ill-equipped to deal with humanitarian aid. Those that ultimately involved themselves deeply in it were flexible enough to work with both Vietnamese and Washington officials in building some trust out of mistrust. They usually had international offices with strong international endeavors and citizen exchanges already in place, and they viewed ending the war in Vietnam as part and parcel of their ongoing endeavor to create a safer and more just world. In the narrower context of the antiwar movement, they were, not surprisingly, groups who generally steered clear of the interminable wrangling that passed for "coalition building" in the antiwar movement, a term often used to exclude those with current or former Communist or Socialist party connections. They were not noisy, not self-aggrandizing, and, perhaps for that reason, not much in the news. Two of these groups were the American Friends Service Committee and the Women's International League for Peace and Freedom, both of which organized long-term humanitarian aid for Vietnam, working either with, or in spite of, the United States Treasury Department. Women Strike for Peace used its very early and continuing contacts in Hanoi to organize mail service between American POWs there and their families in the United States.

North Vietnam ultimately accepted the help of such organizations because, despite reluctance at first to deal with American humanitarian aid and American bombs at the same time, it wanted to establish good working relations with Americans who were friendly. "Friends like you and Norman Morrison have saved the honor of the United States," one Vietnamese official told an AFSC staffer who accompanied a shipment of medical supplies to Hanoi in 1972 (Sullivan 1972b, AFSC).

The first efforts to aid civilians in North Vietnam came in 1965, when a few antiwar groups organized highly charged and publicized donations of money for North Vietnam. The organizers were small, vocal groups on large university campuses. Their goals revolved around domestic revolution, and they used the issue of humanitarian aid to sharpen their confrontation with Washington. The press paid the most attention to these groups, and so did the United States Congress. None of the money ever reached Vietnam. It was sent through a bank in Prague, and the U.S. Treasury Department seized the money there and reprimanded Wells Fargo Bank, which had handled the transactions.

In response to these token supplies, the House Committee on Un-American Activities once again reacted. In August 1966, it scheduled hearings for a bill that made it a felony, punishable by twenty years in prison, for Americans to aid any person from nations engaged in hostilities against the United States. HUAC subpoenaed the most radical student groups that had collected token amounts of money for North Vietnam. Texas congressman Joe Pool, who headed the committee, told the *Times* on 18 August that it was also "a general inquiry into Communism." The committee had little trouble getting the names of students that it wanted—university administrators voluntarily handed over lists of student memberships in the Du Bois Clubs and the Committee to Aid the Vietnam People, which had collected the small donations.[1]

HUAC held four days of raucous hearings, beginning when Pool ordered the students' chief counsel, Arthur Kinoy, arrested for disorderly conduct. Kinoy, a seasoned lawyer who had also represented the Mississippi Freedom Democratic party in 1964, was dragged from the Committee Room and taken to the police station, where he spent the next hours dispensing free legal advice to other detainees. His partner, William Kunstler, took his place.[2]

Some of HUAC's witnesses were friendly, including Edwin Meese, then assistant district attorney of Alameda County in California, and Phillip Abbot Luce, who, it was revealed later, quietly received $1,000 from the committee for his friendly testimony. But the subpoenaed witnesses, young and militant, knew exactly why they had been called, and they determined to give the committee its money's worth. Jerry Rubin, who wanted to be a witness but was not called, turned up anyway in the uniform of an American revolutionary war soldier. Others insisted on being sworn in before giving their names ("otherwise I could say I was James Bond," one of them explained derisively, according to the 20 August *New York Times*) and called committee members by their first name diminutives. Committee members rose to the bait and called the witnesses "a bunch of clowns." When being sworn in, one witness held up his right hand made into a fist except for his middle finger, which re-

1. For a study of earlier university collaboration with the FBI, see Diamond 1992 and Schrecker 1986.

2. Senator Wayne Hays (D-Ohio) said Kinoy's ejection was justified because his name "will be found on any Communist-organized thing." Kinoy's subsequent conviction was later overturned by the Court of Appeals, which ruled that HUAC violated its own rules when Kinoy was cited for contempt. *NYT,* 6 and 19 Aug. 1968.

mained erect. "Everyone pretended not to notice," the *Times* reporter drily noted.

Shouting and scuffling marked the hearings, as witnesses refused to plead the fifth amendment and boasted of the money they collected for North Vietnam, now lying in U.S. Treasury coffers. By the fourth day, more than fifty people had been arrested and dragged from the committee room. When Representative Pool unexpectedly announced at noon that day that the hearings were ended, he said the committee had all the information it needed on how "revolutionary hard-core Communists" in America had aided "the Viet-Cong." Many members of Congress, however, called the hearings a farce. According to the *New York Times* of 21 August, Senator Everett Dirksen, Mr. Republican himself, said that "this spectacle can do the Congress no good," and announced that any bill the committee sent out stood no chance of ever reaching the Senate floor.[3] Still, it was an election year, and it never hurt to vote against communism. HUAC unanimously approved the proposed bill, and it easily passed the House of Representatives, though it never reached the Senate floor. If Pool's bill never cluttered up a statute book, it did serve one purpose: when the hearings began, Joe Pool was considered a poor bet to win reelection in Texas; in November he was reelected handily.

HUAC never called any Quakers to testify, although they were the most diligent and successful in organizing early humanitarian aid to North Vietnam. The American Friends Service Committee was the national Quaker relief organization with a long tradition of humanitarian aid throughout the world. American Quakers traditionally had ministered impartially to all sides during war. The tradition went back to John Woolman, a Philadelphia Quaker who, in 1763, embarked on a journey of reconciliation to Indians at Wyalusing, then considered a center of Indian attacks on settlers. Angry Philadelphians blamed him for "siding" with the enemy, but ever since then, American Quakers had been noted for their evenhanded efforts at alleviating human suffering and encouraging reconciliation. They faced a singular constraint in organizing aid to North Vietnam and NLF areas in South Vietnam because the United States Treasury Department required licenses for humanitarian or medical shipments to these areas, a requirement that the department used to limit se-

---

3. See also "Hullabaloo at HUAC," *Newsweek,* 29 Aug. 1966, 16; "HUAC Hellzapoppin," *New Republic,* 27 Aug. 1966, 6; and "Summer Madness," *Time,* 26 Aug. 1966, 10–11.

verely the quantity and type of goods donated. In 1969, the AFSC had established a prosthetics and rehabilitation program in Quang Ngai, a "pacified" area of Vietnam, and the Treasury Department did not require licenses for material aid and money for this program.

While the AFSC tried to work out these domestic constraints, groups of Friends across the United States started informal associations and organized unofficial relief programs for Vietnam. As early as December 1965, some Friends in New York City sent parcels to the Red Cross Society in Hanoi. The post office accepted the packages, though they apparently never left the United States. When the group tried to mail the next set of packages, the post office in New York refused to accept them, so the group sent the packages to the Canadian Friends Service Committee (CFSC), which forwarded them to Hanoi, *WIN* reported on 5 November.

Groups of Friends in other parts of the United States began to send money for material aid to the CFSC and the Red Cross Society of Vietnam. In some cases they applied to the Treasury Department for licenses, and at first a few of these applications were approved for a fraction of the original request (Chronology, SCPC). The Johnson Administration initially granted these pared-down requests, saying publicly that it hoped Hanoi would permit a permanent Western team to be stationed there to oversee all distribution of humanitarian goods and materials from the AFSC and the International Red Cross, under guidelines approved by the White House. Privately, National Security Advisor Walt Rostow noted that the White House had hoped in 1966 "that this might develop channels through which assistance could be provided to American prisoners of war in North Viet Nam" (Rostow 1967d). In February 1967, after approving a total of $10,300 in funds for the CFSC and the International Red Cross, the White House abruptly ordered the Treasury Department to deny all future licenses, saying that no such relief team was in place and that there was no "assurance that the supplies will in fact be devoted to the non-military purposes intended by the donors" (Rostow 1967f).

The American Friends Service Committee continued working with the White House and State Department to use official channels to send aid to North Vietnam and NLF areas of South Vietnam. At the same time, a group of Quakers already dedicated to practical and symbolic actions against the Cold War resolved to carry out direct action activities that the AFSC was not prepared to perform. They called themselves A Quaker Action Group (AQAG), and described themselves as "an informal association of individual Friends dedicated to confronting the immoral and destructive policies of war and violence while affirming constructive alternatives for the establishment of peace and human brotherhood." AQAG organized humanitarian aid for North Vietnam and NLF areas in the south, saying that, "as heirs of both the Quaker and early American heritage, we consider the giving of humanitarian relief to members of the human family as an inalienable right with which we are endowed by our Creator" (Chronology, SCPC).

A Quaker Action Group decided to send material aid directly to North Vietnam despite White House prohibition. "We are enjoined to love God and our neighbor—to give aid to the suffering and afflicted even if our government should consider them to be our enemy," members wrote to the Treasury Department, explaining their position and intended actions. They decided to fill out the Treasury Department forms but to send their material aid even if a license was denied. If it had become the national interest of the United States to bleed the Vietnamese to death, one AQAG member noted, "then surely the least we can do is put our government on notice that Friends are in the business of giving transfusions"(Flanagan 1967, SCPC).

Cash donations for North Vietnam came from across the nation. AQAG sent them on to the Canadian Friends Service Committee in Toronto, which bought antimalarial medicine and penicillin and shipped it, free of charge, from Montreal to Haiphong Harbor, on the Soviet liner *Alexander Pushkin*. By the time Treasury officials caught up with AQAG, they were able to seize only the last $300 dollar check on its way to Canada. Congressman Joe Pool reintroduced his "aid-as-treason" bill, and the Treasury Department pursued AQAG into Canada, forbidding Canadian subsidiaries of American drug companies to sell supplies to the CFSC for shipment to North Vietnam. That was no major problem. "There seems to be an adequate number of loyal Canadian companies willing to sell to us," AQAG's Ross Flanagan told the *Christian Century* (1 Feb. 1967). The Treasury Department then "suggested" to the Royal Bank of Canada that it seize control of the Canadian Friends Service Committee account and turn over all checks "that involved an interest of North Viet Nam or the Viet Cong," to the U.S. Treasury Department. When the Royal Bank refused, Stanley Sommerfield, chief counsel for the Treasury Department, hinted that there could be "possible severe retaliation" against the Royal Bank for its noncooperation (Schwartz, SCPC).

AQAG was an easier target than the Royal Bank of Canada, and Treasury officials went after it instead, seizing AQAG's bank accounts in New

York and Philadelphia and notifying all post offices in the United States not to accept "from Quakers any packages bound to North Vietnam by way of Canada." Because Canadian Banks refused to interfere in CFSC's bank account, the Treasury Department mailed out letters to over 14,000 American banks, ordering them not to honor any check "payable to or endorsed by the Canadian Friends Service Committee" or to any of the CFSC's officials whose names it conveniently listed in the letter (Chronology, SCPC).

As news of the Treasury Department's actions spread, Quakers in the United States and Canada formed an ad hoc "Quaker Underground" that kept antimalarial medicine and penicillin flowing from the United States to the Red Cross in Hanoi. Friends in Canada with personal bank accounts in the United States sent their account numbers to AQAG, which transferred funds through those accounts to the Canadian Friends Service Committee. Some American Quakers drove their cars to the Canadian border and handed over bundles of cash for the International Red Cross and the CFSC to their Canadian friends on the other side. Money came by wire, money order, and travelers checks, or was changed into British pounds and sent through the mail. By the end of 1966, the *New Republic* reported on 28 January, the CFSC was receiving $1,000 a week through these transfers.

Some members of A Quaker Action Group sent supplies to Canada on foot. They organized "pilgrimages" across the Peace Bridge, which linked Fort Erie, Ontario, and Buffalo, New York. Carrying bundles of cotton, bandages, and surgical instruments, a small group crossed the bridge on 9 October 1966, using their distinct Quaker talent of "friendly persuasion" to win over suspicious U.S. customs agents. Told at the border that customs regulations prohibited goods going to "communist nations," AQAG's Ross Flanagan replied with good humor that he was not aware that Canada was a communist nation. Pleasantries and patience wore down the American customs agents, who ultimately charged them only the customary one-dollar fee. Canadian officials went further, deciding, after some deliberation, to waive all usual fees.

Over the next six months, hundreds of people crossed the border, taking supplies destined for Hanoi to Quakers on the other side. Other groups joined them, including the Catholic, Jewish, and Episcopal Peace Fellowships and Clergy and Laymen Concerned about Vietnam. U.S. Customs officials allowed the pilgrims to cross but warned each of them that they were "violating the Trading with the Enemy act." News of the

Quaker actions were printed in the U.S. Army's *Stars and Stripes,* eliciting some vitriolic responses, including one from an American soldier in Vietnam who wrote, "Assist the Communists all of you Quakers and your children will not be Quakers but Dead or Communist." The U.S. postal service, which refused to deliver Quaker mail to the Canadian Friends Service Committee, was able to deliver this letter addressed only to "Quaker Church (Main) New York" (Flanagan 1966–67, SCPC).

The pilgrimages to Canada were annoying to the administration, but it was difficult to prosecute citizens who sent bandages to the wounded in North Vietnam. And, despite its protestations, Washington did not really want American civilians in North Vietnam overseeing humanitarian relief shipments to civilians there. They might take medical supplies, but they would surely bring back reports of new air assaults and photos of children napalmed, shrapneled, and bombed. Washington's embargo against humanitarian aid to North Vietnam functioned to mute attention within the United States to the reality of the bombing campaign there. The chronology of Washington's changing position on relief shipments to North Vietnam bears this out.

In early and mid-1966, while the American mass media gave scant credence to reports of civilian casualties, Washington encouraged the AFSC to talk with North Vietnamese officials about establishing a permanent presence in the country to oversee humanitarian aid. To congressional critics, Walt Rostow wrote that the White House hoped that "assistance" for the American POWs in Hanoi might be furthered through these channels. Following growing circulation of reports throughout the year of the bombing by Americans who went to Hanoi, and fast on the heels of *New York Times* reporter Harrison Salisbury's widely publicized trip during the Christmas season of 1966, the White House abruptly cut off any prospect that it would permit the AFSC to send humanitarian aid to North Vietnam legally by ordering the Treasury Department to deny all future license requests for medical aid to Hanoi. To justify its new position, the White House said that "the American Friends Service Committee recently sent a representative to Hanoi to discuss a relief program including a request for entry of a Friends Service relief team. The North Vietnam authorities refused to discuss this request" (Rostow 1967d, LBJL). This statement was not true. Russell Johnson, AFSC's Peace Education Secretary for the New England region, had gone to Hanoi in late January 1967 to talk to government officials about beginning an American-run medical program in North Vietnam. The

Vietnamese were concerned about issues of safety—their own hospitals and clinics were being decentralized and hidden in areas that offered some protection from the American bombing campaign—and they were not enthusiastic about foreigners running medical programs in their country. "They made it clear that it would take time to arrange and there were many problems involved," Johnson reported to the White House, "but they did not shut the door on this idea" (Indochina Humanitarian Service, AFSC). The White House, however, was feeling pressure following Salisbury's trip to Hanoi. Te temporary uproar that his eyewitness reports created left no doubt that, if these reports continually streamed out of Vietnam, the bombing campaign there might be threatened. And if the AFSC established a permanent presence in North Vietnam, the reports would surely continue.

The White House was well aware of one upcoming Quaker humanitarian trip to Hanoi when it issued its directive to deny future license requests; A Quaker Action Group was already on its way by sea. In January 1966, AQAG had asked the State Department to validate passports for a sea voyage to Haiphong Harbor to deliver pharmaceuticals. The State Department refused that request, but AQAG members decided to go anyway. They had rented an "activist" yacht, the *Phoenix,* which had sailed into the Pacific nuclear testing zone in 1957 in protest of nuclear explosions there. Its Quaker owner, Earle Reynolds, had been imprisoned for that action, but he was ready to put his ketch into service again.

After AQAG publicized its intention of sailing to Haiphong Harbor with medical aid, it had little difficulty raising the $30,000 it needed for the voyage and medical supplies. By February 1967, Reynolds, who lived near Tokyo, had readied his ketch. He was joined by a crew of five, plus a photographer and a filmmaker.[4] The crew assembled in Hiroshima, where they bought and packed one hundred boxes of medical and surgical goods with the enthusiastic help of Japanese doctors and medical person-

4. Besides Reynolds, the crew members were Betty Boardman, 49 from Madison, Wisconsin, an active member of WILPF; Philip Drath, 53, a contractor from San Rafael, California; Horace Champney, 61, from Yellow Springs, Ohio, a retired editor of the *Antioch Review;* Robert Eaton, 23, a graduate of Swarthmore College, the youngest member; and Ivan Massar, 40, a photographer; Richard Faun, a filmmaker from the Canadian Broadcasting Company; and cameraman William Heick from San Francisco. Heick and Drath spent the previous summer rebuilding bombed churches in the American south. All but Massar and Faun were Quakers, but skipper Reynolds said Massar was a Unitarian and for him "that was close enough."

nel. From there they sailed to Hong Kong to prepare for the final voyage to Haiphong Harbor. In Hong Kong, they gave a copy of their sailing plan to the American Consul General and made one last request to have their passports validated. The consul refused. They faced stiff prosecution for this act, he told them sternly, including ten years in prison and a ten thousand dollar fine. The prospect was unnerving to most crew members. This was a new kind of action, a new kind of embargo defiance, and the voyage itself, into waters at war, was daunting. If they survived the watery trip, other difficulties might await them at home. As a civil rights activist, crew member Elizabeth Boardman had already been to jail. It was only overnight, she wrote,

> but I knew what it looked like from inside. . . . On the other hand, it just doesn't compare with the misery, the suffering, the hunger, the despair that is being bought with my taxes. How could the freedom of one middle class, middle-aged mid-West housewife compare to what was being done to the Vietnamese in my name? If our trip could do any good, could awaken a few more Americans to the dastardly thing they were supporting out of ignorance and apathy, it was worth it. (1985, 11)

The *Phoenix* lay loaded and ready in the Hong Kong harbor but obstacles abounded. They lacked passport validation, and they did not yet have visas for North Vietnam or even clearance to enter Haiphong Harbor. Their cable to the Red Cross Society in Hanoi had elicited a response thanking them for their efforts but expressing "grave concern" for their safety in the Gulf of Tonkin, now dominated by the U.S. Seventh Fleet and its bombers. Areas around Hanoi and Haiphong were being bombed heavily, the cable said, and it suggested they bring in the supplies overland through a third country or by air, rather than by sea. The *Phoenix* had never yet voluntarily cut short a trip—this Quaker navy was not inclined to be the first to do so. The crew waited in Hong Kong while Betty Boardman and Carl Zeitlow flew into Phnom Penh to persuade Vietnamese officials there to intercede with Hanoi to receive the group in Haiphong.

In Phnom Penh, Nguyen Duy Vu, the Vietnamese official with whom they spoke, repeated concerns about their safety but told them that if they decided to go to Haiphong anyway, they would be welcomed. Elated, Boardman and Zeitlow drew up an anticipated schedule of arrival, a description of the *Phoenix*, its markings, the cargo, the radio band they would be using, and a picture of each crew member. Vietnamese officials provided them with general sailing instructions: their radio contact would be Vietnam Ocean Shipping Agency, every hour on the hour, and they would weigh anchor at Buoy Zero, just outside the harbor channel. While Zeitlow flew on to Hanoi to prepare for the *Phoenix*'s arrival, Boardman flew back to Hong Kong and discovered that the *Phoenix* crew was having trouble getting enough diesel fuel for the trip. The American Consulate there had ordered American oil companies in Hong Kong not to sell fuel to the *Phoenix*. Shell, the Anglo-Dutch company, agreed to sell fuel to them, however, and on 22 March, they left Hong Kong for Hanoi.

The week-long voyage from Hong Kong to Haiphong was tedious and difficult. The crew members' schedule gave them little sleep, and boxes of medical goods took up nearly all available space. Quarters were so cramped they had to sleep cradled among the canvas-covered cases of medical supplies lashed to the deck. After a week of scant sleep, spare rations, and cold salt water baths, they were all grateful when the rocky islets off the coast of North Vietnam came into view.

The trip to Haiphong Harbor strained their physical capacity, but it was even harder on their capacity to work together. Reynolds was a good skipper but a poor teacher—his crew was inexperienced and needed training, and he had little patience with their efforts. He worried constantly about all the navigational problems and about the safety of the voyage, and the crew chafed under his criticism. Other problems cropped up: Quakers were accustomed to making group decisions by consensus, but Reynolds insisted, as skipper, on making major decisions himself, even for things unrelated to their sea travel. They were all emotionally involved in the journey, they had to master strenuous physical work, and the trip was dangerous. They grew irritated at each other over small things.

In addition to these stresses, Boardman faced additional constraints. She was the only woman on board and found herself constantly having to prove her seaworthiness. Earle Reynolds's discomfort at having her along was evident from the start, and he made no effort to conceal it. In his notes on the trip, he recorded his "worry" when Boardman turned up: "mother of six with no sailing experience" (Reynolds n.d., SCPC). Other members of the crew had children, including Reynolds himself, and were older than Boardman. Only one, Bob Eaton, had sailing experience, but Reynolds singled out Boardman as cause for worry. Women had worked hard at all points to plan the voyage, raising money, coordinating schedules, and rounding up supplies. But AQAG still reflected too well the larger society; men held all the important titles in AQAG, women rose no higher than "secretary." Boardman felt shut out of the frequent planning discussions, even though the men, peace activists all, considered themselves "progressives" on these issues. "One of the things I couldn't take," she wrote later, "was the roughshod way the men either shut me up or ignored my contributions to the discussions. Several of them spoke very slowly and at great length while all the rest of us hung on their words, but when I got a chance to speak I was quickly silenced." When she finally "blew up" after being interrupted for the second time in as many minutes during a crew meeting, things began to change for the better, but then she felt an uneasy sense of being considered the resident troublemaker for the crew (Boardman 1985, 82).

Boardman addressed these conflicts candidly and self-critically in her book, *The Phoenix Trip*, which provides a rare glimpse of the internal dynamics of a group engaged in a cause larger than themselves. There were many conflicts and disagreements over the day-to-day arrangements and over the larger philosophical meaning of the voyage, and Boardman laid them out unflinchingly. "Here we were," she observed, "trying to stop a war while harboring within us all the elements needed to make war."[5] Still, the crew identified their difficulties, discussed them candidly, and searched together for solutions. Their personal difficulties redoubled their efforts to find points of agreement and to never give up on one another. It was a tribute to their dogged determination to make the trip work and to continue working together even after the sharpest disagreements, that the journey eventually ended with the Quaker navy on warm terms with one another.

As they entered the Gulf of Tonkin on Easter Sunday, 26 March 1967, American jets flew above them, and they worried that they might be deliberately bombed. Their apprehensions increased when an American helicopter hovered over them so closely that they could clearly see the faces of the three men standing in the doorway snapping pictures of them. It flew away just as abruptly, and several hours later the *Phoenix* dropped anchor between a Polish ship and a Soviet freighter at Buoy Zero and waited until dusk, when a small boat, bearing three Vietnamese soldiers and a pilot, came to guide them into the harbor. As they approached the harbor's channel, the Vietnamese pilot warned them to ex-

5. Other firsthand reports of the trip are sanitized of these internal conflicts. See also Reynolds, *Phoenix*, SCPC; Zeitlow 1967; app. B: "Horace Champney's Account of the Voyage from Hiroshima to Hong Kong," in Boardman, 157–74; *NYT*, 25 Feb. 1967.

tinguish their lights—there was an air-raid warning. The skies over the waters were soon filled with American aircraft and surface-to-air missiles. They could hear and feel the concussions of falling bombs across the Gulf. As the crew watched in horrified dismay, one of the antiaircraft missiles struck its target, and an American plane exploded over the darkened sea. "It's hard to describe how we felt when we realized that we weren't looking at a display of fireworks, but at an explosion of a plane containing a pilot and a crew," Boardman wrote. She thought of the men in the plane and of their families who would wait forever at home. "Any death was too much. War was the evil," Boardman reflected somberly (Boardman 1985, 70).

The disagreements that the crew had weathered on the journey returned the moment they docked at the harbor and were met by Red Cross officials, interpreters, and well-wishers who presented them with flowers, greetings, and preparations to take them to a hotel in Haiphong. Several Vietnamese sailors offered to stay on the boat while the crew visited Haiphong City and Hanoi. This offer called for a quick decision. Reynolds had planned that, in keeping with Quaker simplicity, the crew would remain on the boat in the harbor and not be a burden to the Vietnamese who had food and shelter problems of their own. While at sea, the rest of the crew had agreed, but when they realized that the Vietnamese had made arrangements for them to go in to Haiphong City and then on to Hanoi, they concluded it would be more gracious to accept this hospitality than insist on sticking by their prior decision. "We were a pretty disreputable looking bunch," Boardman wrote, "our feet stuffed into tennis shoes without socks, the men unshaven, Horace in short shorts, all of us grubby, with salt water our only wash for nearly a week" (Boardman 1985, 71). Against these conditions, the amenities of a hotel were attractive indeed.

For Boardman and most of the rest of the crew, the situation called for bending their concepts of Quaker simplicity to become gracious guests. From the host perspective, they thought, their insistence on staying on the boat for a week might appear more akin to aloofness than to simplicity. Reynolds did not agree. The single-mindedness that helped carry them through all the obstacles of the trip sailed into Haiphong Harbor with him. Reynolds was determined to maintain the Quaker spirit of simplicity and stay on the boat, but the rest of the crew decided it was better to be accommodating guests and to go into Hanoi with their hosts. They prevailed upon Reynolds to leave the boat for two days to go to

Hanoi later in the week while two of them took his place, but their week in North Vietnam was dampened by their knowledge that Reynolds believed they had all "sold out."

Reynolds's days on the *Phoenix* in Haiphong Harbor were not wasted, he believed, because there he had many visitors "and the opportunity for frank and unofficial conversations lubricated by good Vietnamese beer and snacks from the ship's stores." In long conversations with sailors, workmen, and merchants on and near the docks, Reynolds asked questions and heard their stories, aided by an interpreter with the Vietnam Ocean Shipping Agency. "What do you know about the United States," he asked the mechanic who came to check the yacht's engine. "I know a little," he said, "I know about your early ideals. I know about Lincoln and Washington. And I know that, in their hearts, the American people want peace." One question Reynolds pressed on a number of his visitors was the degree to which their government represented them. Some of their answers were unexpected for him. "In Vietnam it is the peasants who have guns," one of them told him. "The high officials go to work daily, without guards or escorts, riding on bicycles like the common people. They are not surrounded by bullet-proof glass or armed secret service men. If the people of Vietnam did not want this government, these officials would be dead in fifteen minutes" (Reynolds n.d., SCPC, 8).

One day, the manager of the Haiphong hotel came aboard the *Phoenix* and asked permission to serve Reynolds a "typical Vietnamese dinner." His purpose, as he explained it, was that after the war, he believed that many American tourists would be visiting Vietnam. He wanted to know what kind of food they would like. Reynolds accepted the offer, and the next day he received a sumptuous meal. Delicious, he told the hopeful hotelier, but perhaps the sauce was too hot for the average American. The manager sighed. He had been afraid of that. "For your dinner," he said, "I had already reduced the sauce by one-half, but now I must make it even weaker." There on the *Phoenix* in Haiphong Harbor, in 1967, the two men offered a toast to the future success of American tourists in Vietnam.

The rest of the crew spent a day in Haiphong before going on to Hanoi. They toured the city's war museum, where pieces of American planes lay on the grounds outside. Inside were relics of those planes, including the private effects taken from the downed pilots. Boardman did not like visiting the museum. She was looking for experiences that helped the Americans and the Vietnamese transcend the war between their countries, and touring this museum seemed to drag them closer into the conflict. "I hated looking at the pictures of a man's wife and children and the other private objects which were displayed there. . . . How did they expect us to react? I felt that it was unfriendly to take us there. But maybe if I had been under the bombs as they had . . . I would have been a little unfriendly, too" (Boardman 1985, 77).

They saw plenty of places that had been under the bombs during the week they spent in and around Hanoi. Felix Greene, Asian specialist and filmmaker, was staying at their hotel, and he showed them around Hanoi. The Hoang Liet Village on the edge of the city was now nearly demolished and residential areas near the Long Bien Bridge were smashed, though the bridge itself was intact. "They were missing it consistently," the Vietnamese marveled. On the streets of Hanoi, women and men carried rifles as a matter of course. Wherever people worked or gathered in any number, there were stacks of weapons, waiting for the next air raid. The rifles seemed to give people a sense of participation and of fighting back, an antidote to the feeling of helplessness that civilian populations in time of war often experience.

The AQAG team made a point of talking at length to the Vietnamese they met about the larger community of antiwar organizations in the United States. There were a host of groups and organizations in the United States who opposed the war, and many of them requested permission to visit Hanoi. The Vietnamese were not familiar with most of them, and decisions about whom they would host often turned on contacts, however slight, with some Americans who had visited during the early years of the war. Boardman spoke at length to women in the Vietnam Women's Union about the Women's International League for Peace and Freedom, and that group was invited to Hanoi soon after.

All of the crew urged the Vietnamese to invite other Quakers. Norman Morrison was a Quaker, and that alone made Vietnamese officials receptive to the Quaker witness; the AQAG crew used that fact to good effect. They spoke fervently and at length about Quaker history and religious perspective and Quaker organizations such as the American Friends Service Committee. "Everyone seemed interested," a pleased Boardman noted at the end of a two hour "Quaker lobbying pitch" to more than fifty people representing unions, women's organizations, children's welfare, health, education, agriculture, Christian, and Buddhist organizations, and the Vietnamese press. The enduring affection that many people felt for Alice Herz and Norman Morrison was obvious. Photographs of both still filled most of one wall in the Revolutionary Museum. The Vietnamese Women's Union gave Boardman gifts to give to Anne Morrison.

On 5 April, after one last meeting with Red Cross officials and with the film of their days in Hanoi in hand, the crew left Haiphong harbor in a lighter and roomier ketch and sailed back into the Gulf of Tonkin.[6] Their exit from the Gulf was peaceful—the American "photographers" peering out of their helicopters and snapping pictures of their exit even waved. "We leaped to respond," Boardman said, "such a good feeling! They were friendly; they were not going to sink us." Their journey back to Tokyo was uneventful, at least after a typhoon veered away from their sailing route, and the tension among crew members eased under the wide clear skies. "I was euphoric," Boardman wrote. "We had gone to North Vietnam, delivered our medical supplies, talked with many Vietnamese of all classes, learned much about the history, culture, and intentions of the country, and I felt completely satisfied that we had done the best we could for a good cause" (Boardman 1985, 124). Another crew member, Horace Champney, echoed her sentiments. "Perhaps one little sailboat with its handful of Quakers and a few boxes of medicines—though hardly a drop in the bucket of need—could serve as a symbolic witness around the world for a better way of running the planet" (Boardman 1985, 174).

The State Department revoked all their passports as soon as they returned home.[7] The Treasury Department seized the film of the trip and then released it several months later when it could find no legal grounds for confiscation. With their passports confiscated, the *Phoenix* crew could not leave the United States, but they had plenty to do. In the next year alone, Boardman spoke at 208 meetings, from Denver to New York, from North Carolina to Minnesota. She addressed college and university students, Rotary Clubs, churches, elementary and high school students. The *Phoenix* crew went to Washington twice to talk to congressional representatives and officials from the White House, Treasury, and State Departments. The Quaker navy accomplished a number of things. As Carl Zeitlow phrased it,

6. The film of the voyage, entitled *The Phoenix,* is in the Swarthmore College Peace Collection.

7. Their passports remained revoked until the Supreme Court ruled the following year in the Lynd case that such revocations were unconstitutional as long as citizens did not use their passports in restricted areas.

we delivered medical aid in person to the Red Cross society. We established friendly direct communication with the Red Cross and people of
North Vietnam. We came home feeling some personal identification
with the North Vietnamese. Moreover, a number of Quakers and
Friends meetings were moved to act more forcefully on medical aid and
peace projects as a result of our trip. We have had innumerable opportunities to talk to the American people about this war and moral values
through newspapers, radio and television. (1967, 1006)

The *Phoenix* made two more trips to Vietnam. In November 1967, a
crew sailed the ketch out of Hong Kong to Da Nang, South Vietnam, to
deliver medical supplies there. All save the skipper, Robert Eaton, whose
passport was still revoked from the first trip, held United States passports
and South Vietnam visas.[8] When they reached Da Nang harbor, South
Vietnamese officials told the crew that, despite their visas, they could not
come ashore. A gunboat began towing the yacht back out to sea, but
most of the crew jumped overboard and started to swim to shore. South
Vietnamese officers captured all but one, put them on the ketch, and
towed it into the ocean. One crew member, Harrison Butterworth, a professor at Ohio University, made it to shore and was walking to Da Nang
when U.S. Marines captured him and turned him over to South Vietnamese authorities, who deported him. The *Phoenix* returned to Hong
Kong, its cargo undelivered. In January 1968, the *Phoenix* went on its last
mission to Vietnam, back to Haiphong Harbor, and delivered another
load of medical supplies.[9]

The word phoenix later became fixed in the American repertoire of
Vietnam war code words with the Central Intelligence Agency's program
that assassinated "Vietcong suspects" throughout South Vietnam. That
program itself was set up and named in late 1967, after the humanitarian
voyage of the *Phoenix* first linked the word with Vietnam.[10]

8. In addition to Eaton, who had gone on the first *Phoenix* trip, the crew consisted of
AQAG Executive Secretary Larry Scott, AQAG co-chair, George Lakey, Mary Ann Mc-
Naughton, Beryl Nelson, John Braxton, Chris Cowley, Harrison Butterworth, and a Be-
heirin representative, Kyoko Koda.

9. For accounts of these trips see Lakey 1967; "The *Phoenix* at Sea," *CC*, 29 Nov.
1967; "The Second Voyage of the *Phoenix*," *WIN*, 31 Jan. 1968; and Lakey 1968.

10. I could find no information on how the CIA chose this name for its program. According to a former naval officer, AQAG's *Phoenix* and its mission were well-known to
American military personnel in Vietnam because the *Stars and Stripes* carried reports on it.
They had nicknamed it "the Dove," he told me, adding that they used to joke to each other
that "those are the birds we shoot." The *Saigon Post* also covered the *Phoenix* voyages. The

AQAG's initiative in taking humanitarian goods to North Vietnam, despite White House warnings and Treasury Department strictures, helped intensify the issue of aid to Vietnam that had been simmering among American aid organizations and voluntary organizations since 1964. The first *Phoenix* trip coincided with attention that some popular magazines paid to the civilian casualties in Vietnam. In January 1967, *Redbook, Ladies Home Journal,* and *Ramparts* ran feature stories with photographs showing injuries that the bombing inflicted on civilians in Vietnam. These articles drew particular attention to the children wounded and scarred by napalm and conventional bombs. The popular magazines softened the impact, somewhat, by pointing out the work that American medical teams were doing to repair the injuries, but the voices of those medical personnel themselves were not soothing. In reflecting on his work in the war zone, Richard Perry, an American physician, wrote in *Redbook*:

> The Vietcong do not use napalm: we do. This highly incendiary, jellylike substance is dropped in bombs. When the bombs explode, the napalm spews out in all directions like a molten geyser. It sticks to whatever it hits, including human flesh, and burns it black. I have been an orthopedic surgeon for a good number of years, with a rather wide range of medical experience. But nothing could have prepared me for my encounters with Vietnamese women and children burned by napalm. It was shocking and sickening, even for a physician, to see and smell the blackened flesh. One continues for days afterward getting sick when he looks at a piece of meat on his plate because the odor of burned flesh lingers so long in memory. And one never forgets the bewildered eyes of the silent, suffering, napalm-burned child.

At the same time that the *Phoenix* sailed to Haiphong, a collection of physicians, scientists, and religious leaders founded the Committee of Responsibility (COR), an organization devoted to taking some responsibility for the war-injured children in American-controlled areas of South Vietnam. In early 1967, COR sent three physicians to South Vietnam to tour hospitals there. They were not permitted to visit outlying areas, but,

---

Defense Department first officially confirmed the existence of the Phoenix program in a *New York Times* story on 18 February 1970. By then, its existence and its name were already well-known to Vietnamese and Americans in Vietnam. For example, Doug Hostetter, a volunteer aid worker in Vietnam, had discussed the program with Joseph Elder the previous year. See Elder 1969b, AFSC. See also Andrade 1990 and Valentine 1990.

using statistics provided by South Vietnam's own Ministry of Health, they postulated that "at least 10,000 children under 12 years will be admitted to Vietnamese hospitals in 1967 with war-related wounds. . . . At least twice as many will never get to the hospitals to be counted" (Six Who Survived, SCPC). Hospitals made a conscientious effort to care for the civilians, but the numbers overwhelmed them, and napalm and other wounds left injuries difficult to repair. During the course of the next year, the committee brought more than fifty children to American hospitals, where they received care and surgery donated by physicians and staff in American hospitals.

For humanitarian organizations, the necessity of working with both the American military and the Saigon government in the south during the war raised a host of thorny issues about the relationship of their work and the American war effort. Some organizations recognized this more than others. Private voluntary organizations that relied on American government funds could easily find their operations dovetailing with the military goals of the American and Saigon governments because those goals were inextricably linked to the burgeoning numbers of refugees. The pacification program, which relied on forcing villagers to leave their villages and fields for strategic hamlet areas where their comings and goings could be monitored by the military, was a refugee creation program. The refugees were planned, anticipated, calculated.[11]

In an article published in 1974, two church workers with extensive experience in refugee work in South Vietnam during the early 1960s reflected back on the way that refugee and relief work in South Vietnam had reinforced U.S. military objectives. The authors, Doug Hostetter and Michael McIntyre, noted that charitable organizations assumed that the needs of suffering human beings guided the distribution of relief. But, they pointed out, plotting the geographical distribution of relief work in Southeast Asia revealed the depth of politics at work in determining who received charity. Most of the American bombing and shelling fell on North Vietnam and National Liberation Front areas of South Vietnam. Most of the casualties, the hardships, and the destroyed crops, were in these zones. Despite this, Christian churches in the West did not send their aid to these areas; more than 91 percent of their relief activity went

11. For a study of how CARE's operations in Vietnam helped further Washington's military objectives there and of refugee creation generally, see Pergande 1995, Weisner 1988, and Hunt 1995.

to areas controlled by the United States and its allies, areas where the NLF could not and did not, inflict nearly the level of destruction that the American military unleashed. The decision about where to send relief was dictated by political concerns, not humanitarian ones.

The Christian charity that flowed in the wake of American gunboats furthered American military goals in Vietnam by enabling the military to create "humane" refugee camps. A Church World Service team reported from South Vietnam in October 1965 that officials in South Vietnam "seem agreed . . . that the number of refugees will in all probability increase by the end of the calendar year to about one million persons. The team accepts this judgment in the light of what it saw and learned with respect to the terrain, the limited pockets of Vietnamese and U.S. control, and the current strategy of expanding these areas of control to ever larger sectors of the country" (Hostetter and McIntyre 1974, 847).

"Expanding these areas of control" was a euphemism for creating more refugees forced out of their homes and placed in pacified zones. Hostetter and McIntyre pointed out that church agencies seldom asked themselves, "should these refugees be created? should the U.S. seek to expand its area of control?" Rather, the primary question that appeared to concern them was, "how can we collaborate with the U.S. government in helping the multitudes of new refugees which it is planning to create next year?" (1974, 846).

Most United States voluntary agencies in Vietnam tailored their programs to fit the larger goals of the American military there. Village development program goals were defined as "stabilizing" areas so that the National Liberation Front would appear less attractive in light of the money, goods, and services that organizations like CARE could provide. Much of American humanitarian aid functioned to discredit indigenous, broadly supported Vietnamese political groupings in favor of foreign military goals that were designed with classic Cold War interests in mind. To maintain a broad commitment to the Cold War required enlisting broad support among all sectors of American society, even the humanitarian organizations. The level of fear and misunderstanding of communism had to be kept high, particularly when fighting the Cold War meant destroying Third World peasants. American zeal in pursuing the Cold War, even to the smallest hamlet in Vietnam, reeled in charity organizations in its wake.

Americans, many of them young, who worked with humanitarian organizations in Vietnam watched with dismay as their work bolstered the pacification program. Some of them steered their dismay over the twisted trail of charity into constructive action. The largest voluntary organization in South Vietnam was the International Voluntary Service (IVS), begun in 1953, eight years before the creation of the Peace Corps, for which it served as a model.[12] By 1967, there were 170 IVS volunteers in South Vietnam. IVS volunteers, mostly recent university graduates, worked in rural areas on agricultural projects, taught in local schools, and worked with refugees on salaries of eighty dollars a month. IVS was one of the most highly respected American agencies in South Vietnam because its volunteers lived and worked at the village level. They knew Vietnamese life and culture more intimately than any other American group. They socialized primarily with Vietnamese, spoke the language fluently, and spent their days in the web of village life. On 25 September 1967, the *New York Times* quoted U.S. Ambassador Henry Cabot Lodge as saying in 1965 that IVS was "one of the success stories of American assistance in Vietnam," and that it formed part of a development effort "indispensable to success."

In September 1967, Don Luce, then director of IVS in Vietnam, and three field staff members resigned in protest against the war and the role of IVS in it. They were backed by forty-five other IVS volunteers, who sent a letter to President Johnson calling the war "an overwhelming atrocity" that could result in no honor for America. "We have seen enough to say that the only monuments to this war will be the dead, the maimed, the despairing and the forlorn," the letter read in part. "By helping the refugees," one volunteer said, "we are just easing the conscience of the military when they make more refugees." They had already spent months trying to change American policy in Vietnam. "I've made suggestions on our refugee policies, our destruction of villages, our use of defoliants," Luce told a *New York Times* reporter in the agency headquarters in Saigon. "People in USAID [United States Agency for International Development] listen and suggest we write a report and then nothing happens. It's become a land of report writing." Watching the horror grow month after dreary month, Luce, a Cornell University graduate in agricultural science who had lived in Vietnam for eight years, decided it was time to leave IVS. "I could not become part of the destruction of a peo-

12. IVS was run by the United States Agency for International Development. A similar volunteer organization, "Crossroads Africa," also inspired the structure and mission of the Peace Corps.

ple I love," he concluded. "It's become unbearable to witness the destruction of Vietnamese family life, the home, the agricultural system, the transportation. We're defeating ourselves here."[13]

Relations between IVS volunteers and the U.S. State Department and the Saigon government continued to deteriorate. By mid-1971, there were only thirty-one IVS volunteers left in the country. Just before the elections in South Vietnam, scheduled for October, the Saigon government expelled the rest. Hugh Manke, director of IVS in Vietnam, was quoted in *Christian Century* on 29 September as saying that the few remaining volunteers, by virtue of their placement throughout the country, would have been in positions to spot irregularities during the elections; expelling them got rid of a troublesome group and allowed the American government to declare the elections "fair."

For United States–based organizations that tried to send humanitarian aid to Hanoi, dealing with their own constituencies, with Washington, and with Hanoi was a daunting enterprise that overwhelmed most of them. The small donations that some campus groups organized in spring 1966 were designed more to annoy Washington than to help Vietnam. Other groups stopped their exploratory efforts when they ran into White House objections. Still others abandoned the effort when they could not readily work out arrangements with officials in Hanoi.

The Fellowship of Reconciliation, which devoted most of its fact-finding missions to the Saigon area, tried, in 1967, to organize a trip to Hanoi for that summer, to take medical aid there. Alfred Hassler, FOR's executive secretary, began by organizing a nationwide fund-raising campaign called "Meals of Reconciliation" to raise money for medical goods for North Vietnam. The program quickly raised over $50,000 (Hassler 1967b, SCPC). FOR was concerned about Treasury Department prosecution for sending the aid, and decided to enlist "relatively prominent figures within the religious world" for a trip to Hanoi, in hopes of decreasing the probability of prosecution. Hassler secured tentative commitments from Daniel Berrigan, Robert McAfee Brown, Rabbi Jacob Weinstein, and Edwin Dahlberg for the proposed trip. Dahlberg, former

13. See Luce 1968; Luce and Summer 1969; End This War," *Nation,* 9 Oct. 1967, 322–23; *NYT,* 20, 24, and 25 Sept. 1967; and *CC,* 11 Oct. 1967. In 1969, Luce returned to South Vietnam with the World Council of Churches. He later exposed the tiger cages of Con Son Island. In April 1971, he was expelled from Saigon. See "The Tiger Cages of Con Son," *Life,* 17 July 1970.

president of the National Council of Churches who had gone to Saigon with FOR in 1965, was reluctant to commit himself fully to the journey. He was seventy-four years old, he reminded Hassler, "and if a long prison term should be at all likely, I would have to think about this pretty realistically" (Dahlberg 1967, SCPC).

Dahlberg never had to make that ultimate decision because Hanoi did not encourage the trip and by late fall 1967, FOR abandoned efforts to send a team to Hanoi and looked instead at ways of funneling the money it had raised through the World Council of Churches and the Vatican's Caritas Internationalis, which had publicized plans to build a 350-bed hospital in North Vietnam. In searching for an explanation as to why his efforts to get to Hanoi were not immediately successful, Hassler concluded that the Vietnamese had "great difficulty in discriminating" among the heavy load of requests they continually had for permission to visit Hanoi, and that they favored people

> whose influence on the general populace of the United States is extremely limited, but whose position is interpreted by Hanoi as one of "total solidarity." I have labored with them repeatedly the importance of establishing communication with those whose concern about the war cannot necessarily be interpreted as a commitment to the NLF point of view, but who also have much greater access to the American public. They express appreciation and understanding for this point of view, but up to now it is not translated into action (Hassler 1967a, SCPC).

Just whom Hassler was referring to in his letter is not clear. Travelers to Hanoi that year included A. J. Muste, Pastor Martin Niemoller, Rabbi Abraham Feinberg, Bishop Ambrose Reeves, an American Friends Service Committee representative, two AQAG groups, and a Women Strike for Peace delegation, hardly people Hassler considered on the fringe. Hanoi could not host visitors constantly, and there were so many requests that many would-be visitors were disappointed. Vietnamese officials took with equanimity Hassler's advice on how to choose the international visitors they hosted. Other groups continually let the North Vietnamese know their recommendations for these journeys too, and they all reported a good reception to their advice, but sensed that it had little impact on the Vietnamese officials, who made their own decisions on these matters. The Vietnamese refused to advise the Americans on their own domestic antiwar strategy, and they just as steadfastly set their own course in hosting Americans in Hanoi.

Throughout these efforts to take regular shipments of humanitarian aid to North Vietnam, the American Friends Service Committee persisted in trying to win White House approval for sending humanitarian aid to North Vietnam. The administration adamantly opposed it, and, to achieve its goal, the AFSC had to win over Washington's hearts and minds. They had already established humanitarian programs in government-held areas in South Vietnam. Their largest program was a prosthetics and rehabilitation center staffed by volunteers in Quang Ngai province in South Vietnam, where, as early as 1966, there were an estimated 100,000 refugees. The prosthetics were made almost entirely with locally purchased or locally constructed materials. In running the program, the AFSC refused American military protection; in fact, it relied on Americans as little as possible. An essential ingredient in the program was training Vietnamese to replace the few Americans that were there. By 1969, the Quang Ngai center was producing and fitting sixty-five prosthetic cases a month.

Stephen Cary, an AFSC representative who made frequent visits to South Vietnam during the war, worried about the "danger of identifying ourselves with the generally held image of America as a military power to be tolerated but hardly respected," in South Vietnam. Their ability to decide their own course of action was constrained. Theoretically, Cary observed, following the AFSC tradition of nonpartisan aid would be possible, but in the case of Vietnam, "this would hardly be permitted by our own government." The only possible way an agency could work in South Vietnam, Cary concluded, was to work within the framework of the United States government and hope to "establish an identify separate from the government and the military, although it may not be understood by those at a distance." The AFSC's inability to work on both sides in Vietnam "may convey an impression of partisanship contrary to the spirit of AFSC," one of his reports noted (Cary 1965, AFSC).

The American Friends Service Committee had three different, and sometimes very difficult, groups to balance in organizing aid for Vietnam. Its own Quaker constituency was composed of members who ranged from the avidly antiwar to adamant believers that their government, an elected one, after all, should always be obeyed. Some Quakers compared the aid for North Vietnam that was routed through Canada to the tradition of the Quakers who, in the days before the Civil War, actively aided and abetted runaway slaves on the Underground Railroad despite the federal Fugitive Slave Law. Others saw it as "unpatriotic" because it defied current government proscriptions. AQAG, though not an official Quaker organization, was the subject of heated controversy in Quaker circles and tore apart more than one Friends' Meeting. An October 1966 article in *Friends Journal* recounted the internal dissension engendered by AQAG, noting that at a recent Meeting in Philadelphia one "weighty" member had said he would resign if the Meeting contributed one penny to AQAG. Other Quakers believed that their faith was remiss if they did not minister to those suffering the depredations of the military might that their own tax monies made possible.

Negotiating responses that alienated neither of these positions within its own faith was a task sufficiently exacting, but it required simultaneous balancing with the White House and with the State Department. The American Friends Service Committee took its positions of peace and reconciliation seriously, and endeavored to apply them evenly to all with whom it dealt. The White House was informed of everything it did; AFSC even compiled and handed over a list of all its contacts with the National Liberation Front when the White House asked for one (Contacts 1968, AFSC). Whenever the AFSC Board made a deliberative decision to send aid to Vietnam after the Treasury Department denied it a license, the White House was fully informed, not only of the decision, but of the goods in question and how they would be transported. No matter how definitive Treasury Department denials were, the AFSC never gave up. Without rancor or bitterness, it pursued the White House as calmly and rationally as it pursued peace in Vietnam. Even when Richard Nixon coupled references to his Quaker heritage with a defense of his war policy in Vietnam, Quakers used it to educate Americans about traditional Quaker beliefs, letting them judge for themselves whether the president's Quaker heritage had left him, as he told C. L. Sulzberger of the *New York Times* on 26 January 1969, "a deeply committed pacifist."

Hanoi's response to the AFSC's humanitarian aid efforts was at first mixed, partly because of the symbolic import of the aid. For Americans concerned over the harm of the war, aid for the enemy was a powerful symbol of dissent. For the Vietnamese, taking aid from Americans was a symbol too, representing tangible proof that Washington officials faced opposition, not only throughout international circles, but within their own country. Still, contact with Americans, denizens of the territory that organized and paid for the war in Vietnam, could carry a distasteful element; aid from the enemy, even a dissenting "enemy," was a mixed blessing. Americans in Hanoi, however opposed to the war, bore a mere fraction of the costs of the war that the Vietnamese carried. No matter how often they were forced to huddle in a roadside ditch when the planes came over, their position under the bombs was entirely voluntary. They could, and would, go home to a nation secure within its own borders from Vietnamese attacks. The value of hosting Americans, escorting them throughout the country, putting up with the questions some of them insistently posed in the name of "complete impartiality" about why there was not the "democracy" in North Vietnam upon which America prided itself, could appear small. The Vietnamese struggle for national political independence also involved ideals of self-direction in all levels of decision-making. Americans had their own ideas about what kind of help Vietnam needed—that was evident in the South—and even the most well-intentioned aid process could be designed as much to assuage American consciences as to provide what the Vietnamese believed they needed most.

International meetings in Europe first provided AFSC staffers with direct contacts with North Vietnamese officials. At a September 1967 meeting of antiwar groups in Bratislava, Vietnamese representatives spoke frankly to American Quakers Bronson Clark, Russell Johnson, and Ross Flanagan about their reluctance to welcome AFSC-run programs into North Vietnam and NLF-controlled areas in the South. Nguyen Thi Dinh, head of the NLF delegation, and Ha Thanh Lam, the NLF representative in Prague, spoke warmly of the Quakers. They had not known much about them in the past, Dinh said, but Norman Morrison's death had left a respect for the Quaker spirit throughout Vietnam. She told them of plaster plaques, now ubiquitous throughout the NLF south, she said, containing the bas-relief of two faces—one American and one Vietnamese. On one side was the face of Nguyen Van Troi, who had attempted to assassinate Secretary of Defense Robert McNamara and had been executed by Saigon. The other figure on the plaque was that of Norman Morrison. Dinh had read the Quaker pamphlet *Peace in Vietnam,* she said, and had learned from that about the Quakers. "We are moved by the actions of the Quakers in their understanding of our struggle," she said, and she appreciated their humanitarian work "irrespective of your work with the Saigon government." Because of that, the NLF would always try to protect Quaker workers in the south, she said, "although that is extremely difficult in a fiercely fought war situation" (Clarke 1967, SCPC).

Still, the NLF delegates told the group that they could not welcome an AFSC medical program at that time. Ha Thanh Lam raised questions about the nature and consequences of the Quaker work in the Saigon south. "As a Buddhist," Lam told Clark, "there is a similarity between Buddhism and Quakerism where there is a concern and a feeling of charity for the innocent." But, he went on, the work that the Quakers did in South Vietnam was aiding the pacification program, and he objected to that:

> Your nursery school in Quang Ngai for refugee children helps the Saigon government make an appeal to refugees to "flee communism" and indicates that the Saigon government will give them help by having them attend schools. We know you are operating from good motivation but the Saigon government is able to tell people that they are able to provide hospital service such as your prosthesis program in Quang Ngai as well as your school. Frankly and sincerely I have spoken directly on this point to you. (Clark 1967, SCPC)

It was this very connection between private humanitarian efforts and the "success" of the pacification programs in South Vietnam that was, at that time, moving IVS volunteers to resign their positions there. The fact that their work could act as a magnet to draw people away from NLF areas and into the Saigon areas was one reason the State Department supported the AFSC's work in the south. The AFSC believed that the need for medical goods was far greater in areas under direct U.S. attack, but their own government forbade sending humanitarian aid to those very areas, and the AFSC was under considerable pressure from some American Quakers not to step outside any government-imposed boundaries of "permissible" humanitarian work. In this sense, Lam believed, the AFSC was drawing too narrow a distinction between its own work and the work of the American military. The Quakers abjured violence, but their humanitarian work in areas controlled by American forces by force helped to legitimate the American policies, which were built on violence. Lam pointed out that "whenever voluntary agencies choose to establish relief operations in cooperation with Saigon, they inadvertently encourage and enable the U.S./ARVN forces to evacuate and destroy nearby contested villages and herd people toward new 'approved' locations adjacent to the relief facilities" (Flanagan 1967, SCPC).

Despite its rebuff at Bratislava, the AFSC did not give up. Following these discussions with National Liberation Front representatives, the AFSC decided to contribute $25,000 worth of penicillin and disposable syringes to the Front for its hospitals and clinics. It spent months applying for a United States government license to purchase and ship these supplies. In December 1968, the State Department denied the AFSC's license request because, it said, Saigon claimed jurisdiction over the NLF areas where the goods were destined, and it would be an "affront" to Saigon if Washington granted the license.

The board of directors of the American Friends Service Committee deliberated at some length over Washington's response. In view of their historical commitment to ministering impartially to all civilians, they decided to proceed with the gift, viewing it as a matter of religious compulsion. Gilbert F. White, the board's chair, met immediately with William Bundy of the Department of State and informed him of the board's decision. At the same time, David Stickney, the director of the Quang Ngai Center in South Vietnam, met with Saigon officials and told them of the AFSC's decision and its reasons for donating medical materials to the NLF. He reported back that he found "a ready understanding" of the AFSC's purposes on the part of Saigon officials with whom he talked. The medicines were delivered to NLF representatives in Phnom Penh in three shipments in early 1969 (Indochina Humanitarian Program, AFSC).

The AFSC continued occasional medical shipments to the National Liberation Front, contributing eventually about 15 percent of what it sent Saigon-controlled areas (Sullivan n.d, AFSC). It was not the even-handed approach for which the AFSC strove, but that was not for want of effort. Washington did what it could to obstruct even this humanitarian aid, and the NLF, caught up in its independence fervor, was determined not to bring in Americans to help with its medical programs. The Vietnamese took quiet pride in their own blending of traditional and modern medicine during this period, and Americans who inquired about helping them with their medical needs soon learned that the Vietnamese believed that it was the Americans who had much to learn from Vietnamese medical expertise. At Bratislava, in fact, when the AFSC's Bronson Clark told Dr. Nguyen Trinh Co, vice director of the National Medical Institute in Hanoi, that the Quakers would be interested in setting up a prosthetics program in North Vietnam, similar to their training center at Quang Ngai, Co responded that perhaps the training could go the other way— perhaps the AFSC should send their personnel to Hanoi to learn about rehabilitation work from them.

While it was organizing some small medical aid shipments to the National Liberation Front, the AFSC continued its contacts with Hanoi. In May 1969, it sent Joseph Elder, a member of AFSC's board of directors and professor of Sociology at the University of Wisconsin, to the Stockholm Conference on Vietnam. The conference was called by the International Confederation for Disarmament and Peace, and the American contingent was the largest. Within the American contingent, the Friends had the largest representation. Bronson Clark, the patient and persistent AFSC executive secretary, set up meetings between the Quaker contingent and Vietnamese officials to discuss aid issues. From Stockholm, Elder was going to Phnom Penh to talk with Vietnamese officials there, and the AFSC hoped to send him on to Hanoi as well, to get a list of priority medical needs there. By now, many of the Friends and the Vietnamese at Stockholm knew of each other from other meetings and had come to trust each other enough to speak frankly about their disagreements and remain on good terms. The Quaker delegation included Bob Eaton, who had been on both *Phoenix* voyages to Haiphong, and he had with him pictures of other Quakers who had been to Hanoi. Most of the Vietnamese delegates there had met some of those people, and they were all eager to see pictures of other Quakers they knew of, including pictures of Anne Morrison attending antiwar vigils outside the White House.

The careful cultivation of personal ties paid off. When Bronson Clark made a specific proposal at Stockholm of a donation of medical goods of about $25,000, and coupled it with an assertion that the Quakers saw this as a way for them to learn something from the Vietnamese experience in dealing with medical problems during war, the Vietnamese delegation "seemed to come to life," he said (Clark 1967, SCPC). Xuan Oanh, the translator who had hosted the first Americans in North Vietnam and who was now posted to the delegation at the Paris Peace talks, offered to contact Hanoi about securing a visa for Elder. He knew the Quakers by now, he said; he knew about their "views on giving within a human context," and he was ready to advocate a medical exchange with them (Elder 1969a, AFSC).

Elder's visa for Hanoi came through in Phnom Penh, and he spent a week in Hanoi in June 1969. At his request, the Ministry of Health drew up an itinerary that provided a look at Vietnam's health care system firsthand. French colonial rule had left a system of health care geared for urban elites; the Vietnamese were moving the health care delivery system to the village level, a process speeded up by air attacks on the visible medical infrastructure. A ranked series of public health services began with first aid centers in hamlets, clinics and small hospitals in larger villages, and district level teaching hospitals that trained midwives and medical cadres to work in hamlets and villages. Specialized hospitals were situated at the provincial level. The system meant that most of the medical care that villagers required was available at the village level and nearly 70 percent of the wounded from air attacks could be treated locally. Dispensaries and hospitals appeared well-stocked, Elder noted, and medical research continued apace on ways to control contagious diseases by providing safe drinking water and effective latrines in rural areas, as well as into tuberculosis treatment and polio vaccine procedures. Many doctors combined traditional and modern medical practices, using indigenous materials like bamboo splints for fractures and stocking traditional powders to treat minor injuries (Elder 1969b).

The list of needed medical supplies that Elder received from doctors in Hanoi was not quite what the AFSC had expected. Some of the items on the "wish list" were antibiotics and antimalarial medicines, but the largest item was a request for open-heart surgery equipment for the Viet-Duc Hospital in Hanoi, the principal teaching hospital for surgery in North Vietnam. Dr. Ton That Tung, the hospital's director, was a research scientist of international renown with professional ties to colleagues in France and other European countries. Even American medical texts cited his research.[14] Still, requests for the latest in heart surgery equipment was not what Americans might expect from medical personnel in a country struggling with war and contagious and parasitic diseases. It could seem like a poor, almost frivolous use of resources. Dr. Tung's list was detailed, specifying exact oxygenators, mitral valves, and manometers. It caught the AFSC off guard. Elder contacted French surgeons who knew Dr. Tung and had been to Hanoi, and asked if they believed that the Viet-Duc Hospital could indeed make good use of the equipment. The French physicians pointed out that in Vietnam, rheumatic fever was common among adults, and surgery to replace damaged heart valves was frequently the patient's only hope.

A reassured AFSC presented the list to the Treasury Department, now under the guidance of a newly elected Nixon administration, which was eager, at first, to establish cordial ties with AFSC representatives. In

14. See, for example, Rhodes 1970, 924, 946. An oral interview with Dr. Tung is in the video *Vietnam: A Television History: "America's Enemy."* For a report on Dr. Tung's work at Viet-Duc hospital, see Lewis 1972.

an abrupt change from its previous denials, Treasury approved the list and quickly issued a license. In August, 1969, Elder flew to Phnom Penh with some of the equipment, expecting to go on to Hanoi to deliver it. Instead, officials in Hanoi asked him to postpone his trip until later that fall. Throughout August, half the scheduled International Control Commission (ICC) flights into Hanoi were canceled. Ho Chi Minh was dying. Officials in Hanoi did not want foreign visitors filling up its one hotel when the moment arrived to handle a sudden influx of international diplomats to mourn the passing of Vietnam's national hero. On 2 September 1969, twenty-four years to the day after he had first proclaimed Vietnam's independence, Ho Chi Minh died.

After Ho's death, Elder returned to Hanoi with the first shipment of AFSC's medical aid. He had new goods to take into Vietnam as well. Media accounts of his June trip to Hanoi, along with reports that he was returning there, brought mail to him from families of Americans captured or missing in Vietnam and Laos. Mary Winn, whose husband, David, had been shot down over North Vietnam, came from Minneapolis to see Elder. She brought mail and a list of questions: Did Elder think the Hanoi government would let the relatives of imprisoned servicemen go there to live to be near their men? Could they write to the Catholic archbishop in Hanoi to intervene on their behalf? Could wives of men whose bodies had been recovered go to Hanoi to claim the bodies? Would giving the American prisoners typewriters make it easier to get mail out? She had one question that Elder could answer immediately: Could wives of missing servicemen send vitamins to children in North Vietnam with him? Mary Winn's idea sounded like something the State Department would have a hard time turning down, particularly because she was not one to keep such a refusal private. Indeed, the State Department responded quickly, calling Elder the following day to say it had no objection to a shipment of vitamins for Vietnamese children. Winn provided one hundred dollars, and in October Elder flew into Hanoi with open-heart surgery equipment and bottles of vitamins funded by a few families of American prisoners in Hanoi (Elder 1969d).

Three months later, the AFSC's Louis Schneider took additional heart surgery equipment to Hanoi, and in May 1971, the AFSC sent more with Charles Read. Each trip in took letters for American POW's in Hanoi as well, and each trip out brought their letters home. The success of these missions encouraged the AFSC to solicit funds for future medical donations and enlist medical specialists to deliver them to Vietnam. Dr.

George Perera, retired Associate Dean and Professor of Medicine at Columbia University's College of Physicians and Surgeons, delivered the AFSC supplies to the Viet-Duc hospital in July 1972. Like other scientists who began to go to Hanoi after 1970, Perera was asked to lecture to students and other scientists in his area of specialty. As the war wound on and Vietnamization or "de-Americanization," as the Vietnamese called it, proceeded apace, Hanoi became especially receptive to American scientists and the intellectual exchanges brought by these visits (Indochina Humanitarian Program, AFSC).

The AFSC's attention to building ties of trust with Hanoi and Washington simultaneously was ultimately rewarded. The organization's persistence, its careful cultivation of strong personal contacts, and its decision to send humanitarian aid to the NLF despite Washington's refusal to issue a license, convinced officials in Hanoi to begin humanitarian exchanges with the AFSC. The AFSC's existing network of international offices was crucial in fostering the personal contacts that broke through Vietnamese reservations about long-term ties with an American pacifist organization that was simultaneously running medical programs in South Vietnam in some cooperation with the American government. Careful attention to openness and honesty gave the AFSC everything in Hanoi that White House diplomats lacked: growing personal ties of respect and friendship despite ideational differences, access to government officials, developing contacts between professionals in the education and medical establishments, and the firsthand observations necessary to make informed judgments about Hanoi's goals and intentions.

5

Prisoners and Politics

Traveling to Hanoi continued to be most difficult. Washington authorities delayed issuing passports and seized others that, it charged, had been carried into North Vietnam. During the air war, there was also the logistical problem of flying into a country undergoing relentless bombing. Meeting with North Vietnamese officials in the United States was nearly impossible because Washington routinely denied visas to Vietnamese from North Vietnam or those affiliated in any way with the National Liberation Front. In response, antiwar activists planned international conferences where Americans and Vietnamese had the opportunity to meet in a setting at some remove from both the immediacy of the air war in Vietnam and the political climate of the Cold War in the United States. These conferences were also a natural outgrowth of the commitment to a broad internationalism that some activists maintained even during the height of the Cold War. The opportunity for the very first American visit to Hanoi, after all, came directly out of a 1965 international conference in Moscow. The international gatherings held in Canada and Europe during the war in Vietnam were valuable for activists in the United States because they brought together disparate elements of the antiwar movement in a setting where the Vietnamese presence helped keep the focus on that specific war.

The largest of these international gatherings took place in Bratislava, Czechoslovakia, in September 1967. This meeting resulted in the first prisoner of war release to American peace activists. Only a few captured American military personnel had been released before, and some of them were subsequently charged by the U.S. Army with "aiding and abetting the enemy," a move hardly designed to encourage the National Liberation Front to offer further releases. The Bratislava-inspired releases were the first of a series of new releases, most of them from Hanoi, to peace activists. The Pentagon greeted these releases with a shifting strategy whose only constant was to render subsequent releases less probable.

The Bratislava Conference was initiated to exchange reports on antiwar activities in the United States and "make peace efforts more effective." From Hanoi came Nguyen Trinh Co, a professor of surgery, Nguyen Minh Vy, editor of the Vietnamese newspaper *Thong Nhat*, Do Xuan Oanh of the Vietnam Peace Committee, and Vu Thi Hao, a teacher in one of Hanoi's technical schools. The eleven NLF representatives included Nguyen Thi Dinh and Phan Thanh Van of the Women's Union, Ha Thanh Lam, a Buddhist social worker and NLF representative at Prague, Dinh Ba Thi, a trade unionist, and Tran Van An, an economist and member of the Vietnamese Student Union. Thirty-eight Americans attended the conference: two Episcopal priests; three Quakers; journalists with the *Saturday Review, The New Republic, National Guardian,* and *Ramparts;* representatives from the Southern Christian Leadership Conference, Students for a Democratic Society, and the Student Nonviolent Coordinating Committee; professors from various universities; and other activists from across the antiwar spectrum.[1]

The American groups reflected diverse interests and perspectives. The American Friends Service Committee came to Bratislava to discuss its ongoing efforts to provide humanitarian aid to Vietnam. Others came out of a need to know America's enemy and so understand America itself better. Some members of Students for a Democratic Society came to Bratislava believing they could find there a strategy to revolutionize American society. The Vietnamese kept pulling the discussions back to the social realities of Vietnam itself. The pervasive corruption and prostitution that had come with American men, money, and arms to South Vietnam were phenomena that Americans acknowledged; it was even becoming the stuff of hesitant news reports in the United States. Americans tended to see these developments as anomalies, conditions not inextricably linked to the nature of the American presence. At Bratislava, Vietnamese delegates em-

1. For a listing of all the Americans attending see "Final Prague List," in "International Conference," Bratislava, SCPC. Some of the Americans at Bratislava were Malcolm Boyd, Carol Brightman, Bronson Clark, Ross Flanagan, Russell Johnson, David Dellinger, Betty Dellinger, Tom Hayden, Norman Fruchter, Carole King, Vivian Rothstein, Rennie Davis, Eric Weinberger, Christopher Jencks, John Pairman Brown, Robert Brown, Carol McEldowney, and John Wilson.

phasized that they saw it otherwise. They saw it as emblematic of the cultural and social loss in their country that the presence of the Americans and the war had engendered, and they found that Americans were not good listeners on this subject. In his report on the conference, journalist Christopher Jencks (1967) noted that "conversation kept returning to the brothels and music halls which cater to Americans in Saigon, a subject which moved the Vietnamese in Bratislava more than it did the Americans." NLF delegates made it clear that one of their goals was to end the corrupting influence that foreign control, both French and American, had wrought in Vietnam. Jencks noted that they pointed with pride to the fact that northern universities were run entirely by Vietnamese, in Vietnamese. Southern universities, on the other hand, relied on foreigners and were conducted in French and English, the language of the colonizers.

An event at the conference's beginning illustrated the very different experiences that shaped the sense of urgency and world view of these two groups. The American delegation arrived in Bratislava after twenty-two hours of air travel across the Atlantic and Europe. Some of them were exhausted and asked to cancel the opening session, at which they were to present the first reports, in favor of time to sleep and organize their remarks. After telling members of the Vietnamese delegation of their travel weariness, the American travelers learned that all of the Vietnamese had begun their journey at least two weeks earlier, and some of them had been on the road for two months. Somewhat embarrassed by their lack of stamina, they agreed to commence proceedings on schedule.[2]

All the Americans had come to Bratislava hoping to discover insights about Vietnam that they did not receive through their own media. They found this information in abundance. American firepower was at its height in Vietnam; the Vietnamese did not minimize the destructiveness of that power, but they looked at the meaning of that destruction from the inside out. Madame Dinh began her report by briefly reviewing the history of the war in a global context, but she then went on to look at the war from a perspective that began within Vietnam and moved outward to American force around the world. Seventy percent of American ground forces worldwide were tied up in the war, she believed, and 40 percent of the American navy and 60 percent of its tactical air power were organized

---

2. Some of the Vietnamese had traveled the entire length of Vietnam, crossed China by train and taken the Trans-Siberian Railway to Moscow. The Soviets required hard-currency payments for travel from foreigners, and the Vietnamese, who had very little of it, traveled cheaply by necessity (Clark 1967, SCPC).

against Vietnam. One million troops, American, ARVN, South Korean, Australian, and Filipino, were "bogged down" in Vietnam. And still, she continued, the Vietnamese were defeating American purposes there. Despite the enormous commitment America had made to winning the war, it was the NLF that was steadily expanding in control and influence in South Vietnam, she concluded.

Nguyen Minh Vy followed these observations by pointing out the desperate uses to which Americans put their famed productive capabilities. Currently, the Americans were dropping one ton of bombs on North Vietnam each minute, he said. The damage was widespread and severe, but he noted that the American mania to destroy had reached the point where "the Americans seem willing to exchange an F-105 fighter plane for a container of petrol." He described one instance where American pilots had succeeded in destroying a small bridge, but in destroying that bridge (which was quickly rebuilt as a "movable" bridge), they had lost three American planes along with their crews. This appeared to Minh Vy more a strategy of desperation than one born of military confidence (Clark 1967, SCPC).

These kinds of analyses removed the Vietnamese as "victims" of American aggression and depicted them as already victors in their struggle for an independent Vietnam. It was not the perspective to which many Americans, including antiwar activists, were accustomed in 1967. Even those who sympathized with Vietnamese nationalist aspirations viewed the Vietnamese as somewhat impoverished underdogs who needed all the help that they could get in order to hold on until American forces withdrew and a negotiated settlement could be reached. The confidence with which the Vietnamese at Bratislava viewed their future, and the commitment that prompted it, surprised many of the Americans there. The AFSC's Ross Flanagan touched on one such aspect in his report on the conference:

> At Bratislava I was reminded of how cheap words are—how easily we Americans intellectualize the war and ignore our real responsibilities for ending it. Talking with the Vietnamese, one couldn't help but be struck by the contrast between the total commitment of their lives and the shallowness which has typified so much of our own protest. There is hardly a family in South Vietnam which hasn't been directly touched by the war, we were told, while here in America we complain about the traffic on the way home from our Day of Protest. "I'm prepared to suffer through the war in Vietnam if that will bring people to a realization of the futility of war," remarked one Friend recently, urging his Yearly Meeting not to act lawlessly by extending relief to all parts of Vietnam. (Flanagan 1967)

At the end of the conference, Nguyen Thi Dinh of the Vietnamese Women's Union suggested that the National Liberation Front could release some American prisoners if someone at Bratislava would go to Phnom Penh to pick them up. None of the Americans had come to Bratislava prepared to go on to Hanoi, much less return from Southeast Asia with American prisoners of war. The NLF delegates asked Tom Hayden and four other SDS members, Carol McEldowney, Vivian Rothstein, Rennie Davis, and Norman Fruchter, to go to North Vietnam from Bratislava. Along with them went former air force sergeant turned Episcopal priest John Pairman Brown and journalist Robert Brown. It was a difficult trip for them all. Vivian Rothstein, who had spent the summer of 1964 registering voters in Mississippi, wrote from her hotel room in Bratislava that she was

> very scared and upset about the trip. I feel as if when we land in Beirut I would like to get a ticket straight to NY and forget about the whole crazy adventure. I'm afraid it's a bigger step politically than I realize. That my passport will be invalid. . . . I am also scared about the bombing . . . going to Mississippi was a strain, and involved fear and a political decision which was hard to erase. But this even more involved a change which is irreversible. (Hayden, 1988, 212)

The group went directly from Bratislava to Hanoi and spent eighteen days in North Vietnam. Hayden was struck by the increased intensity of the bombing, compared to that of his December 1965 trip to Hanoi. Their travels throughout the country always included time spent crouching in ditches by the side of the road as American F-105s streaked overhead. They hoped, Hayden said, that the pilots up there would not see them as just another target on their radar screens.

When the rest of the group returned to the United States, Tom Hayden went on to Phnom Penh, where he waited three weeks for the National Liberation Front's prisoners, Daniel Lee Pitzer, James Jackson, Jr., and Edward Johnson, to arrive from South Vietnam's delta area. The day after they reached Phnom Penh, the four flew out of Cambodia for the United States. That same day, American military officials in Saigon, who had had no contact with the three POWs, released a report claiming that the men had been "brainwashed."

The former prisoners winged their way home, with media stories from the Pentagon of their "brainwashing" following them as they landed in New York on 13 November.

The evidence for brainwashing advanced by the American military in Saigon lay in statements made by Phung Van Tuong, a self-professed former NLF agent now working with psychological-warfare advisors to the American government in Saigon. He claimed to have held "indoctrination" sessions with these American prisoners in their camp near Camau. After the early and widely reported news of "brainwashing," more detailed news accounts, such as that in the *New York Times* on 14 November, revealed that Tuong, a slight twenty-five-year-old, said only that he had spent a number of hours talking to the American prisoners about "the revolution in Cuba, about the Negroes in the United States, about the Vietcong victories." Tuong spoke very little English, reporters soon noticed, and the prisoners did not understand Vietnamese. How did the "brainwashing" take place? Tuong explained that he had brainwashed the POWs by reading English words, which he barely understood, from a written text.

With even the media skeptical now, the State Department issued its own report, saying that the prisoners "probably" had not been brainwashed, but by then the damage was done. On the plane home with Hayden, all three men had spoken in measured tones of their captivity, of how they disliked some of their guards but found others likeable, of the English classes they had conducted for the enthusiastic Vietcong cadre, of their dislike for the monotonous food, of the tedium and despair of confinement, of the respect they had for the stamina and commitment of their captors, and of how they had greeted with flat disbelief many of the things the Vietnamese had told them. For example, Pitzer, who had been captured in 1963, told Hayden that he had refused to believe, for two years, his captors' assertion that President Kennedy was dead (Hayden 1988, 232). All three were still plainly skeptical about the existence of an antiwar movement in the United States because they had heard of it only from the Vietnamese.

As the homeward-bound former POWs read the press reports alleging brainwashing, their memories of captivity shifted. The allegations of brainwashing were particularly vile for Pitzer. At the U.S. embassy in Beirut, he called his wife and, for the benefit of the embassy officials standing around, immediately launched into a tirade against the Vietnamese and "the goddamned communists who are trying to take over that country, and we've got to keep fighting there. . . . I hate those red bastards. They tried to brainwash me, but they couldn't. . . . America is the greatest country in the world" (Hayden 1988, 235).

The Pentagon's campaign to discredit the National Liberation Front prisoner release worked well. When the NLF had released George Smith and Claude McClure in November 1965, the two had criticized the American role in the war at their first press conference and had spoken of their captors generally as humane and fair. Military officials then shut the two up by taking them to Okinawa, threatening to court-martial them for aiding the enemy, and holding them under house arrest for five months. The Pentagon had no evidence to back up its charges, however, and eventually released the two. On the day that Pitzer, Jackson, and Johnson were released in 1967, military officers, apparently fearing that they, too, would oppose the war, leveled charges of brainwashing, hoping to silence any intended criticism immediately or to browbeat them into changing their minds. Such charges of brainwashing, which originated with American military officers in Saigon, began a military pattern of injecting propaganda charges into, or deliberately interfering with, each prisoner release thereafter that took place outside American military supervision. The prisoners were weary and homesick, some of them ill, and all of them carried loads heavy enough without the burden of the Pentagon's point-scoring.

The Pentagon had its own plans for the prisoners, and carefully scripting their return home was a major part of it. Denied total control of that process, Pentagon officials greeted prisoner releases with demands that demonstrated fear of dissent within its ranks more than confidence in its purpose. Future prison releases under these circumstances were due more to the persistence of antiwar activists than to encouragement from the Pentagon.

There were more prisoner releases in the works, however. Two months after the November releases, and after a string of activists had visited Hanoi and urged officials there to follow the National Liberation Front's example, Hanoi initiated its first prisoner release. With several hundred American prisoners in Hanoi by then, the question was whom to release. By that time, early 1968, the American POW population in Hanoi ranged from the fiercely prowar to those who openly opposed the American war. Both of these groups were minorities within the prisoner of war population. The majority of POWs fell between these two camps— neither vehemently for nor against the war, but seeking to make their own way through the larger morass. They were mostly career officers, after all, with years of service, pensions, and future employment to protect. It was mostly from this broad middle group that Hanoi officials chose the twelve prisoners it eventually released before the end of the war.

The first inkling of Hanoi's plan to release prisoners came in January 1968, when the Vietnam Peace Committee sent a telegram to David Dellinger saying that "in celebration of our New Year Tet holiday, we are preparing to release three captured American pilots to the American peace movement. Please send responsible representative for reception and discussion" (Berrigan 1968). Dellinger called historian Howard Zinn at Boston University and Jesuit priest Daniel Berrigan at Cornell University. One of them, he hoped, would be willing to go. They both were. The two men met for the first time the next day when they left Kennedy Airport for Copenhagen, the first leg of their race to Laos. They hoped to reach Vientiane by Friday afternoon, in time to catch the weekly ICC flight to Hanoi.

Before they left New York, a State Department official called them and offered to validate their passports for North Vietnam. Zinn and Berrigan declined. Neither one recognized the government's efforts to regulate, for political purposes, its citizens' international travel. But the State Department official had a more pressing concern: Washington wanted the fliers brought back on a military plane, not on a civilian airliner. Zinn and Berrigan, thinking then that the release itself would be much more important to the Pentagon than the mode of transportation home, told the official that they would leave the route home up to the pilots (Zinn 1968).

When media reports publicized the upcoming trip, relatives of some POWs prepared letters to send with Zinn and Berrigan. Two women from North Carolina who were married to officers missing in North Vietnam flew up to Kennedy airport just as the two activists were leaving New York. They brought letters for their husbands imprisoned in Hanoi along with letters from other women with missing husbands. They asked the two activists to carry the letters to Hanoi and deliver them to officials there. Carrying a thick packet of letters, the two men flew to Copenhagen and then to Frankfurt, to Rome, to Teheran, to Karachi, to Calcutta, to Bangkok, and at last to Vientiane, only to learn that the plane for Hanoi had already come and gone—they would have to wait until the following week.

Late on Friday night, 9 February, the plane returned to Vientiane and carried them on to Hanoi, where they slept soundly in their austere hotel until the dawn's early air raid. Their hosts were the same ones who had hosted earlier antiwar groups—members of the Vietnamese Peace Committee who had come of political age after World War II in resistance groups fighting the French. Zinn and Berrigan asked them why were they releasing the pilots. Because it was part of building an understanding with the people of the United States, Do Xuan Oanh replied. They knew there was an enormous difference between these pilots and the men who refused the draft in the United States, Xuan Oanh said, but the information available to both groups was the same. Perhaps the return of the pilots could help convince the American people that they and the Vietnamese had something in common after all. But even if it did not, Oanh concluded, "relations between you and us remain the same." Berrigan noted ruefully, "They had not lost all hope in the American public, a phenomenon which struck us as somewhat rarer at home than in North Vietnam" (Berrigan 1968, 43).

Zinn and Berrigan spent a week in Hanoi waiting for the next plane out, visiting museums in the city, touring villages and cooperatives outside Hanoi, and talking to Vietnamese officials. Wherever they went, people asked them the same question: "Did you know Norman Morrison?" His image still served, the Vietnamese insisted, as a symbol for potential future relations between Vietnam and the West. Zinn and Berrigan both spoke French, and when they met with Premier Pham Van Dong they needed no translator. The premier thanked them for coming to Vietnam and then said:

> Your visit here is of some importance, and we thank you. Our countries have been at war for some time. The war, however, will continue as long as Johnson and Rusk wish. It remains difficult for us, as well as for the Americans, to know the meaning of this war. But we ask, as a result of this visit, that you clarify the meaning of the war for your fellow Americans. Because you are a people by and large intoxicated by the war, it is almost impossible for you to know what is really happening here in North Vietnam. And yet, there are signs of hope. For if one compares the situation of the United States when the air war began with the public sentiment of today, one indeed marks a great change in the climate. And so one is justified in continuing to hope. (Berrigan 1968, 126)

President Johnson would increase the troop levels in Vietnam, the premier believed. He also expected an American ground invasion of the north. But these actions, coming on top of an already enormous American commitment to Southeast Asia, only proved that the United States was already losing the war. "It is an atrocious war," the premier told them, "it will grow worse." Still, they were all responsible for their own countries, he continued.

> We expect to win our victory here on our battlefront. And we also wish you much success in your struggle within your own country. But that is your struggle and responsibility, a duty resting upon you. I have confidence in Americans. In the eighteenth century they gave the world an example of a true revolution, and we have quoted in our own constitution phrases from your Declaration of Independence. Certainly one of the great results of our mutual struggle will be the beginning of entirely new relationships between Americans and Vietnamese on the basis of respect and peace. (Berrigan 1968, 130)

Zinn and Berrigan spent one afternoon in the war museum in Hanoi, which offered a genealogy, of sorts, of the American arsenal since the war began. Berrigan's description of the museum demonstrated how the air war had changed since the first American toured the museum in 1965. The cluster bomb canisters in the war museum had grown ever larger over the years. Their pellets went from steel to fiberglass, impossible to x-ray. American technology depicted in the war museum progressed from jellied gasoline to napalm laced with polystyrene to make the deadly gas hotter and more adhesive. The museum also carried captured gas masks issued to the American pilots with instructions for their use printed in English, should they fall beneath the range of their own weapons.

Comparing museums of war in Vietnam and the United States pointed to the difference between the view from the ground and the view from the sky. American public sites of weaponry during the 1950s and 1960s invited viewers into the cockpits of the fighter planes. Some of them offered programs that simulated the experience of flying above the earth. The uses to which the planes were put were not part of the displays. The view from under the planes scarcely existed. The imagined terrain beneath appeared empty, bereft of habitation or vegetation, inviting the observer-participant to presume that these planes were not utilitarian, that they served only the sheer delight of flying, and that the significance of their existence and activities was confined to the cockpit. In the war museums of Vietnam, the significance of the planes' purpose was inescapable. The view from the cockpit was there, too, in the gas masks and instruction sheets to the pilots, but they inverted the expected identification with cockpit artifacts, serving as studied reminders that even the cockpit was not immune to the weapons of the plane. In that sense, even the cockpit was below the bombs. The museum artifacts kept viewers below the plane and too close for comfort to the weapons of death: the canisters, the pellets, the napalm. Sometimes the bombings' wreckage constituted the museum itself. In some rural areas, village museums were constructed within the bombed homes and their surrounding gardens, where the artifacts were simply wreckage from the blast. These museums were usually local affairs, created by the villagers themselves and tended, for a time, by the numbed survivors. Photographs of those dead, along with pieces of clothing they once wore and pages of the books they once read, placed the viewers themselves squarely in the path of the bombs. "One bombing brings hundreds of social problems in its descent," a Vietnamese journalist told Berrigan as he reflected on the horrific conditions in which villagers who survived a bombing suddeny found themselves (Berrigan 1968, 77).

No one was left unmoved by these exhibits. Many Americans in North Vietnam hardly knew how to react—the perspective was beyond their own historical experience, and it brought them up close to moral issues that they were accustomed to intellectualizing from a safe distance. Stopping "the seventh war from now," encouraging the Vietnamese to adopt a "nonviolent" strategy, and arguing over issues of communist exclusion from peace organizations, appeared as simply more imperious luxuries indulged in from the home territory. "Numbed and appalled as we were," Berrigan wrote,

> I think we knew beyond any doubt that America would be accountable to history for a genocidal war, in violation of every international convention from The Hague in 1907 to Geneva in 1929 and 1949. . . . I thought also of an eminent American churchman who asserted in the last months that it is probably a better tactic for the peace movement to concentrate upon 'broad areas of United States tactical and diplomatic and military mistakes, rather than upon individual instances of cruelty or civilian destruction.' I only wish he could have been with us on this night. Perhaps he would have come to a realization that it is exactly there, in the flesh of the innocent, that the true measure of the war must be taken. (Berrigan 1968, 68–69)

There was another view from the ground that Zinn and Berrigan found in the villages of Vietnam. It was a view designed to educate villagers on survival tactics. Many villages could not afford to build large concrete-lined bomb shelters. Instead, they dug holes in the earth large enough for one individual and laid a lid of heavy woven bamboo over it for shelter. To demonstrate how effective even these small shelters could be against heavy bombing raids, an instructor would bore small holes in the soft earth with a single finger, up to the second joint. Then the instructor would stand above the small holes in the ground, up in the "view from the cockpit," place one hand with fingers spread above the holes, and with the other hand, pour rice through the fingers as if trying to strike the small holes. The holes seldom suffered a direct hit. By encouraging people on the ground to view their total environment from the view of the cockpit, Berrigan noted, the village instructors could help organize the fear that welled up in villagers when they heard the sound of the planes coming through the open skies.

On Friday evening, just before the weekly plane from Vientiane landed in Hanoi, Vietnamese officials released three American pilots, Major Overly, Captain Black, and Lieutenant Methany, to Zinn and Berrigan. The two activists immediately informed the pilots of the State Department's wishes that they travel home by military jet. They pointed out that if the pilots chose to travel by military jet they could both avoid the press and reach home sooner. On the other hand, Hanoi had released the three explicitly as an independent gesture in response to pressure from the American antiwar movement and could view their traveling by American military conveyances as another Pentagon success in flaunting its freedom over the Asian skies. The pilots told Zinn and Berrigan that they had the clear impression that their own release and their route home were linked, insofar as the Hanoi government was concerned, to possible future releases. Out of consideration for their fellow prisoners, they wanted to travel home on a commercial flight with Zinn and Berrigan.

With this understanding, the five flew out of Hanoi and on to Vientiane. But at the Vientiane airport, the United States ambassador, William Sullivan, and three attachés boarded the airplane. The ambassador crisply reminded the newly released prisoners that they were first and foremost members of the armed forces. The Department of Defense wanted them to travel on military aircraft, he told them—indeed, he added, the decision "comes from the White House" (Zinn 1968, 435). Lieutenant Methany objected, raising the issue of future prisoner releases. Ambassador Sullivan said he doubted that Vietnamese officials had really indicated a preference to Zinn and Berrigan that the pilots travel home by commercial transport. Major Overly assured the ambassador that the two activists were right—the three pilots had been told exactly the same thing before their release. But, Sullivan replied, it could be equally harmful to future prisoner releases if they "met the press and said the wrong things." For nearly an hour they remained on the aircraft, the pilots trying to reach a compromise with the ambassador that could result in further prisoner releases. But Sullivan was insistent—"the best minds in Washington have been involved," he said—and finally the three pilots agreed to go with the ambassador on an air force jet. The three pilots went back to their military duties in the United States and never held a press conference (Zinn 1968, 436).

Berrigan left Vientiane believing that the United States should prepare itself for defeat. "Snatching" its own pilots, he thought, was a sign of how precariously the military was beginning to view its own image. "Some 250 years of national history have not prepared us for the possibility of so unthinkable a thing as defeat," Berrigan wrote on his way home.

> Defeat, moreover, at such hands! Hands which are neither large nor well fleshed out, nor white, nor skilled in the multiple uses and misuses of technological power. It is not to be wondered at that two forces of pride, one of dismay at the death of young Americans abroad, and the sense, cold as the hours before dawn, that we are about to lose a war for the first time in our history—that these two have induced an unparalleled deepening of national consciousness. Americans, perhaps for the first time in their history, are about to have their measure taken by those whose stature, by every Western standard, is less than our own. (1968, 71, 72)

Hanoi's first prisoner release was framed by the Tet Offensive, which also was the occasion for the capture of two American women working in the south. Marjorie Nelson was a medical doctor working at the American Friends Service Committee's rehabilitation center in Quang Ngai, and at the end of January 1968, she had gone to Hue to visit a friend, Sandra Johnson, an International Volunteer Service teacher at the high school there. The weekend stay she had scheduled for Hue turned into weeks when National Liberation Front soldiers attacked the city during the Tet Offensive and took up positions near Johnson's residence. After bombs destroyed the house, the NLF cadres announced that, because of the continuing bombardment, they would be taken out to the mountains, and "when peace was restored," they could return to their families. They were prisoners, Nelson realized (1968, AFSC).

In the evening darkness, they set out with a group of soldiers and walked through the night until they reached a small village, where they ate breakfast. They continued walking all day until they reached a mountain camp late that evening. There they discovered twenty-five American GIs who had been captured in Hue. The American GIs were closely guarded, some of them injured and ill and, to Nelson, appeared disoriented and depressed. None of them spoke Vietnamese. They could not communicate with their captors, they had no idea where they were going or how long they would be prisoners. One told Nelson that he did not ever want to "feel" like a prisoner—this was far from the life of action he had expected in Vietnam. It was "the greatest learning experience of his life," he said. Some of them had children about whom they now thought incessantly. "I felt in a very uncomfortable position with them," Nelson said, "They'd been sent to Vietnam while I'd come of my own volition. Here they were, stuck; very likely many wouldn't survive." Conditions were rough for all of the GIs in the camp, Nelson noted, but they lived under the same circumstances as the NLF soldiers, who appeared to Nelson to have high morale and cheerfulness to spare in the days after Tet, in 1968 (Moran 1971, 31).

The American aid workers' experience was tempered by the fact that, unlike the GIs, they spoke Vietnamese. Nelson had been in Vietnam only four months when she was captured, but she had worked hard at learning the language and now had basic proficiency; furthermore, she and Johnson were eager to learn the language and to learn something about the National Liberation Front. The NLF cadres were incredulous that the women could speak their language. They seized the opportunity to ask them endless questions: How old are you? Are you married? Do you have a sweetheart? Are your parents living? How did you get to Vietnam? In America, do you cook with wood or coal? The women wanted to stay busy during the long days of captivity. "I repeatedly offered to work," Nelson said,

> certain that with all the fighting going on there were many injured people who could use a doctor's help. The answer was always the same: "We have enough Vietnamese doctors and nurses; we don't need your help." This was not true but they were tremendously proud and determined to be self-sufficient. I had to respect this spirit even though I felt frustrated because I couldn't serve in a situation where I was sure I was needed. (Nelson 1968, 4–5)

At one point the camp cadres asked them to write statements covering their reasons for coming to Vietnam, the work they did there, and their views on the war. Nelson wrote what she would have written regardless of who asked her—that she had opposed the war before coming to Vietnam and had seen nothing there to change her mind. Her brother, Beryl Nelson, had even been to Hanoi the previous September—as a crew member on the second voyage of the *Phoenix* to Haiphong Harbor. Excerpts from their statements were later broadcast on Radio Hanoi.

After a week in the first camp, Nam, the cadre in charge of the prisoners, told them that all the prisoners would be moved to a camp about ten days walk away, where conditions were better, the food was more varied, and they would even have soap, towels, and showers. When they reached the new camp, Nam told the two women that he would be going back to the first camp. Nam and Nelson had spent many hours talking; she had helped him learn English and he had helped her build her Vietnamese vocabulary. He clearly regretted leaving someone he now seemed to consider a friend and gave Nelson a medallion as a "keepsake" to remember him by. Then he handed her a slip of paper with an address on it, adding, "Here is the address of my sister who lives in the North. When you return to the United States I want you to write and tell me what's happened to you." Nelson said, "I was touched by this, because I felt that despite culture, language, and ideological barriers some communication had really taken place" (1968, 5).

The two women stayed at the second camp until the end of March. There were two rules for everyone at the camp, they were informed shortly after arriving: they must not try to escape, and they must be friendly and greet everyone. Easy rules to follow, they both agreed, as they had no idea where they were, and talking to everyone was the best way to hone their language skills, something they could use to stay busy in the absence of other work. There was plenty of food "if you like rice," Nelson noted, adding that "sometimes they had peanuts to go with it, but seldom more than that" (1968, 5). When Nelson suffered through one week-long bout of dysentery, a locally trained nurse provided regular visits and treatment. The camp radio brought in news from Hanoi and from the American Armed Forces Network. From the latter, Nelson and Johnson heard that they were missing from Hue and that American Marines were looking specifically for them. This was, to them, more alarming than hopeful because a rescue attempt could easily create more bloodshed.

With little to do, Nelson and Johnson talked to the cadres at the camp at great length, about their families, their children, education, medicine, farming methods, and religion. One of the young cadres planned to become an engineer when the war was over. He was delighted that Nelson had studied chemistry and that Johnson taught algebra. The three spent hours writing out chemical formulas and algebraic equations with sticks on the ground. The cadres at the camp were greatly interested in the Society of Friends. Once, when they were discussing people they admired, one of the Vietnamese named Norman Morrison. Nelson pointed out that he was a fellow Quaker. Startled, the cadre exclaimed, "I thought he was a Catholic, like me" (Moran 1971, 32).

Near the end of March, the camp cadre told Nelson and Johnson that they would be taken out of the mountains and returned to a highway near the bus line where they could catch a bus back to their homes. They had perpetrated no violence against the Vietnamese people, the cadres told them. They had come to Vietnam to help, not to harm, and so they would be returned to their work. Their personal effects, including their money, passports, cameras, and wallets, were returned. The only missing item from her wallet, Nelson noted, was a picture of her family. That evening in the bomb shelter, the cadres threw a farewell party for the two women, replete with canteens of tea and a basin filled with peanut brittle. The soldiers gave them aluminum combs made from metal salvaged from napalm canisters, and lectured them on the preferability of combs over napalm canisters as a use for aluminum. They walked that night down the mountain in the company of three soldiers, who turned them over to a local family. After breakfast with the Americans, the Vietnamese family took the women down a path to the highway, where they caught a bus to Hue.

If ever a case was ripe for becoming a metaphor refurbishing the entrenched image of the perils of the old American frontier, this was it. Two white women, dedicated to serving others, without male protectors, captured by an enemy depicted as vicious and bloodthirsty, carried off into the "wild" mountains for weeks—the script called for them to be harmed, perhaps killed, by the cruel enemy, or rescued by heroic American males whose courage and faith would reveal the stark perfidy and faithlessness of the captors. Had a sustainable hint of any of this story emerged, the case would have been seized by the press, the public, and the American president, as embodying the contrast between civilization and barbarism, between the respect that males in the West accorded females and the contempt with which the enemies of the West held them. It could have provided an emotive and visceral rationale for the entire war effort in Vietnam.

Instead, the case fit the reality of the American "frontier" more than the myth, and so it quickly disappeared from the media's and public's consciousness. The women did not need or want a military rescue, they used the occasion to learn more of the language of "the enemy," and they struck up friendships with the cadres. The American men with them could not be symbols of heroic victors because they were themselves prisoners of war and needed the women's language skills for the most elementary communication with their captors. Not only were the cadres unthreatening to Nelson and Johnson, but they looked out for their welfare. While walking along a dense part of the forest, one of the soldiers noticed that Johnson's long hair repeatedly got caught in the underbrush. He gave her his own hat for protection, Johnson said, "a gallantry for which his buddies teased him at great length"[3] (Moran 1971, 35).

The Tet Offensive, during which three American prisoners were freed in Hanoi and Nelson and Johnson were held in captivity, also framed President Johnson's announcement that he would not seek reelection. Many antiwar activists worked to elect a peace candidate in the fall. But assassination followed assassination in the United States that year. The death of Martin Luther King, Jr., came as a blow to reformers of all persuasions and fed a growing disenchantment with broad nonviolent action. Robert Kennedy's death chilled the hope of an antiwar victory in the fall elections. Richard Nixon's campaign promises to end the war by some unspecified plan, and his subsequent election and announcement of "Vietnamization," augured a slow withdrawal accompanied by air power sufficiently heavy to avoid the appellation of defeat. Nixon's Vietnamization was not original with his administration. It was a faithful imitation of the French strategy of *jaunissement* (yellowing) that Paris had vainly adopted in 1952—assigning more of the burden of combat to Vietnamese troops in its client state while withdrawing its own troops, in a broader strategy of shifting from direct to indirect rule. Still, the political debate over the war changed in 1968. Neither of the two major candidates, Richard Nixon and Hubert Humphrey, promised to win the war;

3. Glenda Riley points out that the enduring myth of white women and American Indian males was that women were weak and vulnerable while Indian males were savage and rapacious and that "contact between the two groups was almost always calamitous" (1984, 249). In fact, Riley shows, relations between the two usually were pleasant and collegial, and white women often opposed aggressive actions against American Indians on the frontier.

both promised "peace," which, though undefined, signaled the end of victory rhetoric.

In July, Hanoi offered to release three more American prisoners to members of the antiwar movement. The State Department announced immediately that it planned to fly the released prisoners home on military aircraft, and Ambassador Sullivan held a press conference in Vientiane to inform the world that the POWs would be ordered to transfer immediately to a military aircraft when they reached Laos. With this preemptive strike already hurled, Stuart Meacham of the American Friends Service Committee, Anne Weills Scheer of Women Strike for Peace, and Vernon Grizzard of Students for a Democratic Society flew to Hanoi on 10 July. There, Meachum urged Hanoi officials to release the POWs despite Sullivan's announcement, and they did, freeing James Frederick Low, Fred Neale Thompson, and Joe Victor Carpenter from a city prison camp on 18 July. When the American visitors first met the POWs, they were braced for some hostility. "It was an emotional meeting," Meacham told the *New York Times* on 4 August. "We didn't know how they'd react to us or how we'd react to them. After all, we represented a movement that was totally opposed to what they had done." But the activists and the newly released pilots quickly discovered that any potential differences were far outweighed by the fact that they all wanted the exchange to work in a way that could encourage further releases before the end of the war.

The newly released prisoners appeared healthy and in good spirits when they addressed foreign correspondents in Hanoi. They spoke of their long trek to Hanoi after being shot down, of their life in prison, and of their hopes for an early peace in Vietnam. The war caused a lot of destruction, Thompson said in reflecting on the lessons of his own captivity. "It cost a lot of lives on both sides That's why it must be ended as soon as possible," the *New York Times* quoted him as saying on 19 July. After that press conference, Ambassador Sullivan summoned another in Vientiane and announced that he would, without consulting the pilots, put them on medical evacuation planes when they reached Laos.

Sullivan waited in vain when the next plane from Hanoi arrived in Vientiane. The newly freed pilots and their American entourage were still in North Vietnam, where they stayed for the next two weeks while Hanoi officials sent a message to Paris asking Ambassador Harriman for assurance that the pilots would, at least, be given a genuine choice in deciding how to return to the United States. On 31 July, a cable came from Paris

with Harriman's assurance to that effect. When the next plane out of
Hanoi arrived in Vientiane, Sullivan's hours at the airport were partly rewarded, for his quarry was aboard. This time, the pilots refused to go
with him, arguing that further prisoner releases might be jeopardized.
After a heated, hour-long discussion between the pilots and Sullivan, the
disappointed ambassador exited the plane and the three pilots flew on to
Bangkok and there boarded a Trans World Airlines jet for New York
(*APW* 1971, 222). When the released prisoners arrived at Kennedy International Airport in New York two days later, air force officials were waiting for them and took them immediately to the hospital at Andrews Air
Force base for "evaluation and administrative processing" before receiving new orders. They were not allowed to meet with press officials. Pentagon spokesmen told the *New York Times* that the three did not want to
do so.

Soon thereafter, Stuart Meacham received a letter from Do Xuan
Oanh of the Vietnamese Peace Committee, telling him that two of the re-
leased pilots were now assigned to train new pilots in the air force. Releasing POWs so that they could teach others to bomb Vietnam was not
Hanoi's intent, Oanh protested. Meacham had been unaware of the released pilots' new assignments, but news reports confirmed Oanh's letter.
During a trip through Paris on his way to Hanoi the following December,
Meacham brought up the matter with Averell Harriman. Harriman told
Meacham to tell Oanh that he, Harriman, had ordered that the pilots be
reassigned. Meacham carried the message to Oanh, who asked that he
provide confirmation of the reassignment. When Meacham tried to confirm the reassignment with Harriman, the Paris negotiator refused to
commit himself and let Meachum know in "a very guarded reply" that he
wanted to wash his hands of the whole matter (Meacham and Collett
1968, AFSC).

Washington's policy on the American prisoners of war appeared piece-
meal, in a reaction to the initiatives of antiwar activists and POW releases.
The Pentagon encouraged the very first released POWs to meet with the
press, but antiwar sentiment seeped early into prisoner of war camps, and
by 1965 the Pentagon could not trust its own to emerge from those
camps committed to the American cause. George Smith's and Claude Mc-
Clure's frank criticism of the war seemed to stun military officials in Vietnam, who responded by placing them under arrest and threatening to
court-martial them both. Smith and McClure had had no contact with the
antiwar movement before their press conference; if they could not be

trusted to let their experiences as prisoners of the enemy vindicate American purpose in the war, the subsequent release of prisoners directly to the antiwar movement alarmed military officials, who sought to forestall further criticism by calling the men "brainwashed." When that tactic backfired, the Pentagon began pressuring returning POWs to place themselves under military orders immediately upon release and not to speak at all to the press. The Pentagon's priority was protecting its own image, and as the nation turned increasingly against a military solution to the war, the fate of the prisoners of war became subordinate to that priority.

The administration's prisoner policy took an unexpected twist in 1969, when Alfred Hassler of the Fellowship of Reconciliation pursued the prospect of a "third force" in South Vietnam that could rally broad support for an alternative both to the National Liberation Front and to the regime in Saigon. The prospect for the kind of Buddhist-led third force that Hassler had envisioned in Vietnam in 1965 had receded by 1969, though hope for it was still strong among certain segments of the antiwar movement in the United States. The prospect had dimmed as the level of support given by Washington to the Thieu-Ky regime increased— the third force concept ultimately relied on America's voluntary withdrawal of support from its heavy commitment to the Saigon governments of the past years in favor of the third force coalition. As such, it was a solution as dependent on Washington as was Thieu.

Still, Hassler continued to hope for this alternative and, in May 1969, he led a Fellowship of Reconciliation delegation to Saigon to "identify the variety of religious forces in South Vietnam and the range of political expression there." The team took with them retired rear admiral Arnold True, Congressman John Conyers (D-Mich.), and John Pemberton, executive director of the American Civil Liberties Union.[4] The study team's initial mission was to explore the range of religious and political sentiment in South Vietnam, and it became apparent that the "variety of religious forces" and the "range of political expression" in Saigon were well represented in its prisons and detention camps, where many of the third force business leaders, intellectuals, and students were now held. The team

4. The other team members were James Armstrong, a Methodist bishop; Anne Bennett, a WSP member who served on the General Board of the National Council of Churches; Allan Brick of FOR; Robert Drinan, dean of the Boston College Law School; and Seymour Siegel, professor at the Jewish Theological Seminary of America (Armstrong and Conyers 1969, 1307).

then asked the State Department for help in determining the grounds for detention in Saigon, and in assessing prison conditions generally. Undersecretary of State Elliott Richardson assured the team that its trip was "unnecessary" because there were "diminishing few" political prisoners in South Vietnam (Hoa Binh 1968–70, SCPC).

Official figures on prisoners in Saigon were hard to come by because there was no central agency in Saigon that tracked prisoners. Numerous agencies had the power to arrest; so many people were imprisoned without official charges that the State Department said it could only guess at figures. In addition, prisoners were listed simply as "Communists" or "civilians related to Communist activities," both labels euphemisms for a wide range of activities, including government critics generally. The Director of Correctional Institutions in Saigon, Colonel Nguyen Psu Sanh, told the study group that 69 percent of the 35,000 prisoners in the country's forty-one correctional centers were so classified. Their numbers, according to William E. Colby, Deputy of Pacification, had gone up and would continue to go up as the pacification program developed (U.S. Study Team 1969, 8).

The study team was not allowed to see any of the prisoners they had specifically requested permission to see, but they were granted tours of three of the four Saigon-run prisons: Chi Hoa prison in Saigon, Thu Duc, an all-female prison, and Con Son Island prison. The warden of Chi Hoa, often described as a "showcase prison" because American advisors were setting up rehabilitation programs there, reported that about half of his prisoners were "criminals" and the other half "communists." All of the prisoners wore colored badges indicating their classification: red tags indicated "communist" or "communist sympathizer," yellow tags indicated "criminal activity." One hundred and twenty of the prisoners were Buddhist monks, according to a 15 October *Christian Century* article. The warden of Con Son Island prison told the delegation that nearly one thousand of his seven thousand prisoners were soldiers from the South Vietnam army who were accused of being National Liberation Front agents. Another three thousand were civilians accused of working directly with the NLF, and over two thousand prisoners had never been charged. At Con Son, there were fifty prisoners between the ages of four and eight and another four hundred between the ages of eight and eighteen. The team saw no rehabilitation accommodations for the young prisoners— they spent their days in large bare rooms with sanitary facilities at one end. The team also learned that, at that time, the U.S. government was donating a million dollars to expand Con Son to provide for an expected influx of prisoners from Operation Phoenix (U.S. Study Team 1969, 10).

The number of unsentenced prisoners was highest at Thu Duc, the women's prison. There, the team was again struck by the "extreme youthfulness" of many of the prisoners. Ninety were under the age of eighteen. The younger they were, the more likely they were to be charged with "leftist tendencies." But older women could be "leftists" too. The team met one slight, aged woman who, according to her dossier, was serving a fifteen year sentence for "passing VC letters" (U.S. Study Team 1969, 8).

The study team members' report was detailed and sober. They considered legitimate the "suppression of political freedoms . . . of those actively engaged in conducting war against the government." Hassler's primary concern was that the sweep of dissidents was so wide it caught up in it the makings of a third force, of religious and political dissenters, "of loyal nationalists who advocate forming a coalition government with N.L.F. representatives," and that the chilling effect of these internments alienated ever larger segments of the population. One of the young prisoners the team interviewed told them that in his "secure" rural province, a majority of the males his age experience "arrest and detention at least once." FOR's report highlighted the arbitrary nature of arrests and the various levels of torture in the Saigon government's detention centers. "U.S. officials," the report stated, "agree that there is torture, but insist that it does not take place in the correctional centers but in the interrogation and detention centers where the prisoners are taken first." American involvement in the interrogation centers was less direct than in the correctional centers, and the torture at that level was attributed to the Vietnamese. But the American military continued to turn over all the suspects they rounded up in village sweeps to the interrogation centers, where they knew that torture was regularly used to extract potential information.[5]

The study team's report attracted wide attention in the United States. Team members testified about their findings before Congress in hearings that the media picked up and covered in some detail. The new Nixon administration had confidently predicted that it would escape the fate of its predecessor, end the war with honor, and restore American prestige. "Give us six months," Henry Kissinger had told an AFSC dele-

---

5. For other accounts of procedures at interrogation centers see Orville Schell 1968 and Truong 1985.

gation shortly after Nixon's first inauguration. "If we haven't ended the war by then, you can come back and tear down the fence." They did not generally tear down fences, the Quakers told him, but they would keep his timetable in mind. Nearly six months had passed from that day until Undersecretary of State Elliot Richardson reluctantly met with the study team upon their return in June 1969, a meeting they characterized as "stiff, formal and unsympathetic." Richardson sent their report to the American mission in Saigon for comments, and he prepared a response from the State Department. The response contained no specific refutation of the many charges of the team report. It agreed "in general" that "shortcomings" existed in the detention and penal system in the south of Vietnam, but Richardson said the State Department gave greater "recognition to the efforts of the Vietnamese Government to acknowledge and correct these deficiencies," which did not "represent a deliberate policy . . . to suppress legitimate political opposition" (Richardson 1969, SCPC). The "shortcomings" of South Vietnam's prison system, the administration said, mostly reflected the problems of "modernization, severe wartime pressures," and the fact that the legal system in Saigon was "based more on the French Napoleonic Code than on American or English practice" (Comments, SCPC).

FOR's fact-finding trip to South Vietnam's prisons, and its subsequent report, spurred Washington to change its posture on American prisoners of war and to use the POWs as a resource to trump reports about the political prisoners in Saigon. The most damning information about Saigon prisons was the torture used to extract confessions. Washington set out to overwhelm that knowledge with allegations that American prisoners of war were routinely tortured too. After FOR's study team notified the White House of its upcoming trip to Saigon's prisons, and after they had told Undersecretary of State Richardson of their plans to investigate politics and prisons in South Vietnam, the Nixon administration responded by calling a press conference and alleging that Vietnamese torture of American prisoners in Hanoi was routine and systematic. Allegations of POW torture also functioned to portray Americans who made an issue of torture in the south, and of United States complicity in it, as naïve enemy sympathizers—they should have been devoting their energies to attacking the Vietnamese for torturing their fellow Americans.

Against this backdrop, Hanoi offered to release three more prisoners to antiwar activists who, in face to face meetings, continually pressed Vietnamese officials for information on, and contact with, prisoners of war. In early July 1969, David Dellinger received a telegram from the Vietnamese delegation in Paris requesting that he meet with them there to discuss arrangements for a possible prisoner release. Dellinger was then under indictment as one of the Chicago Seven and needed federal permission to leave the country. Hasty meetings with federal judge Julius Hoffman and the office of the attorney general secured the necessary permission, and Dellinger flew to Paris with assurances from army and navy officials that the prisoners would not be "snatched" as they had been under the Johnson administration, but would be allowed to return home directly to their families, and that they would not be used in any subsequent war activities against Vietnam.

On his return, Dellinger arranged for a four-person delegation to go immediately to Hanoi for the prisoner release. In the group were author Grace Paley, another defendant in the Chicago Seven case; Rennie Davis; Linda Evans of SDS; and James Johnson, one of the Fort Hood Three war resisters. Three filmmakers, Norm Fruchter, John Douglas, and Robert Kramer, accompanied them, filming the trip as they went.[6] The group arrived in Hanoi on 18 July, and while they spent the requisite week in Hanoi awaiting the next plane out, they took a trip south near the seventeenth parallel that divided Vietnam into two sections, to the town of Dong Hoi in the misnamed "demilitarized zone," which the Vietnamese called "the land of fire." The bombing there had been halted the previous November, but there was little left to view along this route. Even the Catholic churches were all destroyed. The French, at least, spared the churches, one of the survivors in Dong Hoi told Grace Paley nostalgically. "I don't know why it was customary for us pilots to dump all unexpended ordnance on Dong Hoi," Paley quoted an air force captain as saying to her later. "It wasn't an order. It was just customary" (Paley 1971, 31).

The road south took them through town after bombed-out town. "We were not military men," Paley wrote, "not even people who'd been

6. According to the *New York Times,* 15 Aug. 1971, when the group returned to New York, the State Department seized all their film, citing a statute prohibiting importing pictures "advocating or urging treason or insurrection against the United States, or forcible resistance to any law of the United States." The film was not yet developed when confiscated. Customs officials developed the film and then returned it, saying they had found nothing "subversive." Robert Kramer went back to Vietnam twenty years later, interviewing and filming many of the same people interviewed on the first trip. That film, *Starting Place,* was released in 1993 by Interama.

to wars, we weren't bored by the repetition; we didn't even get used to it." Bomb craters, thousands of them, rocked the landscape. The last standing bridge the group saw was the Ham Rong Bridge near Thanh Hoa. Sometimes there were pontoons to replace the bridges; more often the riverbed was raised with stones and they drove across it.

Even villagers far from the beaten path had been driven underground to live in tunnels. In the demilitarized zone, children had grown up attending underground schools and going to underground hospitals. The villages all had their Houses of Tradition, where they placed the artifacts of the war: deactivated pellet bombs and scraps of planes that had been shot down. One village near the sea had buried a pilot named "Dixon" and placed a white cross over his grave, "in case his mother should want to come see it after the war" (Paley 1969, 8). One survivor of repeated bombings recalled later that the roar of the B-52 explosions repeatedly tore eardrums, leaving many villagers deaf. A hit within half a kilometer would collapse the walls of bunkers, burying alive the people cowering inside. Into these blasted areas American pilots had tumbled out of burning planes and floated down into villages furious at the bombardment. "It is a peoples' war," Paley concluded.

> Some people do not like the word genocide and we will leave the word alone—still, in this kind of war, every person takes part and the next thing a logical military brain hooks into is the fact that every person is a military target or the mother of a military target and they live in the same house, and since all military targets must be destroyed, it follows that the whole people must be destroyed. (Paley 1969, 8)

Back in Hanoi, the American delegation met the three American prisoners scheduled for release: navy lieutenant Robert Frishman, air force captain Wesley Rumble, and Seaman Douglas Hegdahl. There was tension among the three POWs from the beginning because senior officers in the Hanoi prison camps had by then forbidden all POWs to accept early release. For some reason, those senior officers had taken a particular liking for a young seaman's apprentice, Douglas Hegdahl, who, at nineteen years of age, had fallen off his ship, the guided missile cruiser USS Canberra, into the Gulf of Tonkin on 6 April 1967. Vietnamese fishermen picked him up, and he quickly found himself in the POW prison in Hanoi, where he was immediately assigned a room with senior officer Richard Stratton. The senior officers took Hegdahl under their wing and, in the single exception to their rule, eventually told him to accept early release (Hubbell 1976, 378). When Hegdahl, Frishman, and Rumble left Hanoi, Hegdahl was the only one to do so with the blessing of the senior officers. Hegdahl recalled that when the three gathered at the Hanoi airport, he reminded the other two that they, unlike himself, were leaving the prison without authorization. Neither of the two military officers answered the apprentice, whose "reminder" put them both on notice that they were going home with reputations that, as far as some senior POW officers were concerned, required some burnishing.

The entire group left Hanoi on 5 August and flew to Vientiane where the American chargé d'affaires, Charles Rushing, boarded the aircraft and asked the officers to transfer to a waiting military plane for the journey home. The trio made it clear they wanted to fly home by commercial aircraft in order not to compromise further prisoner releases, and Rushing soon gave up trying to convince them to change their minds. This prisoner release offered the Pentagon the opportunity it sought to silence, or at least dampen, charges by activists of mistreatment of prisoners in South Vietnam and at the same time rally support for its presence in Vietnam during an era when it was plainly committed to withdrawing from there under pressure. These interests fit in with any opportunity that Frishman and Rumble sought to allay charges that they had "cooperated" in exchange for early release.

For a month the three were kept from the national media, and then the navy scheduled a news conference at Bethesda Naval Hospital, where Frishman launched an avalanche of charges against the Hanoi government for its treatment of prisoners of war. It was "an ordeal of horror," he said. He was not fed enough. Beatings were random and frequent, solitary confinement was the rule. The prisoners were routinely deprived of medical treatment. He reported only one specific instance of abuse against a specific prisoner: Richard Stratton, Hegdahl's roommate, Frishman said, had had his fingernails torn out. The charges made front page news around the nation, and Frishman was encouraged to travel the country and hold other news conferences.

Frishman stayed in the navy, quickly becoming its spokesman on POW issues and spending a good deal of time coordinating the activities of POW wives' groups. Journalists who followed Frishman's claims soon noticed that his statements were contradictory. At the Bethesda interview, for example, he had declared that almost all of the prisoners were consistently held in strict isolation, but in other settings he spoke of prison conditions as though everyone had at least one roommate. Others who had seen Richard Stratton recently said his fingernails were intact. Pressed on this point, Frishman eventually denied he had ever said anything about fingernails.[7] Douglas Hegdahl soon caught up with Frishman, speaking at Pentagon-organized press conferences about how he had been kept in solitary confinement for more than a year during his sixteen months in captivity and had lost sixty pounds from insufficient food. Before Hegdahl began speaking at these press conferences, however, he had told his hometown reporter a different story: that he had gone on a "hunger strike" in Hanoi after he lost his roommate and ate only part of his daily food in protest until he got another one. That was why he lost weight, he told the reporter. His food "would have been adequate" if he had eaten all of it.[8]

The White House used Frishman's and Hegdahl's tales at first to dampen criticism of its client-state's prison policies in South Vietnam, but the prisoner of war issue began to take on a life of its own. Washington encouraged assertions of cruel, pointless torture in Hanoi to dampen criticism of Saigon's own prisons, but those assertions later rendered credible, for Americans, eventual allegations that Hanoi was keeping American POWs behind after 1973 and subjecting them to ongoing torture. The POW issue, cultivated in Washington for political ends, eventually imprisoned subsequent administrations in a posture from which they had to struggle for extrication for years to come.

In the beginning, Washington's use of the POW issue for political purposes was an open secret. In fact, after the White House had learned of FOR's intended visit to Saigon to study prison conditions there and had prepared its own media briefing alleging torture in Hanoi POW pris-

7. The Defense Department allowed Frishman wider latitude in speaking out than any other released prisoner, even publishing a first-person account of his captivity in the December 1969 *Reader's Digest*. Seymour Hersh concluded that Frishman's accounts, taken together, were vague and contradictory and that evidence of systematic abuse of prisoners had always been missing. A government official told Hersh that Frishman "was under strain when he was released. He had been interviewed many times. He played ball the most and therefore was the most torn" (Hersh 1971; see also Van Dyke 1971).

8. The most comprehensive accounts of the American prisoner of war experience in North and South Vietnam are Gruner 1993 and Howes 1993. For some of the prisoners' own accounts see Alvarez and Pitch 1989; Brace 1988; Coffee 1990; Denton 1976; Dramesi 1975; Guarino 1990; Grant 1975; Ben and Anne Purcell 1992; Risner 1973; and Jim and Sybil Stockdale 1984. See also Hubbell 1976, which focuses exclusively on the stories of the hard-core officers and on the very early years of imprisonment.

ons, the Pentagon sent private explanatory letters on the briefing to wives and parents of captured and missing American pilots because it feared the charges would unnecessarily alarm them. The letters concluded with this remarkable sentence: "We are certain that you will not become unduly concerned over the briefing if you keep in mind the purpose for which it was tailored." After FOR's study team report, Pentagon officials began to tell family members of POWs how to talk to the press. Women married to POWs were told to stress Vietnamese "violations" of the Geneva conventions and the impact of their husbands' imprisonment on their own private lives. They should not "discuss the situation in terms of national policy or politics as relates to our involvement in Southeast Asia. . . . Policy and politics are not germane to the disregard of the Geneva convention by the enemy." In an atmosphere inflamed by White House duplicity, family members began making unfounded but widely publicized claims that prisoners routinely had their fingernails pulled out, their bones broken and rebroken; "in some places they just dig holes in the ground and drop them in. They throw food down to them, and let them live there in their own waste" (Hersh 1971).

The prisoners in Vietnam suffering the greatest systematic mistreatment remained those over whom the American government had some control: the captives in South Vietnam. The FOR study team was the first American citizen group to investigate systematically the treatment of prisoners in South Vietnam. They interviewed numerous prisoners past and present, prison administrators, and American officials. The testimony of prisoners was corroborated by Vietnamese officials themselves and, in bits and pieces at first, by American GIs involved in, or witnesses to, torture.[9] When the Nixon administration encouraged American POWs returning from Vietnam to fabricate and exaggerate their own stories of mistreatment, it did so with the knowledge that systematic torture in Vietnam came from its client-state's prison apparatus and that American citizens were initiating their own investigations of conditions there.

The myth of the systematic torture of American pilots in Hanoi fed into traditional myths of American nationhood. It evoked the myth of savage American Indians slaughtering peaceful settlers and inverted the increasingly troublesome real scenes coming out of Vietnam: General

9. Memoirs of the war written by American officers will almost casually describe torture techniques they used on Vietnamese during the war. See, for example, DeForest and Chanoff 1990, 55; Anderson 1982; and *New Republic,* 19 Dec. 1970.

Nguyen Ngoc Loan shooting a prisoner at point-blank range on the streets of Saigon; American GIs rounding up terrified villagers, raping them, and burning their homes. Substituting images of tortured American pilots made their status, captured while on expensive bombing missions over the towns and villages of Vietnam, equivalent to that of relatively ill-equipped Vietnamese troops fighting on their own soil against an enormously weapon-wealthy nation, and to that of the villagers who aided them. It created additional American contempt and hatred for Vietnam at a time when the war was unpopular and "Vietnamization" was fated to become a substitute for victory. The emotive issue of POW torture required no knowledge of the war, its context, or its course. The physical distance between the pilots and their civilian targets washed their killing clean. Before Grace Paley went to Hanoi, she received a call from the wife of a pilot who had been missing for more than two years. There had been no word from him during that time. She asked Paley to try to find out if he was in Hanoi. When she returned from Hanoi and her journey through the blasted countryside, Paley called the woman to tell her that none of the American prisoners she talked to, or the Vietnamese, knew anything of her husband. The distraught woman asked Paley why the Vietnamese insisted on keeping the pilots.

> I explained that they were considered war criminals who had come 10,000 miles to attack a tiny, barely armed country in an undeclared and brutal war. She said, "Well, they're airmen. They're American officers." I told her about Nien Trach, Dong Hoi, Vinh Linh, the dark tunnels, the people seared by napalm, shattered by pellets, the miles of craters, the bloody mountains. She said, "Oh, Mrs. Paley, villages and people! My husband wouldn't do that." (Paley 1971, 33)

The tale of the lives lived by American prisoners of war in Hanoi is not difficult to unravel, though no single POW memoir offers much in the way of an overview. By comparing different accounts with each other and with interviews during the POW homecoming in early 1973, a clearer image emerges. The tenor of the POW experience that the American public heard was set early by some of the first pilots who were shot down over North Vietnam and who carried with them a zealous adherence to the military Code of Conduct, a list of rules purporting to define rules for organizing one's life as a captured soldier. The Code was a document calling on soldiers to carry the war into the prison camps: their first duty was never to surrender of their own free will, never to accept early release, continually to resist and always endeavor to escape, answer no questions save for name, rank, serial number, and date of birth, refuse all cooperation with camp officials, organize all prisoners in a strictly regimented military chain of command, and follow only those orders given by senior POW officials. The Code was not official military policy and its stipulations carried no military penalties. Its provisions were extreme, and most POWs found themselves in violation of the first one at the outset—refusing to surrender when shot down and surrounded was suicidal, as were efforts to escape. Most prisoners ignored the Code, adhering only to stipulations against divulging military intelligence.[10]

Some of the first officers shot down over North Vietnam, or the hard-core POWs, as they came to be known, were, in the first years, bent on carrying out the Code to its utmost, devising forms of resistance that appeared, at times, more juvenile than principled. Motivated by the allegations of brainwashing leveled against American POWs in Korea, and determined never to be so labeled, they carried the war with them into the camps, even "provoking" torture, as they put it, if need be. They refused to get up when the camp gong sounded in the morning, they refused to make their beds, they refused to bow in greeting the guards or they offered exaggerated bows with contemptuous smiles, they refused to use the toilets in the prescribed way, throwing food into them to clog the sewer lines, they banged on doors or buckets to create noise, they looked for ways of breaking any camp rules and sabotaging any equipment they could. "We learned to reverse everything the guards said," one of the hard-core officers told a reporter later; they kept their spirits up by "keeping the Vietnamese infuriated." Another wrote with some satisfaction later, "We were all troublemakers, hard core, diehard . . . constant irritation . . . incited others to resistance." Jeremiah Denton, one of the best-known prisoners, told a reporter in 1973 that "we forced them [the guards] to be brutal to us." Any punishments that followed were considered, by these hard-core prisoners, to be torture.[11]

10. For the view of the Code of Conduct to which the hard-core officers adhered, see Coffee 1990, 80.

11. After their release, the hard-core prisoners themselves used the term "juvenile" to characterize their resistance. Prisoners, like everyone else in Hanoi, were also not supposed to put toilet paper into the toilet, but into a separate container because toilet paper clogged the small sewer pipes. It was then, and still is, a not-uncommon procedure in urban areas in many third-world countries. Some of the prisoners, for example took satisfaction in deliberately stuffing toilet paper into the toilets anyway, infuriating many guards who had to clean

Some of the pilots carried their will to remain at war in the prison camps to other extremes, refusing to write letters home or to accept medical treatment. As a matter of principle, James Stockdale refused to let a Vietnamese doctor operate on wounds on his leg from ejection injuries. Sam Johnson also refused treatment for ejection injuries, but camp officials took the resistant pilot to the hospital anyway and treated him, a procedure that he admitted helped his fractured vertebrae. Eventually most of the hard-core prisoners did accept medical treatment. Some of them admitted that it saved them. Sam Johnson noted that when one deeply depressed POW, Ron Storz, slashed his wrists with a razor, a camp guard gave Storz an emergency transfusion directly from his own arm (Johnson and Winebrenner 1992, 183).

The hard-core pilots hailed any success at prison sabotage as a victory over the Vietnamese. One of them recounted with satisfaction watching another prisoner, Douglas Hegdahl (the prisoner who was released in 1969), as he swept the street in front of the prison, unscrew the gas cap of a truck parked nearby and pour dirt into the fuel tank while no one else was watching (Hubbell 1976, 185). When some of the hard-core prisoners who had been isolated because of their behavior were allowed to exercise in the main prison yard again with the majority of POWS, they immediately and clandestinely disconnected all the electricity to the main prison, even though that action inconvenienced their fellow prisoners most (Johnson and Winebrenner 1992, 194). Even James Stockdale (1984, 447), whose writings convey the impression that torture was the rule for all prisoners, estimated that 10 percent of the POWs received more than 90 percent of the "punishment."

The first pilots to be shot down were certainly expecting harsh treatment. Their American military training included a POW "course," which provided, in the words of one trainee, "a taste of what to expect in a POW camp, especially a camp run by Asian communists" (Watson 1993, 100). The trainees in the United States Navy–run mock POW camp were "captured" by older American officers, who subjected them to pointless beatings, constant harangues, and fed them watery potato soup—two meals every three days. Their "guards" constantly asked them innocuous questions about their blood type, religion, or other things, which they were not supposed to answer; they were supposed to give only their

---

up the resulting mess (Coffee 1990, 86; Johnson and Winebrenner 1992, 161; *NYT* 30 Apr. 1973).

name, rank, and serial number. If they answered the innocuous questions, more beatings followed. They were strung up in parachute harnesses and swung about until they threw up, they were put into wooden boxes too small for them to stretch out in and left there in utter darkness for hours, they were put into two oil drums welded together and filled with water. The chief lesson of that course, graduate James Watson concluded, was to "save the last grenade for yourself" (1993, 100).

Saving "the last grenade" was not necessary, because the Pentagon supplied pilots flying over North Vietnam with instruments of suicide in the event they were shot down. It was not something new to this war. Paul Tibbets, who bombed Hiroshima in 1945, told the *Columbus Dispatch*, 3 July 1995, that he carried cyanide capsules with him for all the pilots under his command. Francis Gary Powers, who was shot down over the Soviet Union in 1960, carried a poison needle with him down to Soviet soil, and he remarked bitterly after his release that many Americans expected him to commit suicide rather than embarrass his government (Powers 1970, 53, 69). The Pentagon refused to comment on suicide instruments provided its officers, but Americans who toured village museums in Vietnam saw captured American air force kits containing cyanide capsules for pilots to use at their discretion if they faced capture (Myerson, 149). A British WILPF delegate told *Pax et Libertas* (July 1965) that she met an American POW in Thanh Hoa province in 1965 along with the villager who had prevented the pilot from swallowing his capsule. The suicide equipment could account for some Americans who appeared to have survived their initial shootdowns but were never heard from again. At any rate, the mock POW camps, along with the instruments of poison handed out, made American POWs fear the very worst in a real prison camp in Vietnam.

Some officers had additional reasons to expect brutality. James Stockdale was a squadron commander on the *USS Ticonderoga* in the Gulf of Tonkin in 1964, and he knew that Vietnamese boats had not attacked U.S. destroyers in the Gulf as President Johnson claimed. Stockdale was convinced that if Americans knew the truth behind the subsequent Gulf of Tonkin resolution, they would call the war itself into question, and he was determined not to allow his information to become public. Stockdale believed that Vietnamese officials would try to torture the truth about the Gulf of Tonkin out of him. The Vietnamese either did not know of Stockdale's former position or did not care. He said that they never expressed the slightest interest in his side of the Gulf of Tonkin story, but his fears kept him needlessly on guard during his entire captivity (Stockdale 1984, 162, 182–84).

Some of the American POWs were tortured. One of the first was Rodney Knutson, who shot and killed an unarmed villager at point-blank range while trying to shoot his own way out of captivity in 1965. After his release, he described his punishment for this as torture. Some of the other hard-core POWs were, on occasion, harshly punished for infractions large and small for two years until 1967, when the prison system became more centralized. At that point, prison officials decided to handle the refractory prisoners by separating those few senior officers from all the others and isolating them together in another area. After that their infractions were solitary and largely ignored (Hubbell 1976, 91, 430).[12]

Most of the other pilots never tried to bring Washington's war into the Hanoi prison camps and quickly settled into a dreary life as prisoners of war. Their greatest fears, some of them recalled later, came when they were shot down into the villages they had bombed. There, at the hands of the angry villagers, they were often afraid for their lives. Vietnamese authorities not infrequently saved them from death in the villages and took them on a trek to the prison system in Hanoi, where they lived, usually two or three to a cell, in a prison compound. For many of them, especially in the first years, life was filled with loneliness, homesickness, boredom, and sometimes, deep depression.

Still, they managed to carve out some routines and organize in ways that sustained them. There were daily periods for outdoor exercise, even volleyball and basketball, of which they made maximum use. Because there were cigarettes for those who smoked, most of them took up smoking to pass the time. As time went on and they succeeded at developing some measure of trust with camp officials, they gained greater freedom to gather in large groups, work in and around prison compounds, and hold religious services and classes for each other. They formed a Toastmasters International Club, and they built a bread oven and fish pond in one compound and worked at landscaping there. Their meals were adequate, if unvaried: endless rice, a glass of milk, fresh fruit, sometimes, and bread with most meals.

12. According to their own interviews with American journalists in 1973, when they were all released, the great majority of POWs were never tortured, and even for the hard-core group, what torture they did face largely ended in 1967 (*NYT* 20, 23, 28 Feb., 1 May, and 29 Dec. 1973).

They had books: Shakespeare, Dickens, Arthur Schlesinger, Jr., Townsend Hoopes, and Mikhail Sholokhov, among many others. They could read conventional Western literature, but the prison library offered the pilots other books that gave them their first exposure to scholarly studies of Vietnam. Those books were written almost entirely by Americans: George McTurnan Kahin's *The United States in Vietnam,* books by American historian and Vietnam critic Howard Zinn, The American Friends Service Committee's booklet on Vietnam. Eventually, even the *Pentagon Papers* made its way to the prison library in Hanoi. Some of the pilots told American visitors and journalists that these books, for the first time, made them think about Vietnam as a country in and of itself. "Flying is exciting," one of them said after his release, "especially when you're being shot at. There's a great sense of power in flying a jet; there's something almost sexual about it. You don't think about the people you're fighting, you think about the target. Otherwise you don't think about much else except your family, flight pay, and promotion. Only when you're shot down do you ask, 'what the hell was I doing up there?'" (Coffin 1972, 4).

In 1969, the minority hard-core POWs were returned to camp life with the other pilots, where, as senior officers, they again tried to impose the Code of Conduct on the others, adding the stipulation that no prisoner should learn the Vietnamese language or even use Vietnamese words when talking to camp guards. Many of the other pilots resented these hard-core officers, seeing their constant badgering and baiting of the Vietnamese camp officials, as well as their escape plots, as pointless and dangerous. Trying to escape from a heavily guarded prison in Hanoi, for example, appeared to be foolish, particularly because the escape would only be into the city itself and then the Vietnamese countryside. Many of the pilots, who had ejected into rural areas, considered the Vietnamese peasants, who were angry at the bombing, far more dangerous than their prison guards. Some of them accordingly threatened to tell camp officials about any escape plan hatched by the hard-core officers (Johnson and Winebrenner 1992, 249).

The return of the hard-core officers to the camps marked a period of particularly high tension among the pilots. Fistfights broke out occasionally, and one fight culminated in one pilot pulling a knife on another. Vietnamese officials complained often to Americans about the prisoners' inability to get along with one another. One American officer, the *New York Times* reported on 23 February 1973, said that when the hard-core officers were allowed to rejoin the others in 1969, he suffered "much more mental anguish from Americans than from North Vietnamese." These strains and other personality conflicts were severe enough that some pilots, including Everett Alvarez, asked, and were permitted, to be isolated from their compatriots within the camps (Alvarez and Pitch 1989). The hard-core officers generally continued to share cells, and they bitterly denounced others who rejected their confrontational stance. Most of them, however, mellowed as time went on and evidence accumulated that the war was perhaps not worth enormous and self-inflicted sacrifices. Even the hard-core prisoners conceded that, by early 1971, as many as half of the officers were openly disillusioned about the war (Hubbell 1976, 549).

This was not the POW picture that emerged after the pilots returned in 1973, however. The "official" POW story developed within the camps among the hard-core officers. In March 1971, anticipating a release, senior officer Jeremiah Denton developed an account of the POW experience, an account entirely informed by the experience of the minority hard-core officers. This version was given out in the camps as the one that would be presented to the public when the POWs came home. This version depicted the pilots as heroes, embattled constantly by mindless torturing Vietnamese. All the pilots were supposed to learn this story and make it their own (Guarino 1990, 279). When the pilots returned in early 1973, the Pentagon arranged press conferences across the country, spotlighting those few who had bitterly resisted everything in the early years and had been occasionally tortured. It was their story that drowned out all the others in the news media, so that public memory after the war was shaped by the accounts of these few hard-core officers who had been tortured at times between 1965 and 1968, and who stretched their stories, leaving out their own deliberate prison provocations, to cover the entire POW experience. The torture stories were presented without context and were offered as evidence of a cruel Vietnamese character that thrived on torture for its own sake. Any injury a POW had suffered was attributed not to ejection injuries, which accounted for almost all of them, but to torture. These stories also served as proof of American endurance and suffering during a war that, by then, had little else going for it. Jeremiah Denton's official story of torture came full circle; because it served to offer stark proof of Vietnamese cruelty and propensity to torture, POWs who had not been tortured now had to answer as to why they had not been. Not being tortured could imply, after the war was over, that one had functioned as a turncoat, a quisling, an eager collaborator.

The official story purveyed at the POW homecoming was reinforced over the coming years by the POW memoirs. By 1973, when the POWs came home, reputable American publishers had stopped publishing works that were virulently racist. They made an exception for POW memoirs. Written almost entirely by the minority of hard-core officers, who carried their hatreds home with them, these memoirs are filled with invective against all things Vietnamese. They despised the culture, they hated the food, they hated the language, they hated the people. The POW memoirs are replete with racist diatribes at all Vietnamese camp officials, whom they gleefully accorded names like Anus, Bastard, Piss Ant, Dipshit. The Vietnamese people were all slopes, dinks, and gooks. Returned POWs like James Stockdale, who became Ross Perot's running mate in 1992, Jeremiah Denton, who was later elected senator from Georgia, Gerald Coffee, and Sam Johnson, among others, took turns, in the twenty years following their release, publishing books that regularly referred to any and all Vietnamese by these terms. Nothing Vietnamese escaped their hatred— even the Vietnamese language was excoriated as the "primitive" language of people who "weren't very sophisticated and will believe almost anything" (Coffee 1990, 138). The memoirs make clear that these officers despised the Vietnamese before they were prisoners of war, and that they were furious when other POWs did not share their hatred. Some of the other POW returnees, in fact, told a *New York Times* reporter, on 30 April 1973, that they believed that the intense hatred those hard-core officers felt toward the "gooks" caused them to exaggerate their torture.[13]

The hard-core POWs' hostility toward Vietnamese life and culture exceeded that of the larger American culture in quantity, but not in kind. Most Americans believed, as a matter of course, that Vietnamese, and especially "communist," society was barely worth considering. For example, despite the fact that Americans and the media knew practically nothing about Vietnam, *Time* magazine, on 14 April 1967, ridiculed what it called "Hanoi's endemic ignorance of Western idiom, intellect, and ideology." In his study of the media and the war, historian Daniel Hallin noted that

13. James Stockdale later revised his memoirs, and the revision is milder in excoriating all things Vietnamese and those POWs who did not fall in line with himself and other hard-core officers.

never did I hear a journalist comment on the hostility that many American soldiers felt toward all Vietnamese, whichever side they were on,
though one would occasionally hear a soldier use the term *gook* in an interview (this hostility is usually a prominent theme in veterans' recollections of the war). It was sensitive enough to show American troops
burning huts, but the issue of racism was apparently too sensitive to
touch. (1989, 135)

However much venom toward the Vietnamese is found in the POW
memoirs, there is little reflection on any larger cause that brought these
officers to Vietnam. Whether it was anticommunism that sustained those
who wrote the memoirs, or commitment to democracy, or loyalty to their
fellow officers, or defense of capitalism or religion, it is seldom hinted at.
The authors are more likely to break off the narrative to reminisce about
the better days before capture, when they could have prostituted sex
cheaply with Vietnamese women, than to ruminate on any ideology or
larger cause that carried them and their country to Vietnam.[14]

Without a cause to sustain resistance, some of the men seemed to fall
back on an attachment to hatred itself along with a determination to reg-
iment camp life according to their own vision, regardless of its effect on
the other prisoners. Trained to value competitiveness and strict, even
blind, obedience to military rank, the senior pilots who were captured
early in the war set out to mold the prisoner camps into arenas that
demonstrated their ability to suffer and survive—something no ground
soldier in Vietnam ever felt constrained to prove—for until they were shot
down, the war meant no physical engagement for the pilots. In the prison
camps, without their planes, their only weapons were, as one hard-core
officer later put it, "our bodies and our pain," and even the pain could

14. Accounts by American men, both civilian and military, of their life in Vietnam during the war often include blatant and celebratory recitations of their sexual experiences with
prostitutes in Vietnam, and in "R and R" locations in Southeast Asia. In addition to POW
memoirs, see, for example, Charles Anderson (1982) for bemused accounts of gang rape
and endemic sexual harassment of Vietnamese civilian hirees on military bases. Senior officer
David Hackworth (1989) boasted about taking his men en masse to brothels and even, at
one point, insisting to the brothel manager that his men get "double duty" with the employees in return for his unsolicited delivery of a radio to the brothel manager. American
civilian men often seemed to take the right to sex with Asian women just as casually. See, for
example, John A. Parrish's graphic account of his vacation in Thailand (1972), when he was
working as a doctor in South Vietnam. Some American military officers provided the capital
for prostitution enterprises that became lucrative investments for the investors.

enter the zone of competition. Of his own prison experience with torture, Sam Johnson wrote that, as an incentive to provoke it, "the passion of patriotism pales next to the fervor of our competitive ego-driven natures" (Johnson and Winebrenner 1992, 145).

The obstreperousness of the hard-core POWs posed an immediate problem of prison security for Vietnamese officials in Hanoi, but they appeared more concerned about convincing their own public that the pilots should not be put on trial or executed for their bombing attacks. Outrage at the American bombing was the rule among Vietnamese citizens, who viewed the pilots as international bandits. To justify keeping them alive, Vietnamese officials pressed the pilots in captivity for letters or statements in which the pilots would acknowledge that bombing Vietnam was wrong. Many of the pilots complied, writing innocuous statements that expressed their regret at the bombing damage and their hope for an early end to the war. Vietnamese officials used these letters for domestic consumption, allowing egregious syntactical or grammatical errors that some pilots deliberately made, even though they had English translators readily available to clean up the scripts. They read the pilots' statements on Vietnam's radio broadcasts and occasionally translated and printed them in Vietnamese papers. Officials seemed to hope that the public would accept these statements as proof that the pilots were at least somewhat penitent and that the government was acting reasonably in keeping them alive. Hanoi's most concerted effort to convince the public that the pilots were repentant came early in the war, when they forced the pilots into a public march through the streets of Hanoi, telling them insistently to bow to the people crowded on the sidewalks. The image of pilots ostensibly showing public remorse for their bombing seemed to be an effort to dampen popular demands for executing the pilots.

Disdain for the pilots and growing impatience with them permeated Vietnamese society. As the war went on, the relentless bombing embittered some Vietnamese officials, who had developed real friendships with activists and had earlier helped them take letters and packages to the POWs. Do Xuan Oanh, the translator who had once gone to considerable efforts to set up meetings between pilots and activists when the Vietnamese military was most resistant, responded bitterly when some activists, newly arrived in Hanoi, charged that Douglas Hegdahl, one of the prisoners with whom they met, appeared alarmingly eager to please his captors. The Americans told Oanh that they thought it was the result of being browbeaten by the prison guards. What the activists did not know at the time was that Hegdahl, the prisoner who appeared so obsequious to his guards when he met with the activists, was the especial favorite of the hard-core officers, who loathed the activists and wanted to discredit them by any means. According to Hegdahl's later interview with John Hubbell (1976, 202, 354), they had told him to meet with the activists and pretend that he was browbeaten. Hegdahl already had a reputation among the POWs for "conning" the Vietnamese into believing that he was "stupid." Oanh seemed to know this at the time, and he let the activists know that he was less tolerant of arranging these meetings than he had once been. "I can't stand these meetings and sitting and looking at the pilots," he told them, "a month ago, my brother-in-law was killed, five days after his marriage to my sister. I received a card from my sister announcing the marriage, and her husband was already dead. I can't stand looking at these pilots" (Hayden 1988, 222).

As the war ground on and Washington seized the issue of POW torture to dampen criticism of the war itself, American activists continued to travel to Saigon and Hanoi, developing, in the south, friendships with intellectuals, Buddhists, and students in hopes of encouraging a third force that could replace the Saigon regime and seek reconciliation with North Vietnam. In the north, activists continued to urge the government there to release prisoners early. Despite these releases, the Pentagon did little to encourage more of them. On the contrary, it encouraged those few who were released to make charges that could only discourage further releases. Still, activists continued to urge Hanoi to release prisoners and, from their contacts with those prisoners, they began to look for ways to ameliorate the conditions of imprisonment both for the prisoners themselves and for their families.

The *Phoenix* being loaded with medical supplies in Hiroshima, Japan. *Courtesy of Ivan Massar.*

Bob Eaton, Horace Champney, Elizabeth Boardman, and Ivan Massar in a textile mill in Hanoi. Most of the machinery in the mill had been moved to safer rural areas. *Courtesy of Ivan Massar.*

Phil Drath, the mayor of Hoang Liet, and Elizabeth Boardman in a partially rebuilt Buddhist shrine damaged by American bombs. *Courtesy of Ivan Massar.*

A hospital in Hanoi where *Phoenix* crew members saw a baby wounded *in utero* by American shrapnel. Horace Champney, Bob Eaton, Elizabeth Boardman, and Phil Drath seated in a row with Vietnamese doctors across the table. *Courtesy of Ivan Massar.*

Louis Schneider, executive secretary of the AFSC, presents a medical kit for use by paramedics in village health work to a representative of the Provisional Revolutionary Government. *Courtesy of the American Friends Service Committee.*

John Sullivan and Dr. George Perera standing with Hanoi doctors outside a bombed-out hospital. *Courtesy of the American Friends Service
Committee.*

Louis Schneider presents a diesel engine, for pumping water, and medical kits to Vietnamese representatives. *Courtesy of the American
Friends Service Committee.*

6

Carrying the Mail

In late 1969, Women Strike for Peace turned citizen travel to North Vietnam into a conduit for personal mail between American prisoners of war and their families in the United States. Citizen travel to North Vietnam had helped draw attention to the view from below the bombs, and it had directly challenged, and changed, some of the restrictions on travel that the government had placed on all Americans. Traveling activists had won the right to travel even to the heartland of "the enemy." They had initiated and nurtured valuable ties of friendship and understanding with Vietnamese citizens and officials. These ties formed an important positive image of Americans for the Vietnamese who repelled American military force in their country. Travelers who developed the most enduring ties to Vietnamese tended to be those with a strongly pragmatic bent. They sought to craft workable solutions to the problems that the war generated, whether it was dealing with the issue of travel itself, creating an alternative news source on Vietnam, organizing humanitarian aid for Vietnam, or investigating the nature and extent of their own government's complicity in the prison system there. In 1969, they turned their attention to a problem that Washington was beginning to use to generate additional animosity toward Vietnam: poor mail service to and from American prisoners of war in Vietnam.

Travelers to Hanoi could not escape awareness of the difficulty that prisoners and their families had in sending mail to each other. Family members in the United States pressed on them bundles of letters to deliver to POWs in Hanoi and prisoners there asked them to carry mail home with them. Sending mail from the United States to POWs was possible, but it was slow and uncertain and, by the time travelers had won the legal right to travel there, had become mired in the politics of the war. The first pilots shot down over North Vietnam had sent and received letters from home, but the Defense Department used this family mail as a funnel for sending intelligence items to the pilots. In family packages for POWs, the Pentagon placed bars of hollowed-out Ivory soap with secret writing kits inside, Colgate toothpaste tubes with miniature parts for radio transmitters and receivers, and candy with special instructions inside. The Department of Defense prepared inscribed messages inside gum wrappers asking for information on the camps. Prison officials in Hanoi quickly discovered some of these items and laid them out in museums of war for all to see. At the time, the Pentagon denied it had anything to do with these items. Reports from Americans who had seen these items in the museums were "too ridiculous to dignify with a reply," one Pentagon official told the *New York Times* on 28 September 1972. POW memoirs later described these contraband items in detail, and Sybil Stockdale (1984) later explained how she had worked with the Pentagon to get them into the prison system. The goal, Hanoi officials believed, was to identify the POW camps so that the rest of Hanoi could be bombed with impunity.

Vietnamese officials then directed that U.S. mail to the prisoners be routed through the Vietnamese embassy in Moscow. There the mail was inspected for contraband and sent on to Hanoi in sealed containers. There was no official mail route between the United States and North Vietnam, nor was there an international postal regulation in place to divert mail automatically between the United States and North Vietnam via Moscow. The United States had to create a special routing, which the State Department agreed to do for packages, but refused to create a special routing for letters. Hanoi responded to the agreement on packages by allowing each prisoner to receive one six-pound package every two months, and an additional eleven-pound package at Christmas. Families sent clothing, games, reading glasses, pecan rolls, vitamins, dehydrated foods, air mattresses, and medicines (*APW* 1971, 232).

Getting letters to their family members in Hanoi continued to be a problem for families at home. The Pentagon, having refused to authorize a special routing for letters via Moscow, advised families either to send their mail to the Pentagon for transmitting or to send it to "Camp of Detention, Care of Hanoi Post Office," despite the fact that there was no international routing for this address either. Much of the prisoner mail that was addressed directly to the Hanoi post office never made it to Vietnam.

Further, even though most activists kept the Defense Department informed of upcoming visits to Hanoi, the Pentagon did not pass along this information to families as an alternative mail source. In fact, the army and the navy, competitors always, did not even inform each other of upcoming mail deliveries (Elder 1969b, AFSC).

Prisoners' letters sent from Hanoi through the official channel sometimes did not get to family members, either. When, in 1971, the National Liberation Front announced that it was releasing twenty-three-year-old John Sexton, Jr., the Pentagon hastily released a letter that the prisoner had written to his family from a prison camp more than two years earlier. Sexton's father was angry. "We thought he was probably dead for those two years and here they had the letter all along," he said. Pressed for an explanation from Sexton's family, Pentagon officials told the *New York Times* on 12 October that they had been examining the letter to see if it really was from John Sexton, Jr., and if it had a propaganda content. By the end of 1968, only about one hundred letters from prisoners of war had reached their families, those on an irregular basis (*APW* 1971, 231). Hand-carried mail was much surer and faster than channels clogged with propaganda wars, and many families seized on every publicized activist visit to Hanoi to send letters with them.

Nor did officials in Hanoi view mail service to and from the captured American pilots as a priority worth expending much energy on. The colonial partition of Vietnam had halted mail between the north and the south there, and Vietnamese in Hanoi could see no reason to go out of their way to ensure that American pilots had steady mail from home, when colonialism and the war had cut off mail within their own country. One Vietnamese soldier later told Martha Hess "you see, we had no communication with the South. A soldier would take a letter from his knapsack and carry it from Hanoi to Saigon on foot. This would take from three months to a year. I once received a letter from my wife after two years, and because it had been through rivers and rain and hot weather, I couldn't read it, the words were gone. I could only kiss her letter, I couldn't read it. The war was like that" (Hess 1993, 76).

Vietnamese officials and citizens generally viewed the pilots as war criminals with no claim to the Geneva Conventions on prisoners of war.[1]

---

1. North Vietnam signed the Geneva Convention on prisoners of war in 1957 with the explicit reservation that the convention could not apply to war criminals. The United States signed the convention without such a reservation, but testimony from its military forces told

"What would you do to our pilots if we bombed Pittsburgh?" one of them asked an American visitor. They had lost family members and acquaintances directly to the bombing, and to them, the captured pilots often appeared privileged and arrogant. This was nowhere more true than in the areas directly under the bombs. Pilots continued to say that their closest brushes with death came at the hands of the people in the villages into which they parachuted. Vietnamese popular culture drew out the theme of the barbaric American bombers who took delight in killing. Poet Che Lan Vien captured one Vietnamese sense of the pilots in their midst in a translated poem entitled "The Enemy and Us," published in the *Vietnam Courier* in December 1972:

> Be vigilant! Those are killers.
> They don't care about introspection, still-lifes, structuralism,
> colours and sounds:
> They kill.
> They don't care about Chuang-tzu, Kafka, the unconscious and the
> subconscious, Breton and surrealism, Hamlet and "to be or not to be,"
> they just don't care;
> They kill.
> They sweep on us as the twitter of birds greets the coming of dawn
> Or during starlit and love-laden nights
> Or when the sky is at its bluest
> When gardens are fragrant with the scent of flowers
> And the fruit sweet like human lips.

American travelers who visited villages in North Vietnam sometimes encountered this hostility toward all things American. When poet Denise Levertov was touring the bombed dikes along the Red River delta one day, an old woman asked her guide who were the women "from the distant place with whom you are traveling." When the guide, Madame Be of the Vietnamese Union of Women, replied that they were visitors from America, her interlocutor recoiled. "Americans! Yankees!" the horrified woman exclaimed, shifting the weight of the carrying pole balanced on her shoulders. "Why do you want to bring such evil people here?" (Levertov 1973, 18).

Despite opposition from Washington and a decided lack of enthusi-

---

of routine and unpunished killing of the prisoners of war that it held (Vietnam Veterans 1972; Duncan 1966; DeForest 1990; *In the Name of America* 1968).

asm from Hanoi officials, members of Women Strike for Peace decided, in 1969, to set up a clearinghouse for prisoner mail deliveries, using the steady stream of activists to North Vietnam as carriers. Of all the groups who went to Hanoi, WSP was the best suited to play such a role. Women Strike for Peace had, by 1969, spent years cultivating relationships of trust with Vietnamese officials, especially with the Women's Union. Members had met at length with Vietnamese officials in Hanoi, or in international settings, eight times. They had organized the Americans Want to Know fact-finding trip to Cambodia, and many of them had been to Hanoi on other group trips. The matter of POW mail could now be discussed by friends, rather than by officials staking out stark strategic positions. Offering a clearinghouse for mail between American families and captured airmen in Hanoi was a natural extension of the bridge that WSP had sought for years to build between American and Vietnamese societies. It was also intended as a bridge for Americans themselves, connecting the antiwar movement, the wider American society, and families of POWs.

At a meeting in Hanoi in December 1969, a WSP group made up of Cora Weiss, Ethel Taylor, and Madeline Duckles proposed to Vietnamese officials that Women Strike for Peace form a special committee to transmit prisoner mail. The idea had grown out of discussions they had with Vietnamese women officials at an international meeting in Canada the previous July (Taylor 1974, SCPC). Their immediate goals were twofold: to provide a reliable clearing house for timely delivery of prisoner mail, and to compile a list of all Americans held in Vietnamese prison camps. Women Strike for Peace already had a partial list of POWS, based on letters the group had already carried out of Hanoi and on contact with the many prisoners' families who turned to the organization for help in getting mail to and from Hanoi. The Vietnamese officials in Hanoi readily agreed. The clearinghouse would merely make formal the informal transmission of mail that had begun to evolve as a practical solution to a political deadlock between Hanoi and Washington, and it would require little additional effort from Hanoi. The Vietnamese told the WSP delegation that they could put together a provisional list in a few days, and they promised to update it in the near future (*APW* 1971).

Women Strike for Peace returned to New York with the provisional list of POWs, and 138 letters from 132 prisoners in Hanoi. It was a Christmas she would never forget, Taylor said. As soon as she got home to Philadelphia, "my husband and I sat on the phone and called families from all over the country, telling them that their son, husband, or father was alive and I was mailing them a letter from him." For at least 36 of the families, it was the first time they had heard anything from their missing family members. Hanoi officials continued to leave open the channel of mail through the Vietnamese embassy in Moscow.

Mail between the American POWs and their families ballooned after this initiative. Women Strike for Peace called their newly formed group the Committee of Liaison With Families of Servicemen Detained in North Vietnam, a lengthy name that usually became simply, the Committee of Liaison. By 1970, American activists averaged one trip a month to Hanoi, and the Committee of Liaison began informing families with members in the prison camps of each upcoming visit. Letters to POWs were hand-carried to Hanoi, and returning groups brought out packets of letters with them. They were soon transmitting hundreds of letters monthly, and the committee began keeping careful record of the names that passed through their hands, trying to compile a complete listing of the American servicemen held in North Vietnam. They passed on specific inquiries from families with members listed as missing to both Vietnamese officials and to the American POWs whom they visited in the camps.

The committee's efforts to compile a listing of Americans in the prisons in North Vietnam yielded steady rewards. In April 1970, officials in Hanoi turned over to the committee an official list of 335 Americans they held. They also released a list of five pilots who were found dead or who had died after capture. The committee continued to pass on specific inquiries from families and to press prison authorities in Hanoi for more information. They made all the information they received, including copies of the POW lists, immediately available to the State Department. Their efforts to coordinate information about American POWs soon led to what H. Bruce Franklin called "the battle of the lists" (1992, 67), and this battle helped set the foundation for the subsequent myth that Vietnam continued to hold Americans prisoners long after 1973.

Until the Committee of Liaison set out to compile a list, the State Department drew a distinction between the numbers of Americans who were missing over the skies of North Vietnam and those it believed were prisoners there. On 11 December 1969, for example, just before the Committee of Liaison produced its provisional list, the State Department reported that 1,361 Americans were missing in all of Southeast Asia, of which 419, it said, were confirmed as POWs. The figure was deduced by testimony from observers to shootdowns when possible, and included those POWs believed held in Laos and Cambodia. Members of a squadron could observe a plane's downing and arrive at a fairly accurate reading of the crew's chances, based on, among other factors, whether they ejected. After the Committee of Liaison began its work, the administration's figures for POWs began to vary wildly. On 20 February 1970, only six weeks after WSP had announced that an official list of POWs was forthcoming, a Defense Department official charged that "as many as 600" Americans were held in North Vietnam. On 17 March, the Defense Department released to the press what it called "an unpublished list" of POWs in Vietnam. That list contained 372 names. In December 1971, a Defense Department official released a figure of 378 "known" POWs in Hanoi. Soon after, President Nixon declared that there were presently "1,600 Americans in North Vietnam jails under very difficult circumstances" (Public Papers 1971, 389).

When planes went down, the odds were not in the pilots' favor. If they ejected, some ejection injuries were virtually certain and were often severe. Eighty percent of returning POWs reported injuries prior to their capture, and these were the survivors. Many of the pilots had access to Pentagon-supplied suicide equipment if they chose to carry it on their flights. If they survived, angry villagers almost certainly did away with some of them on the spot, though, as one observer pointed out, capturing an American pilot alive was the crowning ambition of every young Vietnamese at the time. In addition, there were reasons in Washington to keep pilots on the missing, rather than killed, list. Benefits for their survivors were better, for one thing, and the Pentagon said it needed stark proof of death, not eyewitness reports. According to some pilots, the standard solution was to keep a downed pilot on the missing list and, if another crew member was quite sure, based on an eyewitness observation, that he had not survived, to quietly let the family back home know that. This ensured continuing financial benefits to the family while simultaneously discouraging false hopes (APW 1971, 289, 110).

After the Committee of Liaison secured an official list of POWs from Hanoi and began to compile its own, the Defense Department also changed its policy of offering separate lists of believed POWs and those missing, in favor of simply lumping both categories together. Just days after the Committee of Liaison returned to the States in December 1969 with a partial list and Hanoi's promise to compile an updated one, the State Department handed the Vietnamese delegation in Paris a list of 1,406 missing personnel in Vietnam, holding them responsible for every individual on the list whether or not he was internally classified by the services as captured or missing. When American officials did draw a distinction in the future between those missing and those in captivity, the latter figure rose steadily at the expense of the former, even during the time when Washington sharply curtailed bombing runs over North Vietnam.

Washington hewed to this line until the end of the war, charging that Hanoi was responsible for each and every American now missing in Vietnam. Its repeated declarations that there were large (and growing) numbers of Americans missing in the war prepared the ground for charges after 1973 that the Vietnamese had deliberately held some back, though for what purposes was never made clear. In hopes of identifying new POWs, the Department of Defense distributed to families photos and film of captured pilots in Hanoi, asking the families to identify them. Some of the prints were quite vague, leading to multiple identifications. In one case, four different families insisted that the face on the photo belonged to them (*APW* 1971, 240). Additionally, the Defense Department, unwilling to make public its bombing campaigns over Laos and Cambodia, informed families of fliers missing over those countries that they had been downed over North Vietnam.

These political and military circumstances made the issue of "prisoner lists" impossible to resolve, as Washington rejected any list the Vietnamese offered as incomplete and fraudulent. The Committee of Liaison sought simply to cut through the specious impasse and provide families with whatever relief was available. Families and prisoners were eager to respond. By the end of its first year, the committee reported that only six known prisoners had not sent any mail through its channel, even though the Defense Department sent out, in its February 1970 newsletter, a warning to all POW/MIA families about the committee. "A new group called the Committee of Liaison with Families of Servicemen Detained in Vietnam was recently publicized," the newsletter said, and went on to

> strongly emphasize that the action of the North Vietnamese in dealing through this and similar groups, rather than at an official government level, is an obvious propaganda ploy designed to promote the credibility of those who oppose US involvement in Southeast Asia. Further, those who use such groups as an intermediary run the very real risk of personal harassment and have no assurance at all that welfare information will be received.

The Defense Department offered no clues as to what "personal harassment" the families might receive, but FBI agents took to visiting

POW families and warning them personally to have nothing to do with the Committee of Liaison. When pressed for a reason by one defiant mother, the FBI agent could only respond that the committee was "felt to belong to the communist group" (*APW* 245, 181).

The State Department tried, sometimes successfully, to get its hands on the prisoner mail. In January 1970, Louis Schneider, executive director of the American Friends Service Committee, and James Forest, secretary of the World Peace Committee, spent a week in Hanoi making arrangements for a shipment of medical supplies for the Viet Duc hospital there. When they left Hanoi, Vietnamese officials gave them a parcel of sixty-nine letters for delivery in the United States under the auspices of the Committee of Liaison. At their first stopover in Vientiane, James Murphy, an official at the American embassy there, met them at the airport and inquired whether they were carrying any letters from POWs. After replying in the affirmative and discussing their trip briefly with Murphy, the two went on to Hong Kong, where the American consul caught up with them with the news that Frank Sieverts at the State Department had worked out arrangements with the AFSC in Philadelphia for the letter parcel to be sent via diplomatic pouch to the United States.

Schneider and Forest knew Sieverts well from their many meetings with State Department officials, and considered him a friend. He assured them over the phone that the parcel would be sent to the AFSC offices unopened. The State Department was simply trying to make things easier for the travelers, he told them. Schneider and Forest were not returning to New York for three weeks, and the offer to expedite the mail delivery was tempting but problematic. Sieverts had always appeared sympathetic to the activists, but he did work for the State Department. A phone call to their Philadelphia office confirmed their suspicions that the AFSC's main office was not as happy with the arrangement as Sieverts had implied. No one was completely at ease about sending the letters through the diplomatic pouch. On the other hand, they had been requested to do so by friendly officials in the State Department and were not interested in appearing obstructionist. Schneider (1970, AFSC) decided, in the end, to seal the parcel with sealing wax, mark on it that it was not to be opened en route, turn it over to the Hong Kong consulate, and hope that all the mail would indeed go through unopened.

In some cases, federal officials seized prisoners' mail from returning travelers at the New York airport. Usually it was returned after several days. The FBI sent its agents to infiltrate the Committee of Liaison and report back any conceivable grounds for prosecution. The CIA opened international mail between the Committee of Liaison and Vietnamese officials in Paris. Neither agency found anything with which to charge the committee, and eventually the CIA paid the Committee of Liaison a cash settlement for its illegal interference with international mail (Taylor 1974, SCPC).

Despite government opposition, the committee worked quietly and efficiently, organizing mail deliveries and pickups, and using its position as a clearinghouse and intermediary with Hanoi to compile its own list of prisoners, which Washington was already preparing to discount. The committee's success was little noted in the national media. It was not showy, self-aggrandizing, or deliberately confrontational, and its every success brought about sure and sharp criticism from the same sources in Washington upon which the press depended for its news feed. In contrast to its scant coverage of the Committee of Liaison, the media awarded generous coverage to other, less successful efforts to direct mail and packages to the POWs in Hanoi. It publicized no effort so grandly as it did that of the strange travels of Texas millionaire H. Ross Perot and his short-lived "United We Stand" campaign in 1970.

Perot's interest in the POW issue had been sparked by the travels of Frishman and Hegdahl as the Defense Department sent them around the country to describe alleged endemic torture of POWs in Hanoi. Perot was a fervent supporter of President Nixon's war in Vietnam, and he had already organized and financed the mailing of twenty-five million postcards nationwide in support of those policies. Perot had a lot of faith in the cause as well as the active support of the White House and its staff. Presidents had ready access to information that was kept secret from ordinary citizens, the young crew-cut businessman was fond of telling reporters, and since every president so far had concluded that the communists must be stopped in Asia, "I must assume that if I knew what they knew, I would have acted the same." Perot's postcard campaign sought to rectify what he described as insufficient press coverage of Nixon's views on Vietnam.[2]

2. The postcards were distributed to veterans and civic groups and were to be mailed to Perot's new organization, "United We Stand." Perot placed advertisements in 110 of the nation's largest newspapers and bought half-hour blocks of local TV time, urging support of Washington's war policies and soliciting funds for "United We Stand." The entire effort cost him one million dollars. See "Minority of One," in *Nation*, 8 Dec. 1969, and *NYT* 15 Nov. 1969. For a look at support that the White House gave Perot during these endeavors, see Posner 1996, 57–65.

The postcard campaign garnered $100,000 in contributions to Perot, and extensive news coverage. In mid-December, he announced larger plans: he would send family members of American servicemen in Hanoi to Southeast Asia on chartered planes in an effort to meet with the servicemen and secure their release. First, though, he would send them to Paris to meet with Vietnamese representatives. Perot organized and paid for fifty-eight wives of American prisoners and ninety-four of their children to fly to Paris in December 1969 to meet with Vietnamese representatives there.[3] He planned to heighten awareness of the plight of the families of the prisoners by tying their plea for their husbands and fathers to the Christmas holiday season. Accordingly, they were scheduled to be in Paris on Christmas Day only, meeting with Vietnamese officials there in an encounter Perot hoped would be well-publicized. On December 22 they sent a telegram to the Vietnamese delegation in Paris announcing their arrival three days later, asking for an interview then. They received no response by the twenty-fourth, but left anyway, arriving at dawn at Orly Airport, where they boarded buses that took them into the city. Paris police stopped the buses a block from the Vietnamese delegation's offices but finally allowed several of the women to walk to the small red brick-and-stone building that served as the Vietnamese embassy. The mission was closed for Christmas Day and the women were told that the following day it would be reopened. They could meet with representatives then. But Perot had arranged for the group to be in Paris on Christmas Day only; no overnight accommodations had been prepared for them in Paris, and some of them had left small children at home. They could not stay even one night. "We had all so hoped, with our children, that this would be a truly meaningful Christmas," one of the women told a *New York Times* reporter after they had resigned themselves to going home without contacting any Vietamese officials.

The group decided to attend Christmas mass at Notre Dame Cathedral on the way back to Orly Airport. There, in the cathedral, as they and their children milled around in the back of the nave, a French police inspector arrived with word that, after finding out that the women were in Paris for one day only, Vietnamese officials had agreed to cut their own

3. In September, four women had gone to Paris to talk to Vietnamese officials about their husbands, all missing fliers. "We don't know whether we are wives or widows," one of them said. Vietnamese officials showed them photos of the aftermath of bombing raids. Some of the photos included dead children. "[The photos] were very bad," one of the women told the *New York Times* on 18 Sept. "We really didn't have a reply."

holiday short and meet with the delegation immediately. The group re-boarded the buses, went back to the mission, and three of the women spent an hour inside with Vietnamese officials. Over tea, Tran Viet Dung, the political counselor at the mission, took a list of names from the women and told them he would send the list to Hanoi but that informa-tion, when it came, would now only come through American peace orga-nizations. Outside, the rest of the group waited quietly on the buses. They flew back to New York late that evening.

Perot's most flamboyant gesture was equally hapless. He chartered two Braniff 707s, naming one "Peace on Earth," and the other "Good Will to Men," and announced he was filling them with 1,400 "of every-thing," including bedding, clothing, and canned Christmas dinners, and flying it all to Hanoi to serve Christmas dinner to the 1,400 American servicemen for whom the White House was now insisting Hanoi was re-sponsible. Five hundred Sears and Roebuck catalogues were added to the pile to distribute to North Vietnamese. It was no small project. The goods weighed seventy-five tons.

The flight was not a smooth one. As word of Perot's intentions fil-tered out through the media, Hanoi reiterated that mail and packages for the prisoners had to go through the regular channels of either Moscow or WSP. The millionaire was undeterred. "If they understand that it would be to their advantage to allow us into their country to carry these supplies to the prisoners, I see no problem at all," he told reporters in Dallas. "Al-lowing private American citizens to bring Christmas directly to these men would be a major step toward improving relationships between our peo-ple." Perot's planned airship odyssey to Hanoi mirrored Washington's dealings with that country. Wealthy, confident, ignorant of the issues in Southeast Asia, he must have seemed to the officials in Hanoi like a small, well-financed country: a diminutive version of America itself.

Perot's first stop was Bangkok, where he met with Vietnamese diplo-mats who, while not flatly rejecting his plans, strongly discouraged his quixotic quest. But the optimistic traveler confidently asserted progress, declaring that Hanoi would at last "cross the barrier of suspicion." Though he knew little of Vietnam's past, he was certain he knew the Viet-namese better than they knew themselves. *Newsweek* wrote on 13 April 1970 that he had told reporters that officials in Hanoi "think of the pris-oners only in terms of practical advantage. If they realize that their treat-ment of the prisoners actually hurts them in the world's eyes, they are likely to vary their position." Despite the firm discouragement Perot received in Bangkok, the chartered "Peace on Earth" flew on to Laos, becoming the second 707 ever to touch down on the short runway at Vientiane, its reverse engines sending up a cloud of red dust a quarter of a mile wide. In Laos, only two hundred miles from Hanoi, Vietnamese officials flatly refused permission to fly his seventy-five tons of material goods to the American prisoners in Hanoi. The businessman tried to bargain. How about donating the Christmas dinners to war orphans in Hanoi? Could his crew fly into Hanoi and serve the meals themselves to children in orphanages? Perot professed to be baffled as to why Hanoi rejected each suggestion, insisting that all mail and parcels for the American prisoners follow the already established channels. "They don't want Americans to hate them because of a minor issue," he told the *New York Times* on 11 April. "They are extremely sensitive to public opinion in this country." The American prisoners were a "secondary matter" to the Vietnamese, he said, and they "were not aware of the importance Americans attached to the problem."

"Peace on Earth" flew back to Bangkok the next day and Perot set course for Moscow, intending, at last, to funnel his materials into Hanoi via the "normal" channel. But Moscow did not want to be responsible for seventy-five tons of goods for the American prisoners in Hanoi, which was likely to be larded with contraband, and Perot's airlift for American pilots met with little sympathy in other international quarters. Burma and India refused the nomadic Christmas airlift permission to fly over their territory to Moscow. So, on its ninth day of wandering, "Peace on Earth" pointed toward the North Pole and flew to Anchorage, Alaska, to give its weary crew a mandatory twelve hour rest before going on to Copenhagen. In Copenhagen, Perot was finally convinced that the journey was over. Moscow still refused permission for his plane to land there. Even a hastily arranged call to Soviet premier Alexei Kosygin went for naught.

On New Year's Day, Perot returned to Dallas, vowing not to give up. His next step, he said, descending from the aircraft, would be to organize "millions and millions" of letters from Americans that would induce Hanoi to provide "better treatment" for the American pilots. "Staying power and singlemindedness of purpose are the most important ingredients to bring into this," he told reporters. In April 1970 he went to Saigon with five women who were married to POWs. Eighty journalists accompanied him on this crusade to visit prisons for captured National Liberation Front soldiers, seeking to collect letters from them to take to Hanoi in exchange for being permitted to visit the American prisoners

there and to "publicize the good treatment . . . enemy prisoners are receiving in the South contrasting it with the harsh confinement . . . prisoners in the North receive," the *New York Times* reported on 6 April 1970.
"If word gets through to the North Vietnamese people that we have letters from their missing loved ones, it is going to put pressure on the government," Perot confidently told reporters.

Hanoi, however, called Perot's peripatetic flights merely a "provoca-
tive" extension of Washington's policies. His prospects of getting to
Hanoi were dimmer than ever. In Vientiane he was now even denied entrance to the Vietnamese embassy. In protest, he staged a seven hour "sit-
in" near the embassy gate. While he was engaged in his sit-in, three
Americans en route to Hanoi, Noam Chomsky, linguistics professor at the
Massachusetts Institute of Technology, Richard Fernandez, a Philadelphia
clergyman, and Douglas Dowd, professor of economics at Cornell, paid a
courtesy call at the embassy, where they met the protester sitting outside
the gate. Perot's activities, embassy officials told Chomsky, were nothing
more than an act of propaganda.

The organization that Perot built to support his activities proved as
short-lived as his travels. When he announced its formation in late 1969,
he had boasted to *Newsweek* (8 Dec.) that, by March of the following
year, United We Stand, Inc. would be "the largest organization in the
United States," with at least fifteen million members. But the organization existed largely on paper, with Perot's individual and flamboyant gestures comprising its primary activities. In August 1970, for example, he
requested that he be allowed to mount a prisoner-of-war display in the
Capitol crypt. Congress readily granted permission and Perot installed
cages of the type in which he alleged that American prisoners in Hanoi
were kept, along with torture tools he said were like the ones to which
they were routinely subjected. The display, a most unlikely depiction of
life for American POWs in Hanoi, remained as a tourist attraction during
that fall.

After that, Perot's public activities on behalf of American prisoners
largely ceased, though at the end of the year he claimed all the credit for
what he said was better food and medical treatment and increased mail
flow to and from the prisoners. He also declared that a massive "Village
Campaign" was at the moment underway across the United States, con-
sisting of letter-writing campaigns in cities and towns everywhere that
would culminate in millions of letters being taken to Vietnamese officials
so that they would finally know that "it is a whole nation that wants these

men back now." Perot went on to urge Americans to remember the prisoners "each time you put on or remove your socks." The Vietnamese
routinely tortured American pilots by withholding their socks, he told the
New York Times on 24 December 1970, and without socks, mosquitoes
would bite their feet, causing their feet to swell to "two to three times
their normal size." POW memoirs do not mention being subjected to this
happening, though some of them refer, in passing, to the mosquito nets
they had over their beds to protect against the insects. Like many people
in tropical areas then, the Vietnamese themselves often did not wear
socks.

Though Perot was convinced he would not be allowed into Hanoi
after his noisy flight around the world the preceding Christmas, he appears not to have given up entirely the idea of financing Yuletide family
visits to Hanoi. In early December 1971, the American Friends Service
Committee received a call from Senator Edmund Muskie's office. The
senator had been approached by an "American gentleman of immense
wealth" who was eager to finance any costs associated with organizing
and carrying out such visits. The individual in question wished to remain
anonymous and, because of "political implications," Senator Muskie did
not want to be personally associated with the arrangement. He was
merely offering his services, he told the AFSC, believing that they were
the only "likely group" to turn to. AFSC declined to serve as an intermediary (Schneider 1971, AFSC). Perot's interest in the POWs continued at
varying levels. In his bid for the presidency in 1992, he chose a former
POW, James Stockdale, as his running mate and Orson Swindle, another
former POW, to head his new "United We Stand" organization.

Perot's well-publicized travels demonstrated the power of money to
dress up an empty flamboyance that revived the media. Press coverage of
his showy trek virtually obliterated the quietly persistent and far more
productive early efforts of the Committee of Liaison to build a reliable
and sustainable system of package and letter exchanges with the Americans in Hanoi. The committee's motivation did not derive from, nor de-
pend upon, media attention however, and they continued their work
steadily, facilitating mail deliveries and compiling a list of prisoners.

Perot was not the only wealthy American to believe that monetary in-
centives would lure Hanoi to alter its policy on prisoners of war. In this
spirit, a wealthy American entertainer offered to "buy" them. Bob Hope
had spent the past five Christmas seasons touring American bases
throughout Southeast Asia, and in 1971 he planned to do the same. But

he first publicly offered Hanoi $10 million for the prisoners. "I think I could make them a financial proposition," the entertainer told the press in Vientiane, where he had gone to ask for a visa to enter Hanoi. Offering some of his own $450 million fortune for the POWs appeared unseemly to the entertainer, and he proposed instead an arrangement whereby he would hold a "charity show" in the United States to raise the money and then donate it to "a North Vietnamese children's charity," whereupon Hanoi would release all the American POWs. Hope also asked to be allowed to perform in Hanoi.

The Vietnamese seemed little impressed by this remarkable effort to purchase political success. As for his proposed entertainment act in Hanoi, Nguyen Van Thanh, the North Vietnamese embassy official in Vientiane, told Hope politely that the Vietnamese people would be happy to see the act after the war was over. It was not lost on Hanoi that Hope regularly used the air war in the north as fodder for his comic repertoire in entertaining the American troops on aircraft carriers off Vietnam's shore. He had once called the air war on the north "the best slum clearance project they ever had," denigrating at once their lives, their villages, their housing, and their culture, while turning the view below the bombs into a joke. Hope never got his visa to Hanoi, nor did he ever perform there. At least as a gesture, he told Nguyen Van Thanh as he abandoned the effort, the Vietnamese should release a few of the captured pilots. But even as he urged that Hanoi release some pilots, the United States was announcing vast new air strikes in the "demilitarized zone" in North Vietnam.

Throughout 1970, the Committee of Liaison built its prisoner of war list, passing on inquiries to officials in Hanoi about specific prisoners who had not been heard from since they went missing, and asking for information about any prisoners who had died after capture. In April 1970, Hanoi handed over to the Committee of Liaison a list of 335 men it held in prison camps. The following November, four more names were added to the list, bringing the total to 339. By that time, Hanoi had also compiled and turned over to the committee a list of twenty-two downed fliers who had died from injuries or whose bodies had been recovered by officials. The State Department accepted the information that the Committee of Liaison continued to hand over while publicly scorning the committee, denigrating its efforts, and continuing to insist, in a novel approach to wartime casualties, that Hanoi was now responsible for accounting for every American pilot missing in Southeast Asia.

The "battle of the lists" gave way to a genuine military operation to rescue the American POWs. On the night of 21 November 1970, during an ostensible "bombing halt," the United States unleashed two hundred fighter bombers over the skies of North Vietnam. These raids were justified as retaliation for the shooting down of an unarmed reconnaissance plane. Secretary of Defense Melvin Laird claimed, at the time, that the Nixon administration inherited from the Johnson administration an unwritten "understanding" with the Vietnamese that reconnaissance flights, accompanied by fighter bombers, would continue unimpeded after President Johnson halted air strikes against North Vietnam in October 1968. The Vietnamese strongly denied ever granting such permission and the administration could produce no notes or documents to back up Washington's claim. The purpose of the air attacks in November 1970 was to camouflage a raid on a camp at Son Tay, about twenty-three miles from Hanoi, where American intelligence told them POWs were being held. A fleet of American helicopters swept into Son Tay, where, for nearly an hour, soldiers dashed from building to building, searching fruitlessly for POWs while fighter-bombers strafed and rocketed the surrounding countryside. There were no prisoners at Son Tay, and all the Americans raiders returned safely. Their leader later told *Time* (7 Dec. 1970) that they had killed thirty Vietnamese in the attack.

The raid came at the same time that two representatives of the Committee of Liaison were in Hanoi to deliver mail. Morton Stavis and Peter Weiss, who was married to Cora Weiss, had picked up letters from 320 prisoners to bring back home. Around 3:00 A.M. on their last night in Hanoi, sounds of distant explosions awakened them. The next morning, in Hanoi, they heard of the raid, and they brought that information back with them when they reached New York the following day.

Washington intended to conceal the unsuccessful raid, which came during the same week that testimony was beginning in the trial of Lieutenant Calley, accused of massacring villagers at My Lai. Hanoi radio broadcasts referred to the raid, however, and the Pentagon was soon caught off guard by unexpected questions. "We do not comment on propaganda broadcasts from Hanoi," a spokesman first asserted, and Secretary Laird, at first unaware that the story could be corroborated, denied that it had ever occurred. He soon had to abandon that route and explain why a raid was ordered on an area that contained no American prisoners. He chose an explanation that brought the Committee of Liaison directly into the picture. Richard Nixon ordered the raids, he told the *New York*

Times on 24 November, after hearing that American prisoners in Hanoi were dying in captivity of inhumane treatment.

Laird based his assertion of dying American prisoners on three lists that the Committee of Liaison had brought back from Hanoi and turned over to the State Department. The lists, provided by Hanoi officials, contained the names of pilots who had been downed over North Vietnam and had been found dead, or had since died, from injuries. The first list of five names was released to the WSP delegation in Hanoi in April 1970. They turned over that list to the State Department, as they did each subsequent list. Two more such lists provided in November 1970, brought the total to twenty-two. After the Son Tay raid, the Nixon administration insisted that these lists constituted proof that American prisoners were dying from mistreatment. No POW memoir, harsh as they are, has ever charged that Vietnamese authorities killed a single POW either through torture or execution.[4]

The raid generated a flurry of charges and countercharges about the American prisoners, their treatment, and the best way to ensure their safety as prisoners. After claiming that there was ongoing brutality in the prison camps and that the Vietnamese were killing prisoners, Washington now had to assure the public of the security of the POWs in the face of this botched raid. The raid failed, Pentagon officials asserted, because, despite excellent intelligence, they had no cameras that could see through roofs to determine whether or not prisoners were actually there.

At the same time, in the kind of twist for which the war was increasingly famous, the raid posed a new and contrary problem for the Pentagon's credibility. If the intelligence identifying Son Tay as a prison camp was wrong, what about the thousands of other targets leveled over the years, accompanied by solemn Pentagon assurances that they were military targets? This was not an area that the Pentagon could credibly discuss, and officials there increasingly tried to turn the focus to the American POWs, justifying more and more of the military activity in North Vietnam as necessary to bring them home.

At the time of Son Tay, the war appeared deeply unwinnable, but no prospect of its end had emerged. The raid came at a point where the American public's exasperation with the war intersected with Washington's sense that the war could be "endless," in the sense that the United

---

4. According to POW Larry Guarino, a deeply depressed prisoner of war, Ron Storz died in prison of "voluntary starvation" (1990, 274).

States had lost control over events in Vietnam. That loss now appeared to extend even to a loss of control over how to end the war. Because prisoners were traditionally exchanged at the end of war, the American prisoners in Southeast Asia seemed to be caught in a cycle of interminable war. The political failure in Washington to reach agreement with Vietnamese nationalists raised the prospect of Americans languishing in endless captivity, and that prospect drove the Son Tay raid. A successful prisoner "snatch" could paper over the larger defeats in Vietnam. In this context, then, the raid's failure seemed like nothing so much as a jarring symbol of the helplessness that all of America's best and most lethal weapons had procured for itself in Vietnam. A charge that Hanoi was killing prisoners could justify this risky endeavor.

The raid's failure generated enormous anger among POW families for putting the prisoners at risk of retaliation. Why was the Pentagon willing to run a high risk of killing POWs while trying to rescue them? Angry family members of prisoners railed against the White House for jeopardizing the safety of some prisoners in a rescue effort that never had a high probability of success. To deflect this anger, the Nixon administration engaged in an concerted effort to persuade family members to join the administration in charging Hanoi with prisoner abuse. The Pentagon worked closely with the newly formed National League of Families of American Prisoners and Missing in Southeast Asia on this issue, helping to arrange press conferences, writing press releases, and providing members with its own description of life in POW camps.

The National League of Families of American Prisoners and Missing in Southeast Asia was formed out of regional groups of women married to missing American officers. Sybil Stockdale, whose husband was POW James Stockdale, was the first national coordinator. Although the Defense Department helped them in many ways, many of the women who ran the league soon came to believe that their government placed its own interests above those of the POWs. The National League itself soon split, with one faction forming Families for Immediate Release, a group that objected to the way that the National League was manipulated by the White House and that called for an immediate American withdrawal from Southeast Asia.[5]

Although the administration refused to discuss the Committee of Li-

5. Sybil Stockdale (1985) detailed a bitter critique of the Defense Department in its relations with POW families. On Families for Immediate Release, see Keenan (1986).

aison in public, it began to take on the committee through the National League of Families. On 8 December, only days after the Son Tay raid, the league ran an article on the editorial page of the *New York Times* that expressed some of the confused anger that not only family members, but also much of the public, felt by then over the prisoners of war. The league's article, written with help from Pentagon officials, deftly moved criticism of the raid from the White House to the Committee of Liaison and to Hanoi for not releasing the POWs. The article first painted a picture of life for American POWs: "For years they have been slowly rotting in barbaric cells, barely subsisting on thin soup and thick bread with nothing to do, no one to talk to, not allowed to communicate by mail with their families." The article quickly moved to the Committee of Liaison, which was, it asserted, "established by Hanoi." The committee's work had not helped establish contact with POWs, the league's article asserted, though it did acknowledge its work:

> Granted, the committee has delivered more mail in the past two years than has come out in all the previous four years, but still only 339 men have been heard from. There have been 790 fliers downed over the North. What happened to the other 451? Information released recently by Mrs. Cora Weiss of the Liaison Committee lists names of many men who, it is said, "have never been identified from pictures or other sources." Now the North Vietnamese say they're not there and have never been there. So where are they? If they have died in prison, the North Vietnamese should be held accountable to the rest of the world. It is an unthinkable criminal act if prisoners of war have been allowed to die, unidentified, uncared for. There is no possible excuse for a civilized country to allow this to happen.

The list of men who "have never been identified" apparently referred to replies to 104 status inquiries that the committee had turned over to Hanoi officials from their families in the United States. Hanoi officials said they had no information on most of the names so submitted, but 22 of these they had reported as found dead after being shot down over North Vietnam. The National League's article generated an expectation, which the Pentagon knew was false, that it was to be expected that all the downed fliers could be identified, and that it was within Hanoi's capabilities to do so. Hanoi's failure to account for all the American pilots downed over Vietnam was attributed to Vietnamese callous cruelty.

In fact, the proportion of Americans unaccounted for at the end of the war in Vietnam was far smaller than it was in World War II and the Korean War. In World War II, nearly 20 percent of the total killed remain unaccounted for, and that in countries that the United States has always been free to search. In Korea, over 15 percent were unaccounted for. In Vietnam, in contrast, the unaccounted constituted less than 4 percent of the total killed. A study later done by the United States Navy in Vietnam revealed that in 40 percent of fatal noncombat crashes, the navy itself could not positively identify the dead, even though their identities were known and investigators arrived on the scene within hours (Franklin, 1992, 12).

The Son Tay raid proved that, as the United States slid further into defeat in Vietnam, the issue of the POWs could provide the one rallying cry for Washington. In fact, getting back the prisoners became a justification for the war. It was, as Jonathan Schell observed, as if Hanoi "had kidnapped four hundred Americans and the United States had gone to war to retrieve them" (1976, 231). The POW story again turned the war in Vietnam on its head so that Americans became the victims, and, for some Americans, the sufferings of the POWs came to match, even exceed, the sufferings of the Vietnamese. Beyond that, the POW story made even the civilian families of American officers in Vietnam victims of the Vietnamese. The counterpart to Vietnamese villagers whose homes, families, and lives were destroyed by American military might was held equivalent, or less than, that of the waiting endured by the families of POWs. "In no other armed conflict in history have families of military men been exploited in this manner," claimed the author of the National League's article. "Why should young women have to exist in a hellish limbo—neither wife nor widow—with no hope of starting a new life and no assurance that her old life, so cruelly torn apart by this war, will ever be mended?" It was a heartfelt question, one that many more Vietnamese faced than did Americans. By the end of the war, in addition to the several million killed, the Vietnamese counted nearly three hundred thousand missing, most, in each case, civilians, the missing "buried" where they fell, their families bereft of both their remains and knowledge of the circumstances of their deaths.[6]

The Son Tay raid marked the decided use of the POW issue to justify

---

6. For a look at the cooperation that eventually emerged in searching for both American and Vietnamese missing, see Michael Ulh 1994. According to James Watson, American troops sometimes booby-trapped bodies of dead Vietnamese, placing grenades under them, set to go off when anyone tried to move the bodies (Watson and Dockery 1993, 204).

a continued American presence in Vietnam. It also resulted in a decrease in the amount of mail from the POWs. At the time of the raid, when the Committee of Liaison had been in operation for over ten months, the committee had delivered over 2,500 letters from 331 of the 339 prisoners on its list. Some letters and many packages continued to make their way through the channel in Moscow. In the first months after the Son Tay raid, there was a dramatic reduction in letters from the POWs. Part of the falloff seems to have come from Hanoi, as an initial protest against the Son Tay raid. Some of the reduction stemmed from a "boycott" of the mail proposed by POW John McCain after the Son Tay raid, as an internal effort to win the propaganda war waged in the international arena. McCain's argument was that Hanoi must be allowing letter-writing only in order to curry favor with the world. The prisoners' duty, therefore, was to fight Hanoi's strategy by refusing to write letters. If little mail emerged from the POWs, according to McCain's logic, Hanoi would be blamed and would lose points in the international community. POWs could help defeat the Vietnamese by refusing to write letters to their own families. Senior POW officers urged the boycott on the rest of the prisoners, and for a time many of them seemed to have complied, but nearly all of them began writing again and, by the end of 1971, the flow of mail through the Committee of Liaison was back to its prior level (Hubbell 1976, 551). Even McCain's own father, Admiral John McCain, sent at least one letter to his son through Committee of Liaison channels. The admiral gave the letter for his son to Richard Rand, an official "counselor" at the American embassy in Vientiane, to be carried by a Committee of Liaison group to Hanoi (Sullivan 1972b, AFSC).

Another factor slowed POW mail after Son Tay. In response to White House urging to think of the war in Vietnam primarily in terms of the POWs in Hanoi, commercial interests in the United States began to organize large-scale mailings to the prisoners in Hanoi. These campaigns usually would publish the names of some of the POWs in newspaper advertisements and urge that letters be sent specifically to them, or they would encourage the public to send mail to the prisoners in Hanoi en masse. Ross Perot sponsored a mail writing campaign of this sort as did profit-making organizations such as the Mountain Bell Telephone Company. It was an effective gesture for Americans eager to show solidarity with the prisoners in Hanoi, but it delayed the mail to the POWs from their families. Because Hanoi inspected general mail for contraband before it was passed on to the prisoners, the large volume of mail that these campaigns generated slowed delivery of mail from relatives. With these impediments operating after Son Tay, the appeal of sending mail through the Committee of Liaison rose even higher. The committee was never bogged down by large-scale, commercially inspired letter-writing campaigns, and, with its mail confined almost entirely to family members, deliveries through it continued to be the fastest and most certain route of mail between prisoners and their families.

With rare exceptions, the POW memoirs, written as they were almost entirely by senior hard-core officers prone to view even writing letters home as "cooperating" with the enemy, treat the Committee of Liaison with unbridled scorn, even though, eventually, even they used its services. Women Strike for Peace, the group that gave rise to the Committee of Liaison, also received especial scorn in these memoirs. There were many antiwar groups composed only of men who visited POWs, and there were many groups composed of men and women. It was the entirely female antiwar groups that aroused the highest level of hostility among the hardcore officers. Women who undertook visible and controversial political activity in international affairs walked a finer line than did their male counterparts. Women were scarcely represented in America's own political life, and they were still "disarmed," barred from any military service that involved combat and killing, those military activities that, by their very essence, conferred on all men an aura of competence and legitimacy in wielding political power. When "respectable" women, wives and mothers, protested wars, the usual hostility against antiwar activists was ratcheted up by the fears that surrounded images of female activists questioning the rationale for war and acting as harbingers of deeper erosions of domestic support.

The Committee of Liaison continued its work until the end of the war, transmitting regular and reliable mail service to and from Hanoi, forwarding status inquiries from families and responses to those inquiries, and providing the Pentagon with official prisoner of war lists from Hanoi. Their work provided some measure of comfort to many POWs in Hanoi and their family members in the United States, and offered a practical solution to an impasse set in place by considerations that placed Washington's own image over the interests of the prisoners and their families. Until the end of the war, the committee continued to work. Recognizing that the issue of prisoner mail remained potentially subject to official obstruction from both sides, the committee deliberately kept a low profile to allow it to work quietly and effectively. The media was not much interested in its work, preferring the flamboyant gestures of H. Ross Perot. The Texas businessman took the media's generous attention as encouragement to form the organization "United We Stand" as a backdrop for his solo effort to do what the Committee of Liaison did with far less money and bluster. By the end of the war, the committee had carried more than seven thousand letters from POWs in Hanoi to the United States, and had taken nearly as many from their families to Hanoi (Taylor 1988, SCPC).

7

War's End

In the last years of the war, hostility toward citizen travel to Hanoi lessened somewhat, and traveling to "enemy" territory appealed to those beyond the traditional categories. Journalists of all stripes now craved visas, American scientists established collegial and research ties with Vietnamese scientists there, and a few business leaders sought out commercial opportunities. All of these travelers offered similar reports: the bombing did not seem to weaken morale, the Vietnamese were still, by and large, friendly to Americans, and Americans, whether journalists, academics, or activists, came away shaken by the extent of the bombing and convinced of its futility.

Throughout these years, the American Friends Service Committee continued to send humanitarian aid to North Vietnam, never approaching its level of humanitarian effort in the south, to be sure, but still making a far greater effort to be evenhanded than did other Western humanitarian organizations. Other activist groups continued steady and regular trips to North Vietnam, bearing witness to the hardships there that the war inflicted. The Committee of Liaison faithfully provided regular and secure mail service between prisoners in Hanoi and their families.

The mainstreaming of travel to Hanoi closely followed the mainstreaming of the terms for ending the war with which the first travelers there had returned: end the bombing and withdraw American troops. These two entreaties culminated in late 1970 in the Campaign to Set the Date, which called on Washington to cease all bombing and set a date by which time all Americans would withdraw from Vietnam. Hanoi officials had indicated that, when such a date was set, they would negotiate the release of all American prisoners. In addition to the traditional antiwar or-

ganizations, the Campaign to Set the Date was endorsed by a wide range
of groups: the U.S. Conference of Mayors, the newly formed Common
Cause, the Union of American Hebrew Congregations, the Modern Language Association, numerous Protestant denominations, Church Women
United, the National Student Association, and Clergy and Laity Concerned. When, in January 1971, a Gallup poll found that 73 percent of
Americans favored an American withdrawal from Vietnam by the end of
the year, Senator Edmund Muskie sponsored legislation to set a withdrawal date by then. In the House, newly elected congresswoman Bella
Abzug sponsored similar legislation.

The National Student Association carried the idea of setting the date
one step further and approved a proposal to send American students to
North and South Vietnam to draft, with their Vietnamese counterparts, a
"People's Peace Treaty." Activists planned to use the treaty at rallies and
meetings as an educational tool to end the war. The students were
blocked from going to Saigon, however, because the government there
now required visas, and it turned down their applications. "Under no circumstances" would any of them be granted visas, a South Vietnamese
embassy official in Washington told the group. Some members of the
barred delegation noted this visa refusal with considerable irony—they
had once been drafted GIs in South Vietnam (People's Peace Treaty
1971, SCPC). But one NSA representative, Douglas Hostetter, had previously spent three years as a civilian aid worker in South Vietnam. He applied for, and got, a visa on his own and unobtrusively made it to Saigon,
where he met with the National Student Union. The students there drew
up a document that they called a "Joint Treaty of Peace Between the People of the United States, South Vietnam and North Vietnam." The treaty
called for a cease-fire followed by a publicly stated date by which all
American military forces would be removed. Hostetter went on to Hanoi,
where he joined the other NSA representatives. The group returned from
Hanoi with the Peace Treaty signed by Vietnamese from the north and
south, and by American students. Copies of the treaty were sent throughout the United States during the coming months and distributed at meetings and rallies as a way of encouraging support for a specific date for
ending the war.

Other American groups traveling to North and South Vietnam began
carrying the treaty with them, steadily adding to it names of representatives of organizations throughout the region. In January, the Women's

International League for Peace and Freedom sent a delegation to both Saigon and Hanoi, and they signed the People's Peace Treaty with women's unions in both areas. At its international meeting in New Delhi the preceding month, WILPF had voted to support the Maternal and Child's Health Institute in Hanoi, and delegation members returned from the visit to Hanoi committed to raising significant funds to that end. Over the next years, WILPF members in the United States and around the world continued their financial support for the institute, according to the January 1973 *Pax et Libertas.*

American scientists also began traveling to North Vietnam in the last years of the war. They were warmly welcomed as researchers whose work and interests meshed with those of their Vietnamese counterparts. Mark Ptashne, a professor of molecular biology at Harvard University, spent a week in Vietnam in late 1970 with chemists and engineers, discussing the latest work in repressors, DNA findings, and gene research. Several months later, Arthur Galston and Ethan Signer, professors of biology at Yale University and Massachusetts Institute of Technology, spent over two weeks in Hanoi, giving a series of lectures and seminars in plant physiology and the genetics of bacterial viruses. They were followed by George Wald, a Harvard professor of biology and winner of the 1967 Nobel Prize in physiology and medicine, who traveled to Hanoi taking recent medical research journals, which were quickly snapped up by researchers there.

Vietnamese scientists came to expect American researchers to offer seminars and lectures in their area of specialty, and they also began to initiate collaborative efforts in medical research. Dr. Ton That Tung, chief surgeon and director of the Viet Duc hospital in Hanoi, had documented a nearly five-fold increase in primary hepatoma at his hospital since 1962, when Americans had begun spraying defoliants over Vietnam. He used the opportunity opened by citizen travel to send some specimens to the Harvard Biological Labs for collaborative research. Matthew Meselson, a research scientist there, confirmed Dr. Tung's findings that dioxin was present in these specimens, and Dr. Tung began to compare the frequencies of other medical abnormalities in areas experiencing different exposures to aerial spraying (Perera 1972, AFSC). These findings, showing that in areas of American aerial spraying there was a high incidence of dioxin in human livers and a sharp increase in the incidence of primary hepatomas, were published that same year in international journals including *Die Naturwissenschafter* and *Comptes Rendus.*

Dr. Tung had once rarely seen primary hepatoma cases, he told the researchers, but they were now the most common cancer he encountered. Anticipating higher levels of primary hepatomas, he set to work to develop an early diagnostic test for cancer of the liver. Tung enlisted the help of the Columbia University College of Physicians and Surgeons in his work, asking George Perera, one of its leading researchers, to confirm the methodology that he was using in developing the test. During his work with Tung, Perera went to Hanoi to offer lectures to doctors and researchers there. He toured hospitals in Hanoi, where he saw things that gave him deeply personal reasons to continue his collaborative work with Dr. Tung: patients recovering from chemical exposures, a boy with fragments of anti-personnel bombs in his skull, a child badly burned by napalm except where his mother had held her hands over his body.

Vietnamese officials began urging Americans to send more scientists and doctors. If scientific and medical delegations should turn out to be the largest and most frequent, it would be something they would be very "happy" about, one of them told the AFSC's John Sullivan. They requested American journals: the *Journal of the American Medical Association, Annals of Internal Medicine, Annals of Surgery,* and *Surgery, Gynecology, and Obstetrics.* Soon, they hoped, delegations composed entirely of American researchers willing to lecture and offer seminars to doctors in Vietnam, would arrive regularly (Sullivan 1972a, AFSC).

The growing interest in scientific exchanges was set back by new air strikes that President Nixon ordered over North Vietnam in May 1972, when B-52s carried out seven hundred raids over North Vietnam, including a sustained forty-eight-hour attack on Hanoi and Haiphong. On 8 May, the president ordered the navy to drop explosive mines throughout Haiphong Harbor. The air strikes coincided with the arrival of another *New York Times* reporter, Anthony Lewis, who spent two weeks in North Vietnam observing the bombing from below. From the ground, he said in a 15 May article, it did indeed look like Washington was engaged in "a cruel act of technological bad temper."[1] Lewis saw hospitals plainly marked with Red Crosses on their roofs that were damaged and destroyed, and patients and doctors driven underground for surgery. A large

1. The phrase, referring to American bombing in Vietnam, was first used by Alastair Buchan, for many years director of England's Institute of Strategic Studies and commandant of the Imperial Defense College (see Anthony Lewis in *NYT,* 6 Jan. 1973).

town square held hundreds of new individual concrete shelters ready for installation along yet more city streets and parks. Foreign diplomats in Hanoi told him about the scenes they had seen just outside Hanoi, of small towns and villages heavily bombed, their clinics and hospitals in ruins.

The news from Hanoi had not changed much since the first American visitors had gone there to see for themselves in mid-1965. Lewis's report, like Harrison Salisbury's before him, contained nothing that American eyewitnesses had not already reported, nor did his report contradict any of theirs. "In the face of bombing and years of war," he wrote, "it is impossible for this visitor to detect any atmosphere of fear." The Vietnamese placed great confidence in their individual bomb shelters and in their ability to improvise their way through the destruction the bombs left behind. "We have no big skyscrapers," one of them told Lewis, "so if the electricity stops we are not stuck on the fiftieth floor." People in Hanoi even had their own grim repertoire of jokes about the bombing. One involved the question as to why bombing was unlikely before nine o'clock on Sunday mornings. The answer was that, on weekends, the American Seventh Fleet pilots believed that they were entitled to coffee first. "Even with sympathy for the men who fly American planes, and for their wives and families, one has to recognize the greater courage of the North Vietnamese people who have been their targets," Lewis wrote later in the *Times* on 6 January 1973.

Inside North Vietnam, statements from the "outside" sounded strange to Lewis. From the Voice of America, which he could pick up clearly in Hanoi, Lewis learned that Vice President Agnew had declared the North Vietnamese Army "demoralized" and that Major General Alexander Haig had told White House correspondents that the political structure in Hanoi was under serious strain and that "prostitution there was growing." Lewis ran the VOA's reportage by Western diplomats in Hanoi. They were amused, he said. Pronouncements from the White House about life in Hanoi reflected more of the unease in Washington than the reality in North Vietnam, Lewis wrote on 29 May. Hearing, over the VOA, the war described in bland and bloodless words by officials ensconced in Washington, a city awash in cherry trees and tranquility, seemed shocking to the journalist who was surrounded by the realities of the carnage in Vietnam. He wrote in the *New York Times* on 22 April:

In the week of this sudden, life-giving spring an American Secretary of State testified for hours about the war in Vietnam without the slightest sign of awareness that American bombs kill Vietnamese when they are dropped. . . . He fell back on pathetic attempts at banter or changed the subject when the hard questions were asked. The Secretary of Defense, whose planes have dropped more than one ton of bombs on Indochina for every minute of the Nixon administration, accused the North Vietnamese of "marauding all over the countryside of Southeast Asia." And he denounced the Soviet Union for lack of "restraint" in aiding North Vietnam—aid that amounts to perhaps one-seventh of what the United States is supplying to South Vietnam.

Soon after the renewed air raids began, a delegation from the People's Coalition for Peace and Justice went to Hanoi for a week to propose a "Hostages for Peace" program to the Vietnamese there.[2] The proposed program called for stationing American volunteers in heavily raided areas where their publicized presence could act as a deterrent to American bombing raids. The volunteers would go understanding the danger, but hoping that their presence might deter American bombing and save the lives of the pilots and of the civilians under the planes.

The delegates experienced seventeen American bombing raids during their time in Hanoi, Nam Dinh, and Haiphong, always traveling at night, and frequently diving from their vehicle for the ditches by the road when American jets roared overhead. Paul Mayer filmed more than 140 bomb craters in Phuc Loc, a village less than one square kilometer in size. Sixty villagers had died, he was told.[3] A high school in Haiphong was leveled; a hospital nearby was bombed one night and again the next morning. As the delegation left the hospital grounds, the air-raid sirens sounded yet again, and by the time they reached the air-raid shelters, they could see the American Phantoms in the clear blue sky dive-bombing the already battered city (Coordinating Committee Report 1972, SCPC).

The Vietnamese generally did not view the "Hostages for Peace"

2. The delegates were Paul Mayer, professor of theology at New York Theological Seminary; Margery Tobankin, president of the National Student Association; Robert Lecky, editor of Clergy and Laity Concerned's *American Report;* and William Zimmerman, a psychologist from Boston with the Medical Aid for Indochina Committee (Returning Delegation, SCPC).

3. Back at home, commentator John McLaughlin dismissed the group's reports as "a discredited 500-word news item" (*NYT* 8 Sept. 1972). The Pentagon denied the raid ever occurred, saying the craters must have been created by "stray SAM missiles."

project as a promising proposal. Tens of thousands of Americans had already died in Vietnam; they had "no illusions" about Nixon's reluctance to kill Americans in this war, they told the group. Paul Mayer noted that "their skepticism concerning the project was also connected to their reluctance to have to take care of large numbers of Americans, and by a certain skepticism regarding the ability of Americans to live (and work) like Vietnamese" (Mayer 1972, SCPC). The group did get to meet with eight POWs, the largest number an American group had ever met. The renewed bombing "seriously jeopardized their own safety and also put off the day of their release," the pilots told the group. They also gave the delegation a letter deploring the massive bombing on the grounds that it endangered still more American pilots, killed civilians in Vietnam, and aroused world opinion although not advancing America's military goals.[4]

The Pentagon countered these reports of civilian deaths by claiming that its new laser-guided bombs had an accuracy of plus or minus six feet. Whether they did or did not was hardly relevant. The overwhelming bulk of the bombing was carried out by B-52s, which carried no precision bombs. "Carpet-bombing" described their task, so the claims of accurately targeted bombing had to be handled gingerly by the Pentagon. If the bombing could be directed with precision, as the Pentagon still contended, then the film of bombed villages, hospitals, and schools that groups like this one brought back constituted evidence that Washington was bombing civilian targets. If, on the other hand, the bombing could not be accurately directed, its indiscriminate use in civilian areas violated international law.

The renewed massive bombing in 1972 raised anew a concern that had once been more muted: the "smart" bombs on which the Pentagon prided itself seemed to be targeting the dikes that held back the Red River from vast areas of Vietnam's agricultural heartland. The bombing damage did not create flooding in the early part of the year—it was the dry season—but the fear was that the targeted bombs, which burrowed in under the dikes at forty-five-degree angles, would weaken the dikes, and they would collapse when the rains came in late summer. The Swedish ambassador to Vietnam, Jean-Christophe Oberg, told American visitors in May

4. The signers were navy commander Walter Wilber, navy lieutenant commander David Hoffman, air force captains Edwin Hawley, Kenneth Fraser, James Cutter, and Lynn Guenther, marine colonel Edison Miller, and navy lieutenant Norris Charles. See Text of Letter 1972, SCPC.

that at first he believed the dike bombings must have been accidental, but his own observations now convinced him they were deliberate. His views on the dike bombings were "not for quotation," he told them. The matter was too politically sensitive. There was still "magnanimity" towards Americans in the North, he added, but if this situation worsened, "hardliners" would take center stage (Sullivan 1972b, AFSC).

The Pentagon Papers revealed that the military had long ago laid out its thinking on the subject of bombing dikes. In 1966, Assistant Secretary of Defense John McNaughton had written a classified position paper saying that massive bombing of population centers in Vietnam would "create a counterproductive wave of revulsion abroad and at home," but, "if handled right," bombing the dikes showed promise, both in starving the Vietnamese people and offering bargaining points to American negotiators. Selective dike bombing would not kill thousands or millions outright, he predicted, but "shallow-flooding the rice . . . leads after time to widespread starvation (more than a million?) unless food is provided—which we could offer to do at the conference table'" (*Pentagon Papers* 4:, 43).

During the height of the bombing that summer in 1972, Jane Fonda arrived in Hanoi to make a film on the effects of the war on everyday life in Hanoi. Although the Pentagon denied it was bombing the dikes, Fonda filmed bomb craters directly on the dikes on the Red River and, like foreign journalists who visited Hanoi that year, and the Swedish ambassador, Jean-Christophe Oberg, she became convinced that the bombings were deliberate. If public protests did not halt them, they could do enormous direct harm to the Vietnamese caught in the path of flooding as well as igniting typhoid and dysentery that massive flooding would bring in its wake.

It was vital that Americans speak out against this bombing, Fonda remarked to a group of Americans and foreigners gathered in a bomb shelter in Hanoi during one raid, because if they were silent, Nixon would ratchet up the damage as his peace plan was stripped of even the illusion of victory. She did not believe Nixon would accept a coalition government in Saigon, Fonda told the group, and Hanoi would never accept a Thieu government after American withdrawal. The Americans in the bomb shelter knew of Jane Fonda as an actress, and they found themselves impressed with the information on the war's course that Fonda had amassed (Sullivan 1972b, AFSC). By 1972, most intellectuals had turned against the war, but, for the most part, figures in the entertainment world were silent on the issue, or supportive of the president. Jane Fonda was one of the first public figures in the entertainment world to take a politically unpopular stand on the war.

Fonda's support of the antiwar movement had begun earlier. She was one of the sponsors of the Vietnam Veterans Against the War's Winter Soldier Investigation held in January 1971 in Detroit. In March 1972, she had created an educational show to tour army bases. The show also drew on the work of Jules Feiffer, Mike Nichols, Donald Sutherland, and George Smith, the prisoner of war released in 1965 by the National Liberation Front. "It's been very disconcerting," the *New Republic* quoted Fonda as saying on 13 March, "to see that Bob Hope, Martha Raye and others of their political ilk have cornered the market and are the only entertainers allowed to speak to soldiers in this country and Vietnam." The military brass was not receptive to Fonda's proposed show, saying that it would be "detrimental to discipline and morale," and they denied the troupe permission to perform on base. The show then moved to coffeehouses near military bases, using live performances and, after Fonda's trip to Vietnam, her film from the war in North Vietnam. By the end of 1972, the troupe had performed at coffeehouses near twenty army bases.

Out of Fonda's educational shows in base coffeehouses was born the Indochina Peace Campaign (IPC), which emphasized a strategy of broadbased public education on the war. The IPC relied heavily on media with which Fonda was familiar: slide shows, films, and graphic displays, and it was kicked off at the Ohio State Fair in August 1972. Fonda turned the footage that she got on her 1972 trip to Vietnam, and on another trip there in 1974, into the film *Introduction to the Enemy*. On 15 November 1974, the *New York Times* film critic Nora Sayre called it a "quiet modest . . . pensive and moving film," as much personal as political, with a "mood of restrained optimism" that "stressed that the Vietnamese do not hate Americans, they want to know more about us." [5]

The furor over Fonda's visit to Hanoi flared up when the hard-core pilots who were shot down on their bombing runs over Vietnam returned to the United States the following year. They singled out for especial opprobrium this young actress who, rather than offering her services to the pilots in the traditional fashion as a pin-up girl for the enhancement of their fantasies, took a political stand and dared to voice unequivocal opposition to the war in the heartland of the "enemy." A photo of a smiling

5. The film was the IPC's first film. IPC Films later produced *The China Syndrome* and *Nine to Five* (Haddad-Garcia 1981).

Fonda standing beside an antiaircraft emplacement especially infuriated them. Many Americans who had witnessed the horrific destruction that American bombers inflicted with near impunity over much of the skies of Vietnam believed, as Fonda clearly did, that antiaircraft equipment was a legitimate self-defense response that could save villagers from the heavy bombing. The image of a young woman who had once played stereo-typed female roles in films, standing literally with the men and the women on "the other side," was a powerful challenge to the patriarchal impulses that traditionally identified men as the defenders of the nation's women and children in wars against the men of other nations.[6]

During summer 1972, travelers to Vietnam, including Jane Fonda, tried to keep the issue of bombed dikes alive. With the full test of "Viet-namization" looming ahead and the presidential elections coming up in November, Nixon was anxious to end the war, at least enough to ensure his reelection, and to appear strong in the face of defeat, a defeat he hoped to turn into "peace with honor." No sooner had the last American combat unit pulled out of Vietnam that summer than Nixon ordered the largest B-52 raids yet over the north. As these raids went on, so did eye-witness accounts of them from visitors to North Vietnam. All testified to deliberate dike-bombing by American planes. In late July, United Nations Secretary General Kurt Waldheim said that "private channels" to Hanoi confirmed that the dikes were being bombed and that, "even in cases where the dikes are not directly bombed, the nearby bombing causes cracking of the earth in the dams and that in this way the result is the same." He appealed to the White House to stop the bombing. Secretary of State William Rogers ordered George Bush, the American ambassador

---

6. Probably few women have been as vilified as Fonda for opposing a particular war since Jane Addams created an international storm in 1915 when, after touring battle zones in Europe, she told *Survey* magazine on 17 July 1915 that the war there "an old man's war," which provided rum and absinthe to the young soldiers to inspire them before bayonet charges. The barrage of criticism directed at her continued long after that war was over, es-pecially from the American Legion. "The trouble with Jane Addams," the *Philadelphia In-quirer* said on 20 July, was that "being a woman, she can't understand how men can possess such courage to charge into a cloud of shot and shell unless soused to the gills." On 15 July, the *New York City Town Topics* called her a "silly, vain, impertinent old maid meddling with matters far beyond her capacity." The offended vice consul of France protested that, for the men of France, "the thought of avenging their womenfolk acts as a much more powerful in-spiration than would absinth" (Vice Consul to Addams 1915, SCPC; Jane Addams 1915, 356–58; *NYT* 12 July 1915).

to the United Nations, to rebut Waldheim's charges. Bush dutifully told Waldheim and the press that American planes did not bomb the dikes. These charges, he told the *New York Times* on 25 July 1972, were "part of a carefully planned campaign by the North Vietnamese and their supporters to give worldwide circulation to this falsehood."[7]

On 29 July, a six-member delegation sponsored by the International Commission of Inquiry into United States Crimes in Indochina arrived in Hanoi. Among the delegates were former United States attorney general Ramsey Clark and Yves Lacoste, a French geographer and specialist on delta systems. The other members were Sean MacBride, former Irish Minister of External Affairs; Frode Jakobsen, member of the Danish Parliament; Inna Kileshnikova, a Soviet surgeon; and Hans Goran Franck, a Swedish lawyer who practiced international law. The day after they reached Hanoi, and only six days after George Bush's denials, the White House issued a statement admitting that there had been "accidental" strikes on dikes and dams in the Red River delta. As if preparing to justify deliberate bombing, it also released a reconnaissance photograph showing three antiaircraft guns on a dam just outside Hanoi, implying that if antiaircraft guns were placed to protect dams, the dams were then legitimate military targets.

The Red River was by far the largest river in North Vietnam, with a flow rivaling that of the Mississippi River, and the delegation focused on it. There were over 2,500 miles of dikes and levees along the Red River. Begun in the highlands during the eleventh century, they had gradually been built down to the coastal areas. There was now a complex system of major dikes with secondary dikes built at right angles, and smaller dikes and canals inside the grid. If these bombings were accidental, Yves Lacoste (1972) reasoned, they would be found near military sites. Instead, most of the ninety-six bomb craters he counted were in heavily agricultural areas, where there was no industry, only villages and rice cultivation. Furthermore, the craters were on dikes without roadbeds and no gun emplacements in sight. The delegation noted that the dike system had been attacked before, in 1965, 1966, and 1967, but during those years the attacks had been halted well before the season of heavy rains began. The concern inside Vietnam in 1972 was not primarily the dike bombings

7. Footage in the video series *Vietnam: A Television History: "America's Enemy,"* clearly shows American planes bombing North Vietnam's dikes.

themselves, to which they were accustomed, but the fact that, for the first time, they were continuing into July and August, when the river began to rise and repairs became increasingly problematic.

Lacoste described the war as the greatest "deluge of fire and steel known to history," and after his trip to Vietnam, he scathingly referred to the American public's reaction to the war as that akin to "a slightly bored theatre audience." Ramsey Clark's delegation and the attention it drew to a kind of bombing that even the jaded found repugnant, drew a visceral response from the White House. Before Clark's delegation returned home, John Mitchell, former attorney general, and Clark MacGregor, chair of the Committee to Re-Elect the President, began to frame opposition to the bombings as one of supporting and furthering "communist propaganda" and undercutting "United States efforts for a just peace in Southeast Asia." Ramsey Clark had been "duped" in Vietnam, John Mitchell told the *New York Times* on 16 August, and he assailed his predecessor for speaking on Hanoi radio and for telling reporters that American prisoners there had told him they were treated relatively humanely.

Concerns over the bombing raids in Vietnam were not limited to the dikes along the Red River. In the ranks of the military, the trickle of protest about the war widened. Hardly had the public furor over Ramsey Clark's trip to Hanoi died down than a young air force sergeant testified before the Senate Armed Services Committee that data on bombing targets in North Vietnam were "routinely" falsified after the fact. On 6 September, the *New York Times* reported that Sergeant Lonnie D. Franks, a twenty-three-year-old intelligence specialist stationed at Udorn Air Base in Thailand, told the committee that more than two hundred officers were involved in the data falsification, which took up to three hours of their time daily. "Everybody was doing it," the sergeant said, "I kept on saying "why?" and they said, "that's the way we do it." Much of the falsified data involved claims after the fact that reconnaissance aircraft were fired upon, thus justifying whatever "unauthorized" targets were bombed. Other officers volunteered other "secrets" to reporters; if reconnaissance planes had more than the usual four escort planes, they were planning, in advance, a "protective-reaction" strike. Some pilots testified that, during periods of official bombing halts, they were routinely ordered to bomb targets in North Vietnam, even when they were not fired upon first. In the end, only General Lavelle, commander of the Seventh Air Force, was held responsible for the strikes. After Lavelle was relieved of his command, the Senate Armed Services Committee dropped its inquiry.

As reports from delegations to Vietnam raised the level of national and international protest over the destruction of Vietnam's dike system, the bombing slowed, allowing the Vietnamese at last to repair damage and avert massive flooding. The bombs continued to fall in other places. In mid-October, American bombs struck the French embassy in Hanoi. France's chief diplomat there, Pierre Susini, was killed. The Defense Department refused to take responsibility for the strike. The embassy may have been hit by antiaircraft missiles, Melvin Laird said, brushing aside a Canadian correspondent's report that he witnessed repeated attacks by American planes over that area in Hanoi at the time that the embassy was struck, an area, the *New York Times* of 14 October quoted that reporter as saying, "with embassies but no North Vietnamese ministries or factories anywhere near."

George Kahin, professor of government at Cornell University, noted that when he went through bombed-out areas in North Vietnam that fall, the bombing appeared indiscriminate. "Each town and city which I passed through," he said, "had been leveled . . . temples, churches, schools, hospitals, marketplaces, houses and public offices. . . . If the destruction I saw was the result of 'precision bombing' of 'military targets,' I can only ask: What in the vernacular of our President and our military leaders is not a military target?" (Vastyan 1973).

In the midst of the bombing, the reelection campaign of Richard Nixon went on apace. Nixon wanted to cut into labor's traditional support for Democrats, and to that end he had already commuted the thirteen-year prison sentence that Jimmy Hoffa, former president of the Teamsters Union, was serving for jury tampering and fraud. Hoffa was out on the street again, but the terms of his parole barred him permanently from any direct or indirect role in Teamster activities. Between the war in Vietnam and President Nixon's political ambitions, the ex-convict concocted a scheme to return to his old place as head of the Teamsters Union. He needed additional presidential attention, and going on a mission to Hanoi struck him as the most promising way to work his way back into the Teamsters Union.

With William L. Taub and Harold Gibbons, the Teamsters vice president, Hoffa flew to the summer White House in San Clemente, California, in mid-July. The three laid before Henry Kissinger Hoffa's plan to climb aboard a labor delegation, still to be formed, that would travel to Hanoi. If Kissinger could round up sufficient support from Washington and put in a word to the Vietnamese negotiator in Paris, Hoffa hoped that Hanoi would release some American pilots to his labor delegation. As a reward for bringing some POWs home from Hanoi, Hoffa expected President Nixon to permit him to return to the Teamsters Union, which had just endorsed Nixon's reelection bid.[8]

On his trip to Paris two weeks later, in late July, Kissinger told the Vietnamese negotiator, Le Duc Tho, that Washington hoped that a proposed labor delegation would be able to visit Hanoi promptly. Hanoi sent an invitation to the labor delegation. In late August, with his invitation in hand, Taub arranged a session with Ralph Erickson, Attorney General Richard Kleindienst's deputy assistant. As a convicted felon now on parole, Hoffa had to stay well within the technicalities of the law. He needed a new passport and proper validation for travel to North Vietnam. A few days later, Raymond Farrell, head of the Justice Department's Immigration and Naturalization Service, advised the State Department's Passport Office that a "hot case" was up for travel validation to Hanoi and they should treat it "discreetly."

Discretion prevailed for a time. On the afternoon of 7 September, Hoffa and Taub went to the passport office and, under expedited procedures, received passports, officially validated for travel to Hanoi. Their departure was set for that evening. But word of the expedited passport issuance and validation leaked out to Secretary of State William Rogers in the late afternoon. He was, according to subordinates, irate, and immediately withdrew the validation, canceled the trip, and made sure that details of these irregularities reached the morning papers.

Recriminations began immediately. Kissinger and Kleindienst denied they had encouraged the trip. Passport office officials blamed a lower-level official not authorized to issue passports for the irregular issuance, though they declined to identify the culprit or indicate what corrective measures, if any, they were taking. Other sources confirmed to reporters that Kissinger and Kleindienst had, without notifying William Rogers, approved the Hoffa trip in hopes of widening labor support for Nixon in the fall elections.

Jimmy Hoffa never got to Hanoi, but Nixon kept the support of the Teamsters that fall, and more POWs did come home. Hanoi officials had already decided to release more Americans, as evidence, they said, that

8. Harold Gibbons had been on a labor delegation to Hanoi in March. For a contemporary report of that trip see *Nation*, 24 Apr. 1972. Taub was not a licensed attorney, though he told officials that he represented Hoffa (*NYT*, 9 and 12 Sept. 1972).

they were not vindictive toward Americans and that they were flexible in negotiating the future release of all of the POWs. On 2 September, Hanoi announced that three American prisoners would soon be released. Later that day, Committee of Liaison members Cora Weiss and David Dellinger called a news conference in Paris to announce that they would soon be flying to Hanoi to bring the three back to the United States.

The last prisoners to be released had left Hanoi in July 1969. Vietnamese officials had repeatedly told American travelers in Hanoi since then that the method by which the American military first "snatched" released POWs, and then turned subsequent releases into vehicles for allegations of torture and mistreatment, closed the door on any further releases. Nevertheless, American activists continued to urge prisoner releases, and Ramsey Clark had repeatedly pressed officials in Hanoi to release more prisoners during his visit there two months earlier. Officials in Hanoi said nothing of Jimmy Hoffa. They indicated to reporters that this last prisoner release was due, in large part, to Clark's intercession as a former high ranking administration official.

The three men released were navy lieutenant Markham Gartley, downed in August 1968, navy lieutenant Norris Charles, shot down the previous December, and air force major Edward Elias, downed in April. All three had met with Americans in Hanoi on previous occasions. Gartley had made a number of antiwar statements during his four years of captivity, Charles had signed the open letter of protest from eight officers that the People's Coalition for Peace and Justice delegation had carried with them back to Washington in July, and Elias was quoted as saying that previous years of bombing had proved that bombing the north did not stop the war in the south, and that the latest bombing merely proved it again.

Hanoi officials invited one family member of each prisoner to come to Hanoi to escort him home. The Department of Defense immediately proclaimed that family travel to Hanoi would not be in the best interest of the United States. The Pentagon would do everything possible to arrange for the returned prisoners to have a prompt private reunion with family members upon their return, officials said, but they sternly warned family members against traveling to Hanoi. Olga Charles, married to Norris Charles, told a bank of reporters as she held their three-year-old daughter that she would go to Hanoi "regardless of what others may think." Minnie Lee Gartley, Markham Gartley's mother and regular antiwar picket outside the White House for four years, said that after five years of not being able to see her son, she was only too happy to go to Hanoi. Only Elias's family decided not to go, citing the Defense Department's statements that such a visit would be contrary to national interests.

On 16 September, eight Americans flew to Hanoi to bring the three prisoners home. Besides the family members, four Committee of Liaison members went to Hanoi: Cora Weiss, David Dellinger, Richard Falk, and William Sloane Coffin, plus two members of a previously arranged delegation, Father Harry Bury and Marianne Hamilton, coordinators of the International Assembly of Christians, a group concerned with the role of the Roman Catholic Church in Indochina. Associated Press reporter Peter Arnett joined the group in Vientiane to cover the trip.[9]

Early the next morning, Olga Charles rose in her Hanoi hotel, ate breakfast and went to a beauty shop in downtown Hanoi to have her hair washed and set. Later that morning, she and Minnie Lee Gartley fought through a wall of international reporters and cameramen to embrace their loved ones. "Hes even better-looking than I had remembered," Minnie Lee said proudly of her son. The *New York Times* reported on 18 September that Elias was clearly disappointed that no family members were there to greet him. "But I will see them very soon," he told the reporters hopefully back at the Hoa Binh Hotel where the delegation was staying.

The entire delegation stayed the requisite week in Hanoi, awaiting the next plane out. They relaxed in the hotel bar and shopped in the small stores and restaurants that lined the streets of Hanoi. They found particularly fascinating the ubiquitous items that looked at first to be fashioned from silver: cigarette boxes, letter openers, combs. On closer inspection they turned out to be made with materials supplied courtesy of the United States Air Force—scrap metal of the planes downed in the countryside of Vietnam.

In the streets of Hanoi, the group attracted little attention—Americans were not an unusual sight—but word that the group included pilots quickly got out, prompting some angry bystanders to come up to the group to tell them of family members they had lost to the bombs. One man brought all his children to the pilots, telling them of how he had lost

9. Bury and Moore went to Hanoi to coordinate plans for the upcoming second International Assembly of Christians in Solidarity with the Vietnamese, Laotian, and Cambodian People. Seven North Vietnamese Catholic clergy attended the meeting, held in Quebec the following month. Clergy from the south could not get government visas for the trip. For Bury and Moore's report on the church in North Vietnam, see the *Christian Century*, 15 Nov. 1972.

his wife in a bombing raid. Father Bury celebrated mass one evening at St. Dominic's Church in Hanoi. Communicants flocked to the rail to receive the sacrament from the hands of the "enemy" priest, the first American to conduct a mass in Hanoi for over twenty-five years.

The week that the group spent in Hanoi was the first week since March 1965 that there were no American military deaths in Vietnam. Vietnamization was working for Americans. By this time, there were only 27,000 American military personnel in Vietnam. During this same week, however, American planes launched more than one thousand air strikes and more than one thousand Vietnamese were killed. The group traveled under some of these air strikes. Their first day in Hanoi included five air raids. On their day trips around Hanoi, they were forced into the ditch by the road several times as American bombers flew overhead. Their hosts still made careful distinction between the American government and the American people. The bomb craters were "Johnson's craters" or "Nixon's craters." Once when their journey was interrupted by American bombers overhead, their young interpreter said "Nixon's flying." Then he laughed. "No give damn," he said. William Sloan Coffin later related the interpreter's words to Prime Minister Pham Van Dong. "Only our English," the prime minister told him, "has been Vietnamized" (1972, 8).

The newly released pilots were well aware that over three years earlier, POWs released to American civilian groups had been intercepted by the American military in Laos and that, after Pentagon debriefings, Robert Frishman had begun to allege systematic torture in the American POW camps in Vietnam. In hopes of forestalling Pentagon ideas about an encore performance, they sent a telegram to the White House requesting that they be allowed to return to the United States with the delegation, and spend at least a few days with their families before returning to military duty. The telegram went unanswered (Coffin 1972, 4).

From Hanoi, the delegation went to Moscow by way of Peking, avoiding the airport at Vientiane, where military officials had boarded previous flights. Had the delegation gone to Vientiane on the regularly scheduled route, they would have found a United States Air Force medical evacuation plane, flown in from the Philippines, waiting for them, and the American ambassador and military officials standing by. The American consul, Richard Rand, had even purchased tickets for himself on the commercial flight out of Vientiane in order to accompany the pilots in case they turned down the military plane.

Having failed to catch up with the pilots in Vientiane, the military tried to catch them in Europe. In Moscow, Adolph Dubs, the American chargé d'affaires, met with the pilots in an airport suite, gave them each a passport, and "formally recommended" that they return on a medical evacuation plane. That was only a half-step away from a direct order, but the three declined. There were two routes home from Moscow, one through Stockholm and one through Copenhagen. American officials requested that Stockholm authorities allow military officers to board the plane there and question the returning pilots. Sweden refused. Such permission would only be granted, Swedish authorities said, if the pilots themselves requested it.

While this matter was still in dispute, the group boarded a plane in Moscow for New York, via Copenhagen. American officials in Moscow then bought tickets for themselves on the same commercial airliner and, with bags full of military uniforms, boarded the plane in Moscow to ride along with the group all the way home. At Copenhagen, Thomas Dunnigan, the American chargé d'affaires, also boarded the plane and told the pilots that an air force jet was available to fly them home. Once again the pilots turned down the offer.

Meanwhile, the White House and the Pentagon appeared alarmed over this prisoner release that they could not command. On 23 September, while the pilots were still in Hanoi, a Defense Department official told the *New York Times* that "the first time they are offered the choice to turn themselves in to U.S. authorities, and they don't do it, they could be considered AWOL." The pressure was on. In Paris, Ambassador William Porter indignantly decried the prisoner release as "impeding" the peace talks. While they were in Moscow, Defense Secretary Melvin Laird called a press conference on 27 September and framed the issue as one of potential treason on the part of the pilots. He contrasted unfavorably the willingness of these pilots to leave the prison in Hanoi with the loyalty of those pilots left behind. The Code of Uniform Military Justice was there to be enforced, the secretary said, and he pointed out that, under this code, any officer could lodge charges of cooperating with the enemy against any other. Laird singled out Elias's family for praise because they have "not taken part in this use of these families, these men, as propaganda tools by the North Vietnamese in violation, absolute violation of the Geneva Conventions." The House Internal Security Committee seized the moment to pass a bill banning all American travel to Hanoi.

The scene at Kennedy International Airport when the pilots arrived late on the night on 28 September was even more conflicted. A military contingent boarded the plane immediately and ordered the men to travel under military escort to their next destination—military hospitals where they would be hospitalized for tests to last at least several days. All three of the pilots were healthy and vigorous, and Gartley told the officers he wanted two days at least with the rest of his family, now waiting for him in the airport terminal. When the military officers refused, Minnie Lee Gartley broke down in tears. "I haven't cried since the day you called me and said my son was shot down," she told the naval officers on the plane. "We just want him to ourselves," she went on, "free of the Government, free of the Navy, free of the press, free of the North Vietnamese, and now we're not going to get it." During the twenty-five-minute shouting match that ensued, military officials shoved reporters from the plane and took Gartley with them to the St. Albans Naval Hospital in Queens for hospitalization.

Norris Charles's family was waiting for him in the airport terminal too, and when they discovered that Norris was headed directly on a military flight to San Diego, they had a similar clash. The family "flipped out," Norris's brother, Dr. Herbert Charles, told the *New York Times* on 30 September. "We screamed and hollered" he said, until the military officials relented and allowed the family an hour together in the airport lounge before flying Charles out to the West Coast to his hospitalization. Elias, whose family had not embarrassed the Pentagon by going to Hanoi to meet him, and the only one of the three to have announced his intention to remain in the service, was also the only one of the three not hospitalized (*Wicker* 1972).

The Pentagon had planned a very different kind of homecoming— one under its stiff control. Known as Operation Egress Recap, and prepared by a team of psychiatrists and psychologists at the Defense Department, the plan assumed that, whenever and however they returned, POWs would come home in "the worst" conditions and would be turned over from the military to their families gradually. The Defense Department planned to conduct extensive interviews with the prisoners, "probing their emotional problems" and debriefing them to "put into proper balance Communist accounts of the extent of anti-war feeling in the United States" (Holles 1972).

Defense Department policy forbade returning prisoners from speaking publicly of their treatment while in custody either of the Vietnamese or of the United States military. They could be stripped of rank and benefits and court-martialed for disobeying this order. They also could not be discharged from the military until they had been completely "processed" under the Pentagon's procedures. Until this procedure was completed, they were under orders not to speak of their prison experience. Many of the pilots were career officers, and as long as they remained in the service after their release, the ban was supposed to be in effect. The policy technically denied all speech about the prison experience equally. In practice, however, POWs who wished to excoriate the Vietnamese for their treatment did so with impunity, even encouragement. Those who spoke of their treatment in milder terms were held to the letter of the law.

Operation Egress Recap grew to include tracking the changes in the lives of individual family members that supposedly would pose potential problems for the returnees. "If his wife has changed the color of her hair or gained weight since he last saw her," such changes were recorded along with "everything that might pose a problem for . . . physical recovery and psychological readjustment" (Holles 1972). But svelte blond wives growing into stout brunette ones was the last thing the Pentagon needed to worry about. The well-publicized scenes of the return of the three pilots in September under civilian direction, and the pilots' clear preferences for immediate reunions with their families, had its impact on other families, who began to put pressure on the Pentagon to dismantle its tightly controlled repatriation plans. They wanted immediate family reunions and extended periods of leave for the prisoners when they came home, and they made sure that the media publicized their demands. When the POWs returned in early 1973, families won their demands for immediate reunification.[10]

In October 1972, just before the fall elections in the United States, Henry Kissinger and Le Duc Tho agreed on the text of a peace treaty. Kissinger planned to fly to Hanoi on 24 October to initial it. On the last day of the month, the agreement was to be signed in Paris. The Committee of Liaison sponsored a delegation to Hanoi in late October. The delegation delivered and picked up mail there and looked forward to being in Hanoi after a peace agreement was signed (Early 1972). South Vietnam's Thieu, however, refused to sign the treaty that the Americans had crafted for him. He knew that his government was weak, and he objected to treaty terms that he believed showed insufficient American commitment

10. The major adjustments for families with a prisoner in Hanoi, as it turned out, involved cases where a spouse wanted, or had already obtained, a divorce, or disagreements about the war itself.

to support its long-term survival after the Americans left. In addition, Nixon's pollster told him that his election victory would be better assured without an agreement; a peace settlement would free "Nixon Democrats" to go back to their own party. Peace was at hand, Kissinger insisted, but while Washington devised a way to convince Thieu to sign the agreement, the war was still on. Rather than celebrating peace in Hanoi, the November Committee of Liaison delegation got to tour the bombed-out Viet Bac region.

Viet Bac stretched north of Hanoi, all the way to the border with China, and it was a favorite target of the B-52s. A Vietnamese poet had described his bombed-out region thus:

> In this land where every foot of soil is human flesh,
> Every blade of grass human hair,
> Where it rains blood,
> Hails bones,
> Life must flower.
>
> (Miller 1972, SCPC)

In America, the poem had seemed a poignant metaphor, Susan Miller (1972, SCPC) wrote, but in Viet Bac she saw the literal truth behind it: schools and hospitals evacuated from more dangerous areas appeared in the middle of fields, the surgery section of a provincial hospital perched precariously on the side of a mountain, fully equipped operating rooms lining whitewashed chambers deep within its natural limestone cave. "Explain to the American people," one farmer told Denise Levertov, "that life here is not turned upside down: the bombing is useless as well as savage" (1973, 18).

In Hanoi, they toured the Bach Mai hospital. The nine-hundred-bed university hospital and research center played a major part in delivering health care to Vietnam's citizens, and it was the pride and joy of its director. The delegation was the last American group to tour the hospital. Bach Mai had barely a month of existence left before it was razed to the ground.

Miller and the rest of the group delivered the November letters for the American prisoners, visited briefly with eleven of them, and collected letters to take back to New York. The withdrawn peace treaty infuriated many Vietnamese. "Since 26 October," the head of the journalists association in Hanoi told the Americans as they were leaving for home, "a new spirit of anger has sprung up among us, for we have never known such treachery as a people before. We do not want to continue the war, but if Nixon does not sign the agreement, we have no other way" (Miller 1973, 6).

The Committee of Liaison sent one last delegation before Christmas to deliver mail to the POWs in Hanoi and to bring their letters back to their families in the United States. Telford Taylor, retired brigadier general and chief United States counsel at the Nuremberg trials after World War II, folk singer Joan Baez, Michael Allen, dean of the Yale University Divinity School, and Barry Romo, a Vietnam Veteran and national coordinator of Vietnam Veterans Against the War, arrived in Hanoi on 16 December, planning to stay a week and be home with their families for the Christmas holidays. Their intended stay stretched into three weeks because of President Nixon's method of pressuring South Vietnam's Thieu to agree to the peace treaty: Washington would unleash one last bombing blitz over North Vietnam to reassure the south that, in the future, America would stop at nothing to prop up a viable government in Saigon.

Throughout the war, citizen diplomats had worked to build ties to "the other side," to offer humanitarian and development aid, and to establish an American presence that would go beyond the war. The cruel ending to the war shocked them, and it came with an unexpected ferocity that stunned even the jaded. A day after the American group arrived, and continuing for two weeks, the United States unleashed its most massive bombing ever over North Vietnam. The bombs fell without rhyme or reason, on places already hopelessly bombed, on towns, villages, and hospitals. Although Nixon used the language of sports to name the bombing, Operation Linebacker II, everyone else called it the Christmas bombing. Nixon rankled at the name, because, as he would point out, he had ordered a halt for "humanitarian reasons" on 25 December, so no bombs actually fell on Christmas Day itself (Isaacson 1992, 469).

The American delegation in Hanoi over the Christmas holidays unexpectedly spent much of its time in air-raid shelters as American B-52s, huge, lumbering, and wildly imprecise, filled the skies over the cities of northern Vietnam. "For the first time in my life," Michael Allen said, "the noise of jet engines ceased to be merely an annoyance and became the sound of death" (1973, 91). The bomb shelters again became the international points in Hanoi. In the shelters they met Canadians, Indians, Germans, Algerians, Bulgarians, Laotians, French, and Spanish officials.

On 23 December, planes struck the Bach Mai hospital. Allen and Taylor reached the site several hours later. "It was a terrible scene," Taylor wrote in a dispatch that appeared in the *New York Times* on Christmas Day, "rescue workers carrying patients piggy-back, cranes and bulldozers and people using only their hands, desperately clearing debris to reach victims still buried in the rubble, and the frantic hospital director running from one building to another." Allen was struck by what the raid had done to the trees surrounding the hospital. Everywhere there were fresh green leaves blown off the trees by the bombs, he wrote, "If only there had been enough leaves to cover the ground and fill the craters and soften the sharp edges of bricks and shattered timbers" (1973, 91). But instead of leaves softening the blow, shattered concrete from a building collapsed over a bomb shelter filled with people. No one got out alive.

News of the bombed hospital appeared on the front pages of the *New York Times* directly beside the famed Apollo 17 photo of the earth as seen from space—the first photo in which no part of the earth was in shadow, the paper said. The coastline of Africa is the dominant geographical feature of the photo. Neither the United States nor Vietnam appears in view; in that photo, both lay in shadows on the other side of the world.

The American delegation had planned to leave before Christmas Day, but the Hanoi airport runway was bombed and cratered, and planes could not land. Instead, Joan Baez and Michael Allen organized a brief Christmas Eve service in their hotel lobby. Baez sang the Lord's Prayer, and, as she reached the phrase, "deliver us from evil," the roar of jet engines rose in the background and the air-raid sirens began to wail. The group moved quickly to the shelter and finished their Christmas prayers there.[11]

The worst raids over the city came on the day after Christmas, when the bombers struck with ferocity, as if to make up for the Christmas Day respite. "Dien Bien Phu in the sky," the people in Hanoi called it (Hess 1993, 20, 61). Kham Thien district, a working-class area of closely packed houses, disintegrated under the wave of bombers over it. The railroad tracks nearby, possibly an intended target, were unscathed. Allen and Taylor had walked through the busy district on Christmas Day. When they returned after the raid, they could see little but rubble—piles of brick, plaster, and timbers, bomb craters fifty feet wide, people searching

---

11. In 1967, the Daughters of the American Revolution had barred Baez from performing at Constitution Hall because of her opposition to the war. Baez then scheduled a free concert next to the Washington monument. The DAR president appealed unsuccessfully to the Department of the Interior to deny Baez permission to perform even there (*NYT,* 15 Aug. 1967).

throughout for family and possessions. The two men had seen unimagined destruction during the preceding days, but in the rubble of Kham Thien they came upon a whole family—mother, father, and two children—dead in each other's arms. "That day was the end for me," Allen wrote, after he saw a woman wandering through the rubble crying, "My son, my son, where are you?" (1973, 93).

In Washington, senior officials were comfortably out of town for the Christmas bombing. President Nixon, whom Kissinger had applauded for his "enormous courage" in ordering the bombing blitz, was at Key Biscayne. Kissinger was in Palm Springs, Florida, and the Secretary of Defense was soaking up sunshine in Hawaii. Pentagon spokesman Jerry Friedheim seemed not to enjoy his assignment, but he mouthed the denials anyway. There was no bombed hospital in Hanoi; the reports coming from there were "heavily laced with propaganda," he told reporters. Telford Taylor's eyewitness report appeared in the *New York Times* the next day. By New Year's Day, the entire American delegation was back in the United States and national newspapers carried their on-site accounts. "By all standards I know," Michael Allen told the *Times* reporter on 2 January, "the hospital was destroyed." The next day, the hapless Friedman abandoned his denials. "It appears that some limited accidental damage has occurred . . . at a hospital the enemy calls Bach Mai," he conceded.

For the United States, the Christmas air raids brought down nearly thirty B-52s, killed sixty-two pilots, handed Hanoi thirty-one more prisoners, and rained down condemnation on Washington from capitals around the world. The *New York Times* reported on 12 January 1973 that even some pilots refused to fly these missions, saying that the war was not worth the killing. The Pentagon tried to see the bright side. The B-52 had redeemed its role as a strategic bomber capable of carrying out its primary mission—penetrating Soviet defenses and dropping twenty-five-ton hydrogen bombs. "The people who might be most alarmed are those in the Soviet Union," an air force general told *Times* reporter John Finney brusquely on 24 December. For Vietnam, the Christmas bombing was more like the looting of equipment and infrastructure that colonial powers engaged in as they were on the cusp of forcible expulsion from their colonies: one last spasm of destruction in the final days, designed to further harry those who resisted.

Still, although the Christmas bombing persuaded Thieu to sign, this best deal that Nixon could achieve bore a familiar imprint. The peace treaty, signed on 27 January 1973, differed little from the one that Saigon had rejected in October. Further, it bore a remarkable resemblance to the Geneva Accords, the same Accords that marked the ignominious French exit from Vietnam in 1954, the same Accords that the United States had then refused to endorse, the same Accords that Hanoi had long insisted were the foundation for any peace agreement in Vietnam. The Paris Agreement of January 1973, Gareth Porter concluded, resulted from "the exhaustion of the Nixon administration's resistance to North Vietnamese terms" (1975, viii). There was one new provision, however: Nixon promised Hanoi "to contribute to the postwar reconstruction in North Vietnam without any political conditions" (Young 1991, 279).

When the peace accords were finally signed in Paris, seven members of the Women's International League for Peace and Freedom were in Hanoi. Two of them were Americans, Dorothy Steffens, and Marii Hasegawa. It was a fitting moment for the group that had sent a delegation to Hanoi two years earlier to sign a peace treaty in the name of citizens in both countries. Louise Lione, a reporter for the *Philadelphia Inquirer*, accompanied the group, reporting for her paper on the festivities in Hanoi surrounding the Peace Accords signing. Along with the POWs, Steffens, Hasegawa, and Lione were the only Americans in Hanoi when the treaty was signed in Paris.

"Everywhere we found a desire for friendship with the American people," Steffens said. For two days Hanoi Radio broadcast over and over the full text of the Paris Accords at dictation speed. Reconstruction was already underway. The one-person circular bomb shelters that lined city streets were being filled in, new tile roofs were going onto the shells of stucco buildings, craters in the road were shoveled in—permanently this time—and over them flowed people bringing into the city straw and bamboo poles to build new homes. The "Nixon bombing raids," as the Vietnamese called them, were over. "The recent war is called the Nixon war to distinguish it from the Johnson war," Steffens (Hanoi Trip, SCPC) noted. The Johnson war was destructive, "but apparently, the Nixon war is considered to have been a much more vicious one."

Reunification was on everyone's mind. "No one can live with a body cut in half," Premier Pham Van Dong told Lione. "We cannot live with our country cut in half. We must have reunification." He expected that relations between Vietnam and the United States would become "more normal." That was why Henry Kissinger was coming to Hanoi, he added. Lione asked the premier if, after Kissinger came to Hanoi, the premier might go to Washington. He reflected a moment and smiled faintly. "Perhaps I shall only be able to visit Washington when a women is president," Lione reported on 7 February.

The WILPF delegation, and others who followed them in the following months, raised money to rebuild bombed institutions, particularly hospitals, and to provide a variety of humanitarian aid. The Hanoi Maternal and Child Health Center that WILPF had supported for two years was damaged in the war. Repairing it was WILPF's priority. When Steffens met with Premier Pham Van Dong, she asked him what other humanitarian contributions WILPF could make. "We are a poor country," he replied, "rich only in—besides courage and intelligence—children. Anything you can do especially for our children, we thank you."

For other antiwar activists, rebuilding Bach Mai Hospital was imperative. On 2 January, Medical Aid for Indochina, founded in 1971 and organized primarily in the medical community and in church groups, announced a $3 million fund raising effort to rebuild and reequip the hospital. Five people, all of whom had been to Vietnam, headed the effort: Ramsey Clark, Bishop John Wesley Lord, Michael Allen, Charles Janeway, Harvard professor of pediatrics, and Pat Simon, whose GI son had been killed in Vietnam. Within days, they had secured pledges for $250,000. Physicians for Social Responsibility sent medical teams to Vietnam to train medical personnel there, to help with eye surgery and prosthetics care. The American Friends Service Committee continued to send pharmaceuticals and educational materials to Hanoi. American visitors, scientists, researchers, and friends, continued to make the trek there and work with doctors and researchers. Dr. Benjamin Spock finally got to Hanoi in April 1973 (Bach Mai Hospital, SCPC; Sheehan 1992).

The money that private organizations raised to help rebuild Vietnam was useful, but it never came close to the sums the Vietnamese believed, when the peace accords were signed, the United States government would provide. When Phoebe Friedman went to Vietnam with a Women Strike for Peace delegation that October, she heard the frequent admonition, "It is the responsibility of the United States to repair what it has damaged" (1973, 628). Guiding an American visitor through the rubble of the Viet-Duc hospital in Hanoi, Dr. Ton That Tung summed up his sentiments by saying "All wars must end. The important thing is what happens afterward. We think the American people should see their duty to help. I have found so many fine things in Americans. American help is necessary. And those who have destroyed should help to rebuild. If the

United States refuses to help, it will be the American soul that is lost" (Vastyan 1973, 389).

When the Saigon government collapsed in April 1975, some members of private volunteer organizations in South Vietnam stayed on. Earl Martin, a long-term volunteer with the Mennonite Central Committee, who spoke fluent Vietnamese, remained in Saigon, mixing with the many foreign journalists who also stayed, absorbing the new side of a Saigon he had never before seen. "Shortly after Liberation," he wrote,

> a wave of Vietnamese self-affirmation swept over Saigon. The common expressions of syrupy deference toward foreigners were suddenly gone. Such self-deprecating language—'America is civilized and modern; we're so poor and undeveloped'—had been commonplace. . . . Long years of dependency on the United States for salaries for the troops, for bullets on the battlefield, for fashions in the beauty salons, for music in the bars and even for rice on the table had taken their toll on the national psyche. But all that crumbled quickly. The smashing of the gates of the Presidential Palace by *bo doi* tanks on April 30 was accompanied by the smashing of an image of American invincibility that had been cultivated for several decades. (1978, 265)[12]

In July 1975, the State Department rejected the American Friends Service Committee's entire request for an export license to ship material aid to Vietnam. If the AFSC shipped its fish nets, powdered milk, rototillers, and yarn, the State Department warned, it could be prosecuted under the Trading with the Enemy Act. The AFSC declared that it intended to ship the goods with or without authorization, but that it would give the State Department time to reconsider. On 10 November, demonstrations against the State Department's decision were held in forty-five cities, while a delegation composed of representatives from the American Friends Service Committee, the National Council of Churches, Church World Service, the United Methodist Church, the United Presbyterian Church, and the Mennonite Central Committee held a vigil outside the White House (after being refused an appointment with White House officials) and then took their case to members of Congress. Four days later, the State Department reversed itself and granted the AFSC its export license (Brink 1975, AFSC; McAuliff 1975).

12. European journalists' coverage of the Saigon government's collapse are also quite different from those of mainstream American reports.

The ferment and wars set off in Southeast Asia by the imposition of colonialism in the preceding century, and the factions and enmities that this latest war provoked, burned on in the entire region, helped along by the determination of the United States to oppose Vietnam at every step and block its international links, even if that meant aligning itself with the Khmer Rouge in Cambodia.[13] As United States policy turned markedly vindictive, it ensured that, for the American war generation, the wounds of war would be slow to heal. An official acknowledgment of concern for the destruction in Vietnam, generous aid for reconstruction, and encouragement of travel and communication between the countries would have gone far toward ending, within America, the sense of guilt, hostility, and myriad lingering hatreds over America's tangled history in Vietnam. By setting out to punish Vietnam after the war, the United States punished itself.

The American government contributed nothing to rebuilding a re-unified Vietnam. Far from providing reconstructive aid, Washington extended the embargo against North Vietnam to the entire country. President Ford vetoed Vietnamese membership in the United Nations, froze $150 million of Vietnamese assets in the United States, and barred Vietnam from participation in the World Bank and the International Monetary Fund. Congress went further and explicitly barred any aid whatsoever for Vietnam. The United States allowed few Vietnamese visitors into the country, and it sharply restricted procedures for legal immigration. The only way now for Vietnamese to come to the United States was to enter a third country illegally and claim political asylum. It was a policy that, like the pacification strategy, was sure to produce refugees.

Other countries provided some help in reconstruction. West Germany and East Germany both sent technicians and helped rebuild hospitals. The Soviet Union provided some help in reconstruction and rebuilding. The Swedish government was generous with material aid, providing personnel and funds for hospitals and schools. The Cuban government provided technicians for rebuilding the country and, for a time, even their food, to avoid "any possible burden" for the Vietnamese (Friedman 1973).

The Committee of Liaison built a coalition organization called Friendshipment to coordinate shipments of medical supplies and agricul-

13. For detailed and wide-ranging accounts of these events see Chanda, 1986, Charny and Spragens 1984, Rowley and Evans 1984, and Young 1991.

tural equipment to the Vietnamese Red Cross. One of its first projects was building a hundred-bed hospital near the site of the My Lai massacre. Another one of Friendshipment's goals was to help establish normal diplomatic relations between the United States and Vietnam. That goal was further away than anyone dreamed possible in 1975. But in the extended absence of formal diplomatic relations, citizen exchanges steadily grew. The American Friends Service Committee continued to maintain a presence in Vietnam and to provide humanitarian materials, and it finally established the permanent presence in Hanoi for which its personnel had worked for so long. Americans with ties to universities, who had gone to Vietnam during the war, continued those contacts. Other church and humanitarian groups joined them. Veterans groups provided contributions for rebuilding projects in Vietnam and sponsored veterans exchanges between the two countries.

These activists continued to lobby the White House for a change in policy toward Vietnam, and to this end they began to solicit help from the business community. "We held lots of meetings in the White House during the 1970s and 80s," activist Joy Carol recalled, "and we continued to send material aid to Vietnam and tried to comply with Treasury Department regulations. They constantly threatened those of us involved with these activities with lengthy imprisonment and heavy fines if any of our material aid contributed to the personal enrichment of any single Vietnamese" (Carol 1993).

The fines that Washington levied for organizing travel tours to Vietnam drove Lindblad Travel out of business in 1989. Lars-Eric Lindblad, whose tour company had pioneered commercial trips for westerners to China and Vietnam when Washington forbade travel to those countries, said he had intentionally violated the sanctions against Vietnam. "I would do it again," he told the *New York Times* on 13 July 1994, after his company folded. "Travel in my opinion is not ordinary trade. Travel is a way of communication. To embargo travel is like burning books or imprisoning journalists."

In the late 1970s, an informal United States task force on Vietnam, begun by Americans who had worked in Vietnam and had visited Hanoi during the war years, began to hold annual meetings to exchange news of Vietnam, provide accounts of organizational work there, and encourage new contacts. Members of the task force solicited the involvement of American corporations, some of whom donated money to various humanitarian projects in Vietnam. The corporate community then began to send representatives to the annual task force meetings. Activists built on the contacts they had made with White House and State Department officials, and, though they took starkly opposing positions on the issue of resuming normal diplomatic ties with Vietnam, they began inviting those officials to the annual task force meetings. By the mid-1980s, administration officials were regular observers at these annual meetings that brought together American activists, commercial interests, and government officials. By 1988, the activists found that their meetings with White House officials were "easier," and there was less official opposition and harassment of their work in Vietnam. In 1988, the informal task force became the United States Nongovernmental Organization Forum on Vietnam, Cambodia, and Laos. Its 1993 annual meeting in Arlington, Virginia, drew representatives from two hundred organizations, corporations, and institutions, along with officials from U.S. government agencies. That year, despite official opposition, according to a 9 July 1993 *New York Times* report, private American humanitarian organizations provided over $15 million in relief and development assistance to Vietnam.

In early 1994, the United States Congress voted to lift the nineteen-year-old trade embargo against Vietnam. President Clinton signed legislation to that effect and began the slow process of restoring diplomatic relations between the two countries. These first halting steps toward official reconciliation came forty years after the United States government had first begun to send its money and men to Vietnam. It came after the deaths of millions and decades of bitterness on all sides.

The Americans who traveled to Hanoi during the days when their government went to war became the moral witnesses to that war. As their own state went about imposing its will on Southeast Asia by military force, they insisted upon viewing the Other as a subject whose concerns and lives were as legitimate as their own, and whose own present and past had to be understood within its own context. They wanted to bring the reality of the war home from Hanoi, and to this end they put themselves under their country's bombs and wrote of the meaning of the war for the people who lived and died under it. They were the eyes for the millions of their comrades who remained at home, and they published copiously in the antiwar press, which activists read avidly. They ensured that Americans would know about the war, that they would have to confront the humanity of the enemy. The blasted villages, the bloody bodies, the limbless survivors, the "thousand social problems" that each bomb carried with it, were, for them, far more significant than the issues of American credibility or national honor that they heard from Washington. "We were not military men," author Grace Paley wrote after her trip to Hanoi, "not even people who'd been to wars, we weren't bored by the repetition; we didn't even get used to it" (1969, 6).

The travelers to Hanoi incurred the bitterness of their own government as they endeavored to aid their compatriot prisoners of war. Efforts to secure early releases for them and open up avenues of communication between the prisoners and their families won them few friends in Washington at the time, but the services they tirelessly provided helped the prisoners and their families during those grim years and provided evidence that, even in time of war, citizens could be a constructive influence for international reconciliation. The humanitarian aid that the activists organized and carried to Vietnam was a successful effort to mitigate some of the bitterness that the war incited there. It provided real and symbolic evidence to the Vietnamese that Americans were more than just a military force, and it provided Americans themselves with an activity that went beyond the limitations of street protests, an answer to the call of conscience as well as a political response.

In retrospect, even architects of the war have concluded that it was, in the words of former defense secretary Robert McNamara, "terribly wrong" (McNamara 1995, xvi). If the war itself is something that the nation cannot be proud of, the antiwar protest that concerned citizens built is something for which Americans can be proud. Those who worked tirelessly to end the war, unpopular and maligned as they were at the time, gave their nation the gift of a partially redeemed past. Imagining the war in Vietnam without a wide protest movement among America's own citizens makes that war even more horrifying. The American travelers to Hanoi held out to the people there the assurance that the American government did not speak for all its people and that a change in relations between the two nations was possible. The Vietnamese who welcomed them there began to speak of the American public as potentially akin to the travelers in Hanoi. "Friends like Norman Morrison and you have saved the honor of the United States," Tran Lam told the American Friends Service Committee's John Sullivan (Sullivan 1972, AFSC). This assurance, too, was one of the travelers' enduring achievements. They kept alive, in Vietnam, the image of Americans as friends.

References
Index

References

Archives

Swarthmore College Peace Collection (SCPC), Swarthmore, Pa.

Barnett, DeWitt. 1966. Report From Japan. AJM, box 43. 10 May.

Chronology Relating to a Quaker Action Group. 1970. DG-74, box 1, History folder.

Clark, Bronson. 1967. Quaker Exchanges at Bratislava. DG-74, box 2, Bratislava. 5–13 Sept.

Clarke, Mary. 1967. WSP L.A. Folder, series B.1, DG-115, box 3.

Comments on Report of U.S. Study Team on Political and Religious Freedom in Viet-Nam. CEC, FOR.

Coordinating Committee Report. 1972. DG-84, box 3, PCPJ.

Dahlberg, Edwin. 1967. Memo to Alfred Hassler. Medical Humanitarian Aid. DG-13, series G. 19 Apr.

Flanagan, Ross. 1966–67. Letters of Criticism, DG-64, box 3.

———. 1967. On Talking with the Enemy. DG-74, box 2, Bratislava.

Gitlin, Nanci. 1965. Djakarta, Speaking Dates Reports. Series B.2, DG-115, box 2.

Gottlieb, Sanford, and Robert S. Browne. 1965. "Report on Visit to Nguyen Van An, 30 June." CEC, FOR.

Gottlieb, Saul. N.d. Peace Walk: San Francisco to Moscow. DG-79, box 2.

Hassler, Alfred. 1967a. Memo to Daniel Berrigan. Medical Humanitarian Aid. Series G, DG-13. 5 Sept.

———. 1967b. Memo to Robert McAfee Brown. Medical Humanitarian Aid. Series G, DG-13. 2 Oct.

———. 1967c. Report From Saigon. CEC, FOR. 6 Feb.

———. 1967d. Transcript. Tape no. 7. CEC, FOR.

Herring, Frances. 1965. American and Vietnamese Women Join Hands for Peace. Series B, DG-115, Djakarta.

Hoa Binh Ad Hoc Committee. 1968–70. 1968. CEC, FOR. 11 Oct.

Joint Statement on Conclusion of Clergy Visit to Hanoi. 1967. AJM, box 46. 9–19 Jan.

Lyttle, Bradford. N.d. San Francisco to Moscow: The Story of a 6000 Mile March for Peace. DG-79, box 2.

Mayer, Paul. 1972. "Some Reflections on the Vietnamese." DG-84, PCPJ, Box 1.

Memorandum on an Informal Meeting. 1965. Vietnamese and American Women Talk Peace in Djakarta. Series B.2, DG-115, box 2.

Miller, Susan. 1972. "Bombing North Vietnam Back to the Stone Age: Trip to North Vietnam." DG-84, box 3, PCPJ. 4–11 Nov.

Muste, A. J. 1965. Memo to Prathia Hall Wynn. AJM, box 46.

———. 1966. Memo to Martin Luther King, Jr. AJM, box 43.

Participants in Vietnam Project. 1965. CEC Journey. FOR.

People's Peace Treaty. 1971. DG-84, temp. box 4.

Proposal for Trip to South Vietnam. 1969. CEC, FOR. 12 Mar.

Report from Vietnam. Series G. CEC, FOR.

Reports from Saigon. 1966. DG-79, box 8.

Returning Delegation From North Vietnam. DG 84, box 2, PCPJ.

Reynolds, Earle. N.d. *Phoenix Sails to Haiphong.* 4, AQAG History, DG-74, box 1.

Richardson, Elliott. 1969. Memo to Barton Hunter. CEC, FOR. 21 Oct.

Schomer, Elsie. 1965. Report. CEC, FOR, series G. 7 July.

Schwartz, Margaret. N.d. Office of Foreign Assets Control. Treasury Department to Nation's Banks. DG-13, box 1.

Six Who Survived. N.d. Committee of Responsibility to Save War-Burned and War-Injured Vietnamese Children. DG-74, Box 1.

Steffens, Dorothy. N.d. Hanoi Trip. Delegation to the Vietnam Women's Union. DG-43.

Taylor, Ethel. 1974. Inquiry into War Crimes—Vietnam Veterans Against the War. Series A.8, DG-115. Mar. 26.

———. 1988. Vietnam Retrospective. Pennsylvania Historical Association. Series A.8, DG-115, box Vietnam.

Text of Letter from Eight U.S. Pilots Detained in North Vietnam. 1972. Coordinating Committee. DG-84, PCPJ, box 3. May.

U.S. Women to Meet with Communist Vietnam Women. 1965. Newsclippings, DG-115, box 1.

Vice Consul for France to Jane Addams. 1915. The Jane Addams Papers, Reel 113.8. 10 July.

Vietnam Courier. 1965a. "30,000 People Harmed." 15 July.

Vietnam Courier. 1965b. "Bombing of North Vietnam Important Cities." 15 July.

Vietnam Crisis. 1965. Series G. CEC, FOR.

Vietnamese Children. N.d. DG-74, box 1, Aid to Vietnam.

Wilson, Dagmar. N.d. Files. Series A.3, DG-115, box 1.

American Friends Service Committee (AFSC), Philadelphia, Pa.

Brink, Paul. 1975. News Release, Vietnam 1975–1989. 14 Nov.

Cary, Stephen. 1965. Report of AFSC Vietnam Mission. 4 Aug.

Contacts With the National Liberation Front of South Vietnam—1965–1968. 1968. ISD, RPO, Vietnam Government.

Elder, Joseph. 1969a. Letter to Charles Read and Martin Teitel, 20 May.

———. 1969b. Letter to Charles Read, 10 June.

Indochina Humanitarian Program, AFSC—Vietnam.

Krabill, Willard. 1966. Vietnam: Soul-Sick and War-Weary. MCC News Service. 28 Jan.

Meacham, Stuart, and Wallace Collett. 1968. Paris Interviews. Vietnam. 16–19 Dec.

Nelson, Marjorie. 1968. Excerpts from a talk by Marjorie Nelson. AFSC—Vietnam. 21 May.

News Release. 1972. AFSC—Vietnam. 3 May.

Perera, George. 1972. Comments With Emphasis on Health and Medical Aspects of Trip to the DRV. ISD, RPO, NVN Reports. 15–22 July.

Schneider, Lou. 1970. Transcript of conversation with Roger Fredrickson and Charles Read. ISO, RPO, NV Trips. 11 Jan.

———. 1971. Memo to Bronson Clark. 1971. ISO, RPO, NV General.

Sullivan, John. 1972a. Memo to Jane Weston. IDS, RPO, NVN Trips. 2 Aug.

———. 1972b. Report on Mission to Hanoi. International Service Divison, RPO. 16 Aug.

———. N.d. An AFSC Reflection on Guenter Lewy's *Peace and Revolution: The Moral Crisis of American Pacifism*.

Lyndon Baines Johnson Library (LBJL), Austin, Tex.

Ashmore, Harry. Oral history notes.

Bundy, McGeorge. 1966. Memo to Hubert Humphrey. Box 218, EX ND, 19/CO, 312. 11 Jan.

Butterfield, Alexander. 1965. Memo to John Jays. Confidential files, box 76, PE 13 Travel Regulations Per Diem, Office of Secretary of Defense. 27 Aug.

Cooper, Chester L. 1965. Memo to Mrs. Philip Good. Gen ND 19/CO 312, 6/30/65–7/2/65. 2 July.

Harriman, W. Averell. 1967. Memo to LBJ. WR files, NSF, box 7.

Hoover, J. Edgar. 1967. Memo to President Johnson. NSF Country File, Vietnam, Bertrand Russell "Trial." 13 May.

Humphrey, Hubert H. 1966. Memo to McGeorge Bundy. Box 218, EX ND, 19/CO, 312, 12/3/65. 10 Jan.

Jones, Jim. 1967. Memo to the president. NSF. 4 Nov.

Panzer. 1967. Vietnam Information Group, Q & A, Two American Biologists. Office files, Panzer. 4 Dec.

Rostow, Walt. 1966a. Lunch meetings with the president. Box 1, NSF. Apr.–Dec.

———. 1966b. The Thirty-seven Day Pause. Viet Nam—W.W. Rostow, 1. NSF.

———. 1967a. Cable from General Westmoreland to president. Box 7, NSF. 5 Dec.

———. 1967b. Edward Brooke to Lyndon Johnson, NSF. 23 May.

———. 1967c. Memo to president. NSF Country File—Vietnam, Bertrand Russell "Trial." 27 Apr.

———. 1967d. Memo to Robert Giaimo. Vietnam: April–June. NSF, Apr. 7.

———. 1967e. Richard Helms to the president. U.S. Peace Groups—International Connections, NSF Intelligence File. 15 Nov.

———. 1967f. Treasury Department Release. Vietnam: April–June. NSF. 27 Feb.

———. 1968a. Memo to president. NSF Memos, box 32, volume 72. 12–23 Apr.

———. 1968b. Vietnam—January–February. Box 1. NSF.

———. Marigold-Sunflower. Box 1, NSF.

Schultze, Charles. 1967. Subversive Activities Control Board, Report 21 July. EX Box 309, FG 285. Subversive Activities Control Board, 11/2/63–7/21/67.

Schwartz, Abba. 1966. Memo for the Undersecretary, 25 January. PE 13, Travel Regulations, Confidential File, PE 2.

Watson, Marvin. 1968. Memo to LBJ. Gen. FO 5-1 11/22/63, box 52. 27 Mar.

WHCF. N.d. Name Files, SC (Stokely Carmichael), box 1.

Yarmolinsky, Adam. 1965. Memo to Assistant Secretary of Defense for Public Affairs. 1965. Confidential Files, Box 76, PE 13 Travel Regulations Per Diem, Office of Secretary of Defense. 3 Aug.

Students for a Democratic Society Papers (SDSP),
University of Wisconsin, Madison, Wisc.

Booth, Paul. 1965. Letter to Ira Sandperl and Joan Baez. Microfilm reel 19, series 3. 29 Sept.

Clamage, Dena. 1965. Letter to Paul Booth. Microfilm, reel 19, series 3. 14 Dec.

Works Cited

Addams, Jane. 1915. "The Revolt Against War." *Survey* 39 (17 July): 356–58.

Allen, Michael. 1973. "Sharing the Agony of Hanoi." *Christian Century,* 24 Jan., 91–94.

Alvarez, Everett, Jr., and Anthony Pitch. 1989. *Chained Eagle*. New York: Donald I. Fine.

American Prisoners of War in Southeast Asia (APW). 1971. Hearings Before the Subcommittee on National Security Policy and Scientific Developments of the Committee on Foreign Affairs. 92d Cong. Washington, D.C.: Government Printing Office.

Anderson, Charles. 1982. *Vietnam: The Other War*. Novato: Presidio.

Andrade, Dale. 1990. *Ashes to Ashes: The Phoenix Program and the Vietnam War*. Lexington: Lexington Books.

Aptheker, Herbert. 1966. *Mission to Hanoi*. New York: International.

Armstrong, James, and John J. Conyers, Jr. 1969. "Vietnam: Sojourn and Sequel." *Christian Century*, 15 Oct., 1307.

Ashmore, Harry S. 1994. *Civil Rights and Civil Wrongs: A Memoir of Race and Politics, 1944–1994*. New York: Pantheon.

Ashmore, Harry S., and William C. Baggs. 1968. *Mission to Hanoi: A Chronicle of Double-Dealing in High Places*. New York: G. P. Putnam's Sons.

Bentley, Eric, ed. 1971. *Thirty Years of Treason: Excerpts from Hearings Before the House Committee on Un-American Activities, 1938–1968*. New York: Viking.

Bentley, James. 1984. *Martin Niemoeller*. New York: Oxford Univ. Press.

Berrigan, Daniel. 1968. *Night Flight to Hanoi: War Diary with 11 Poems*. New York: Macmillan.

Bigelow, Albert. 1959. *The Voyage of the Golden Rule: An Experiment With Truth*. New York: Doubleday.

Boardman, Elizabeth Jelinek. 1985. *The Phoenix Trip: Notes on a Quaker Mission to Haiphong*. Burnsville, N.C.: Celo Press.

Boyle, Kay. 1966. "Assignment in Cambodia." *Progressive* (Nov.): 19–20.

Brace, Ernest. 1988. *A Code to Keep*. New York: St. Martin's.

Brightman, Carol. 1967. "The Discriminating Air War: The Real Targets in North Vietnam." *Viet-Report* (Apr.–May): 3–38.

Brown, John Pairman. 1968. "A Visit to North Vietnam." *Christianity Today*, 3 Jan., 18–21.

Burner, Eric. 1994. *And Gently He Shall Lead Them: Robert Parris Moses and Civil Rights in Mississippi*. New York: New York Univ. Press.

Cameron, James. 1965. *Here Is Your Enemy: James Cameron's Complete Report from Vietnam*. New York: Holt, Rinehart, and Winston.

Carol, Joy. 1995. Telephone interview by author. 7 May.

Catledge, Turner. 1971. *My Life and the Times*. New York: Harper and Row.

Chanda, Nayan. 1986. *Brother Enemy: The War after the War: A History of Indochina since the Fall of Saigon*. New York: Harcourt Brace Jovanovich.

Chandler, Robert. 1981. *War of Ideas: The United States Propaganda Campaign in Vietnam*. Boulder: Westview.

Charny, Joel, and John Spragens, Jr. 1984. *Obstacles to Recovery in Vietnam and Kampuchea: U.S. Embargo of Humanitarian Aid.* New York: Oxfam America.

Chatfield, Charles. 1992. *The American Peace Movement: Ideals and Activism.* New York: Twayne.

Che, Lan Vien. 1972. "The Enemy and Us." *Vietnam Courier* (Dec.): 15.

Chinnery, Philip. 1989. *Life on the Line: Stories of Vietnam Air Combat.* New York: St. Martin's.

Chomsky, Noam. 1967. "The Responsibility of Intellectuals: An Exchange." *New York Review of Books,* 23 Mar.

———. 1970. "In North Vietnam: A Special Supplement." *New York Review of Books,* 13 Aug.

Clarke, Mary. 1995. Telephone interview by author. 3 Mar.

Clinton, James W. 1995. *The Loyal Opposition: Americans in North Vietnam, 1965–1972.* Niwot, Colo.: Univ. of Colorado Press.

Clodfelter, Mark. 1989. *The Limits of Air Power: The American Bombing of North Vietnam.* New York: Free Press.

Coffee, Gerald. 1990. *Beyond Survival: Building on the Hard Times—A POW's Inspiring Story.* New York: G. P. Putnam's Sons.

Coffin, William Sloan, Jr. 1972. "Three Return." *American Report* 9 (23 Oct.): 4.

Communist Activities in the Peace Movement (Women Strike for Peace and Certain Other Groups). 1963. 87th Cong., 2d sess. Washington, D.C.: U.S. Government Printing Office.

Cooper, Chester. 1970. *The Lost Crusade.* New York: Dodd, Mead.

Crichton, Robert. 1968. "Our Air War." *The New York Review of Books,* 4 Jan., 3–5.

DeBenedetti, Charles. 1980. *The Peace Reform in American History.* Bloomington: Indiana Univ. Press.

———. 1983. "A CIA Analysis of the Anti-Vietnam War Movement: October 1967." *Peace and Change* 9 (spring): 31–41.

———. 1990. *An American Ordeal: The Antiwar Movement of the Vietnam Era.* Syracuse: Syracuse Univ. Press.

DeConde, Alexander. 1966. *The Quasi-War: The Politics and Diplomacy of the Undeclared War with France, 1797–1801.* New York: Charles Scribner's Sons.

———. 1992. *Ethnicity, Race, and American Foreign Policy: A History.* Boston: Northeastern Univ. Press.

DeForest, Orrin, and David Chanoff. 1990. *Slow Burn: The Rise and Bitter Fall of American Intelligence in Vietnam.* New York: Simon and Schuster.

Dellinger, David. 1966. "North Vietnam: Eyewitness Report." *Liberation* (Dec.).

———. 1967. "A. J. Muste Tributes." *Liberation* (Feb.).

———. 1986. *Vietnam Revisited: From Covert Action to Invasion to Reconstruction.* Boston: South End Press.

———. 1992. Interview by author. Columbus, Ohio, 7 Oct.

————. 1993. *From Yale to Jail: The Life Story of a Moral Dissenter.* New York: Pantheon Books.

Deming, Barbara. 1964. "The Spirit of Freedom." *Liberation,* 28–31 Nov.

————. 1966. *Prison Notes.* New York: Grossman.

————. 1985. *We Are All Part of One Another: A Barbara Deming Reader.* Philadelphia: New Society.

Denton, Jeremiah. 1976. *When Hell Was in Session.* New York: Reader's Digest Press.

Diamond, Sigmund. 1992. *Compromised Campus: The Collaboration of Universities with the Intelligence Community, 1945–1955.* New York: Oxford Univ. Press.

Divine, Robert. 1978. *Blowing on the Wind: The Nuclear Test Ban Debate, 1954–1960.* New York: Oxford Univ. Press.

Dramesi, John. 1975. *Code of Honor.* New York: W. W. Norton.

Duberman, Martin. 1988. *Paul Robeson.* New York: Knopf.

Dubovsky, Melvin. 1988. *We Shall Be All: A History of the Industrial Workers of the World.* Urbana: Univ. of Illinois Press.

Dudziak, Mary. 1988. "Desegregation as a Cold War Imperative." *Stanford Law Review* 41 (fall): 61–120.

Duffet, John, ed. 1968. *Against the Crime of Silence: Proceedings of the Russell International War Crimes Tribunal.* New York: O'Hare Books.

Duncan, Donald. 1966. "The Whole Thing Was a Lie." *Ramparts* (Feb.): 12–18.

Early, Tracy. 1972. "Religion in North Vietnam." *American Report,* 4 Dec., 4.

Elder, Joseph. 1969a. Hotel Monorom, 7 Oct.

————. 1969b. Ministry of Health, 12 June.

————. 1969c. Visit to Polytechnic University, 16 June.

————. 1969d. Visit to Revolutionary Museum, 11 June.

————. 1972. "Forty Months of Failure." *Progressive* (Oct.): 12.

Fairclough, Adam. 1984. "Martin Luther King, Jr., and the War in Vietnam." *Phylon* 45 (June): 19–39.

Fall, Bernard. 1965. "This Isn't Munich, It's Spain. *Ramparts* (Dec.): 23–24.

Feinberg, Abraham. 1967. "Mission to Hanoi." *The Progressive* (Apr.): 19–22.

————. 1968. *Rabbi Feinberg's Hanoi Diary.* Ontario: Longmans.

Fitzgerald, Frances. 1972. *Fire in the Lake: The Vietnamese and the Americans in Vietnam.* Boston: Little, Brown.

Foster, Catherine. 1989. *Women for All Seasons: The Story of the Women's International League for Peace and Freedom.* Athens: Univ. of Georgia Press.

Franklin, H. Bruce. 1992. *M.I.A. or Mythmaking in America.* New York: Lawrence Hill Books.

Freedom to Travel: Report of the Special Committee to Study Passport Procedures of the Association of the Bar of the City of New York. 1958. New York: Dodd, Mead.

Friedman, Phoebe. 1973. "Life Today in North Vietnam." *Nation,* 10 Dec.

Frishman, Robert F. 1969. "I Was a Prisoner in Hanoi." *Reader's Digest,* Dec., 111–15.

Galston, Arthur. 1967. "Changing the Environment: Herbicides in Vietnam." *Scientist and Citizen* (Aug.–Sept.): 123–29.

Gerassi, John. 1967a. *North Vietnam: A Documentary.* New York; Bobbs-Merrill.

———. 1967b. "Report from North Vietnam." *New Republic,* 4 Mar.

Goodman, Allen E. 1986. *The Search for a Negotiated Settlement of the Vietnam War.* Berkeley: Institute of East Asian Studies.

Grant, Zalin. 1975. *Survivors.* New York: W. W. Norton.

Griffin-Nolan, Ed. 1991. *Witness for Peace: A Story of Resistance.* Louisville: Westminster Press.

Gruner, Elliott. 1993. *Prisoners of Culture: Representing the Vietnam POW.* New Brunswick, Rutgers Univ. Press.

Guarino, Larry. 1990. *A POW's Story: 2801 Days in Hanoi.* New York: Ivy Books.

Hackworth, David, with Julie Sherman. 1989. *About Face.* New York: Simon and Schuster.

Haddad-Garcia, George. 1981. *The Films of Jane Fonda.* Secaucus, N.J.: Citadel Press.

Hallin, Daniel C. 1986. *The "Uncensored War": The Media and Vietnam.* Berkeley: Univ. of California Press.

Hamilton, Andrew. 1970. "MIT: March 4 Revisited among Political Turmoil." *Science,* 13 Mar., 1476.

Hanh, Thich Nhat. 1965. "A Letter to Martin Luther King from a Buddhist Monk." *Liberation* (Dec.): 18–19.

———. 1967a. *Condemnation.* New York: Unicorn Press.

———. 1967b. *Vietnam: Lotus in a Sea of Fire.* New York: Hill and Wang.

———. 1991. *Peace Is Every Step.* New York: Bantam Books.

Harding, Vincent. 1965. "Other Roads from Selma." *Christian Century,* 5 May.

Harvey, Frank. 1966. "The Air War in Vietnam." *Flying* (Nov.): 38–95.

———. 1967. *Air War—Vietnam.* New York: Bantam Books.

Hassler, Alfred. 1970. *Saigon, U.S.A.* New York: Richard W. Baron.

Haven, Thomas. 1987. *Fire Across the Sea: The Vietnam War and Japan, 1965–1975.* Princeton: Princeton Univ. Press.

Hayden, Tom. 1966. "A Visit to Hanoi." *Liberation* (May–June): 23–55.

———. 1988. *Reunion: A Memoir.* New York: Random House.

Hendrickson, Paul. 1996. *The Living and the Dead: Robert McNamara and Five Lives of a Lost War.* New York: Knopf.

Hersh, Seymour. 1971. "The P.O.W. Issue: A National Issue is Born." *Dayton (Ohio) Journal-Herald,* 13–18 Feb.

Hess, Martha. 1993. *Then the Americans Came: Voices from Vietnam.* New York: Four Walls Eight Windows.

Holles, Everett. 1972. "U.S. Planned More Gradual Homecoming for P.O.W.s." *New York Times,* 30 Sept.

Horne, Gerald. 1985. *Black and Red: W. E. B. Du Bois and the Afro-American Response to the Cold War, 1944–1963.* Albany: State Univ. of New York Press.

————. 1993. "'Myth' and the Making of Malcolm X." *The American Historical Review* 98 (Apr.): 440–50.

Hostetter, Doug, and Michael McIntyre. 1974. "The Politics of Charity." *Christian Century,* 18 Sept., 845–50.

Howes, Craig. 1993. *Voices of the Vietnam POWs: Witnesses to Their Fight.* New York: Oxford Univ. Press.

Hubbell, John G. 1976. *P.O.W.: A Definitive History of the American Prisoner-of-War Experience in Vietnam, 1964–1973.* New York: Reader's Digest Press.

Hunt, Richard. 1995. *Pacification: The American Struggle for Vietnam's Hearts and Minds.* Boulder, Colo.: Westview Press.

Ingram, Timothy. 1970. "The Students Sign a Peace Treaty." *Nation,* 21 Dec., 646–48.

In the Name of America: The Conduct of the War in Vietnam by the Armed Forces of the United States as Shown by Published Reports. 1968. A Study Commissioned and Published by Clergy and Laymen Concerned about Vietnam. New York: E. P. Dutton.

Isaacson, Walter. 1992. *Kissinger: A Biography.* New York: Simon and Schuster.

Isserman, Maurice. 1992. "You Don't Need a Weatherman, but a Postman Can Be Helpful." In *Give Peace a Chance: Exploring the Vietnam War Antiwar Movement,* edited by Melvin Small and William D. Hoover, 22–34. Syracuse: Syracuse Univ. Press.

Jacob, Paul, and Saul Landau. 1966. *The New Radicals: A Report with Documents.* New York: Vintage Books.

Jencks, Christopher. 1967. "Negotiations Now? Reflections on a Meeting with the Enemy." *The New Republic,* 7 Oct., 22.

Johnson, Lyndon B. 1967. *Public Papers of the Presidents of the United States: Lyndon B. Johnson, 1967.* 2 vols. Washington, D.C.: Government Printing Office.

Johnson, Russell. 1966. "Mission to Cambodia." *Liberation* (Sept.): 12–17.

Johnson, Sam, and Jan Winebrenner. 1992. *Captive Warriors.* College Station: Texas A&M Univ. Press.

Julin, Costa. 1967. "Evidence at Stockholm: The Judges Are Everywhere." *Nation,* 5 June.

Kahin, George McTurnan. 1986. *Intervention: How America Became Involved in Vietnam.* New York: Knopf.

Kahin, George McTurnan, and John W. Lewis. 1968. *The United States in Vietnam.* New York: Delta Books.

Katz, Milton. 1986. *Ban the Bomb: A History of SANE, the Committee for a Sane Nuclear Policy, 1957–1985.* New York: Greenwood.

Katz, Neil H. 1974. *Radical Pacifism and the Contemporary American Peace Movement: The Committee for Nonviolent Action, 1957–1967*. Ph.D. diss., Univ. of Maryland.

Kearney, Kevin M. 1987. "Private Citizens in Foreign Affairs: A Constitutional Analysis." *Emory Law Journal* 36 (fall): 285–355.

Keenan, Barbara Mullen. 1986. *Every Effort: One Woman's Courageous Search for Her Missing Husband: A True Story*. New York: St. Martin's.

Koch, Christopher. 1965. "Eyewitness in the North." *Viet-Report* (Oct.): 9–12.

Kraslow, David, and Stuart H. Loory. 1968. *The Secret Search for Peace in Vietnam*. New York: Random House.

Lacoste, Yves. 1972. "Bombing the Dikes: A Geographer's On-the-Site Analysis." *Nation,* 9 Oct., 297–99.

Lakey, George. 1967. "Why I Am Joining the Phoenix." *Friends Journal* (Nov.): 565–66.

———. 1968. "No Port for the Phoenix." *Nation,* 11 Mar., 338–40.

Lakey, George, with Mark Morris. 1968. "The Second Voyage of the Phoenix." *WIN* (Jan.): 3–5.

Levertov, Denise. 1973. "Glimpses of Vietnamese Life." *American Report,* 12 Mar., 18–20.

Lewis, Anthony. 1972. "North Vietnam, A Visit to a Hospital." *Atlantic Monthly* (Aug.).

Lieberman, Robbie. 1992. "Does That Make Peace a Bad Word? American Responses to the Communist Peace Offensive, 1949–1950." *Peace and Change* 17 (Apr.): 198–228.

Luce, Don. 1968. "The Making of a Dove." *Progressive* (Feb.): 13–16.

Luce, Don, and John Summer. 1969. *Vietnam—The Unheard Voices*. Ithaca: Cornell Univ. Press.

Lynd, Alice. 1968. *We Won't Go: Personal Accounts of War Objectors*. Boston: Beacon Press.

Lynd, Staughton. 1966a. "Did Hanoi Respond?" *Viet-Report* (Mar.–Apr.): 18–22.

———. 1966b. "In Hanoi . . . The Peace That Is Not Offensive." *Viet-Report* (Jan.): 3–11.

———. 1966c. "To Speak the Truth." *Liberation* (Mar.): 22–24.

———. 1966d. "What Is the United States Doing in Vietnam?" *Liberation* (Feb.): 6–52.

———. 1993. Interview by author. Niles, Ohio, 25 Jan.

Lynd, Staughton, and Tom Hayden. 1966. *The Other Side*. New York: New American Library.

Lyttle, Bradford. 1966a. "A Neutralist Government Can Stand." *WIN,* 28 May, 8–9.

Lyttle, Bradford. 1966b. "Reports From Saigon." *Liberation* (May–June): 11–17.

Martin, Earl S. 1978. *Reaching the Other Side: The Journal of an American Who*

Stayed to Witness Vietnam's Postwar Transition. New York: Crown Publications.

Mayer, Jean. 1967. "Starvation as a Weapon: Herbicides in Vietnam." *Scientist and Citizen* (Aug.–Sept.): 116–21.

McAuliff, John. 1975. "Aid to Vietnam." *WIN,* 4 Dec.

McCarthy, Mary. 1969. *Hanoi.* New York: Harcourt, Brace and World.

McGrory, Mary. 1962. "Nobody Controls Anybody." *Washington Evening Star,* 14 Dec.

McNamara, Robert, with Brian VanDeMark. 1995. *In Retrospect: The Tragedy and Lessons of Vietnam.* New York: Random House.

Meier, August, and Elliott Rudwick. 1973. *CORE: A Study in the Civil Rights Movement, 1942–1968.* New York: Oxford Univ. Press.

Miller, Merle. 1980. *Lyndon: An Oral Biography.* New York: G. P. Putnam's Sons.

Miller, Susan. 1973. "Vietnam in Struggle." *WIN,* 1 Jan., 6.

Mitchell, Martin. 1966. "From Hanoi." *WIN,* 28 Jan., 12–14.

Moran, John. 1971. "Two Months With the NLF." *WIN,* 15 Feb., 31–33.

Moulton, Phillips P., ed. 1971. *The Journal and Major Essays of John Woolman.* New York: Oxford Univ. Press.

Muste, A. J. 1966. "A Voice Against the Speechlessness of Slaughter." *WIN,* 29 Apr., 5–7.

———. 1967. "Last Words: Report on a Visit to North Vietnam." *Liberation* (Feb.): 8–10.

Myerson, Michael. 1970. *These Are the Good Old Days: Coming of Age as a Radical in America's Late, Late Years.* New York: Grossman.

Nation. 1966. 24 Jan.

"Nation Builds under Fire, A." 1968. Film no. AF1F-160. U.S. Air Force—Air Photographic and Charting Service.

New Republic. 1966. 21 May.

O'Reilly, Kenneth. 1989. *Racial Matters: The FBI's Secret File on Black America, 1960–1972.* New York: Macmillan.

Paley, Grace. 1969. "Report From the DRV." *WIN,* 15 Sept., 4–10.

———. 1971. ". . . I guess it must have been someone else." *WIN,* 15 May, 30–33.

Parrish, John A. 1972. *A Doctor's Year in Vietnam.* New York: Dutton.

Passports and the Right to Travel: A Study of Administrative Control of the Citizen. 1966. Committee on Foreign Affairs, House of Representatives. Washington, D.C.: Government Printing Office.

Peace in Vietnam: A New Approach in Southeast Asia: A Report Prepared for the American Friends Service Committee. 1966. New York: Hill and Wang.

Pentagon Papers: The Defense Department History of United States Decisionmaking on Vietnam. 1972. 4 vols. Senator Gravel Edition. Boston: Beacon Press.

Pergande, Delia. 1995. NGOs and Nation-Building: Village Development by CARE in South Vietnam, 1954–1960. Paper in author's possession.

Phoenix, The (film). Swarthmore College Peace Collection.

Porter, Gareth. 1975. *A Peace Denied: The United States, Vietnam and the Paris Agreement.* Bloomington: Indiana Univ. Press.

———, ed. 1979. *Vietnam: The Definitive Documentation of Human Decisions.* Vol. 2. Stanfordville, N.Y.: Earl M. Coleman Enterprises.

Posner, Gerald. 1996. *Citizen Perot: His Life and Times.* New York: Random House.

Powers, Francis Gary. 1970. *Operation Overflight: The U-2 Spy Pilot Tells His Story for the First Time.* New York: Holt, Rinehart and Winston.

Public Papers of the Presidents of the United States: Richard Nixon. 1971. Washington, D.C.: Government Printing Office.

Purcell, Ben, and Anne Purcell. 1992. *Love and Duty.* New York: St. Martin's.

Race, Jeffrey. 1972. *War Comes to Long An.* Berkeley: Univ. of California Press.

Reynolds, Earle. 1961. *The Forbidden Voyage.* New York: Doubleday.

Rhodes, Jonathan E. 1970. *Surgery: Principles and Practices.* 4th ed. Philadelphia: Lippincott.

Riley, Glenda. 1984. *Women and Indians on the Frontier, 1825–1915.* Albuquerque: Univ. of New Mexico Press.

Risner, Robertson. 1973. *The Passing of the Night: My Seven Years as a Prisoner of the North Vietnamese.* New York: Random House.

Robinson, Jo Ann Ooiman. 1981. *Abraham Went Out: A Biography of A. J. Muste.* Philadelphia: Temple Univ. Press.

Rogers, Alan. 1985. "Passports and Politics: The Courts and the Cold War." *Historian* 47: 497–511.

Rowley, Kelvin, and Grant Evans. 1984. *Red Brotherhood at War: Indochina since the Fall of Saigon.* London: Verso.

Safer, Morley. *Flashbacks: On Returning to Vietnam.* 1990. New York: Random House.

Salisbury, Harrison. 1967. *Behind the Lines—Hanoi, December 23, 1966–January 7, 1967.* New York: Harper and Row.

Schalk, David L. 1991. *War and the Ivory Tower: Algeria and Vietnam.* New York, Oxford Univ. Press.

Schell, Jonathan. 1976. *The Time of Illusion.* New York: Knopf.

Schell, Orville. 1968. "Cage for the Innocents." *The Atlantic* (Jan.): 29–34.

Schrecker, Ellen. 1986. *No Ivory Tower: McCarthyism and the Universities.* New York: Oxford Univ. Press.

Senate Committee on Foreign Relations. 1984. *U.S. Government and the Vietnam War: Executive and Legislative Roles and Relationships, Part 3.* Washington: Government Printing Office.

Senate Committee on Veterans' Affairs. 1983. *Veterans' Exposure to Agent Orange.* Washington, D.C.: Government Printing Office.

Shawcross, William. 1979. *Sideshow: Kissinger, Nixon and the Destruction of Cambodia.* New York: Simon and Schuster.

Sheehan, Neil. 1992. *After the War Was Over: Hanoi and Saigon* New York: Vintage Books.

Small, Melvin, and William D. Hoover, eds. 1992. *Give Peace a Chance: Exploring the Vietnam Antiwar Movement.* Syracuse: Syracuse Univ. Press.

Smith, George E. 1971. *P.O.W.: Two Years With the Vietcong.* Berkeley: Ramparts Press.

Sontag, Susan. 1969. *Trip to Hanoi.* New York: Farrar, Straus and Giroux.

Stockdale, Jim, and Sybil Stockdale. 1984. *In Love and War: The Story of a Family's Ordeal and Sacrifice During the Vietnam Years.* New York: Harper and Row.

Swerdlow, Amy G. 1982. "Ladies' Day at the Capitol: Women Strike for Peace Versus HUAC." *Feminist Studies* 8 (fall): 199–243.

———. 1984. *The Politics of Motherhood: The Case of Women Strike for Peace and the Test Ban Treaty.* Ph.D. diss., Rutgers.

———. 1993. *Women Strike for Peace: Traditional Motherhood and Radical Politics in the 1960s.* Chicago: Univ. of Chicago Press.

Taylor, Telford. 1971. *Nuremberg and Vietnam: An American Tragedy.* New York: Quadrangle.

Thies, Wallace J. 1980. *When Governments Collide: Coercion and Diplomacy in the Vietnam Conflict, 1964–1968.* Berkeley: Univ. of California Press.

Thompson, James Clay. 1980. *Rolling Thunder: Understanding Policy and Program Failure.* Chapel Hill: Univ. of North Carolina Press.

Thurber, Sherry. 1968. "Reports From Saigon." *Liberation* (May–June): 18–20.

"Tiger Cages of Con Son, The." 1970. *Life,* 17 July, 27–29.

Tilford, Earl H., Jr. 1993. *Crosswinds: The Air Force's Setup in Vietnam.* College Station: Texas A&M Univ. Press.

Tolles, Frederick B. 1950. "Unofficial Ambassador: George Logan's Mission to France, 1798." *William & Mary Quarterly* 7 (Jan.): 3–25.

Tolles, Frederick B. 1953. *George Logan of Philadelphia.* New York: Oxford Univ. Press.

Truong, Nhu Tang, with David Chanoff and Doan Van Toi. 1985. *Vietcong Memoir: An Inside Account of the Vietnam War and Its Aftermath.* New York: Harcourt Brace Jovanovich.

Ulh, Michael. 1994. "Searching for Vietnam's M.I.A.'s," *Nation,* 14 Sept., 573–76.

U.S. Study Team on Religious and Political Freedom in Vietnam. 1969. *Congressional Record,* 17 June.

Vagts, Detley F. 1966. "The Logan Act: Paper Tiger or Sleeping Giant?" *The American Journal of International Law* 60 (summer): 268–302.

Valentine, Douglas. 1990. *The* Phoenix *Program.* New York.

Van Dyke, Jon M. 1971. "Were They Tortured?" *Nation,* 6 Oct., 334–35.

Vastyan, E. A. 1973. "Medical Needs and Moral Obligations in Vietnam." *Christian Century,* 4 Apr., 388.

Vickery, Michael. 1983. *Cambodia 1975–1982.* Boston: South End Press.

Vietnam Veterans Against the War. 1972. *Winter Soldier Investigation: An Inquiry into American War Crimes.* Boston: Beacon.

Watson, James, and Kevin Dockery. 1993. *Point Man.* New York: Morrow.

Weisner, Louis. 1988. *Victims and Survivors: Displaced Persons and Others War Victims in Vietnam, 1954–1975.* New York: Greenwood.

Wells, Tom. 1994. *The War Within: America's Battle over Vietnam.* Berkeley: Univ. of California Press.

Whitfield, Stephen J. 1991. *The Culture of the Cold War.* Baltimore: Johns Hopkins Univ. Press.

Wicker, Tom. 1972. "How Free the Prisoners?" *New York Times,* 28 Sept.

Wiegersma, Nancy. 1988. *Vietnam: Peasant Land, Peasant Revolution.* New York: St. Martin's.

Young, Marilyn. 1991. *The Vietnam War, 1945–1990.* New York: HarperCollins.

Zeitlow, Carl. 1967. "Hanoi and the Trek of the *Phoenix.*" *Christian Century,* 2 Aug., 1004–6.

Zinn, Howard. 1968. "The Petty Route Home." *Nation,* 1 Apr., 432–37.

Index